HILDE LARSEN

Know the Truth and
Get Healthy

A Step-By-Step Guide to
True Health and Vitality

KNOW THE TRUTH AND GET HEALTHY
A Step-By-Step Guide to True Health and Vitality

iUniverse books may be ordered through booksellers or by contacting:

iUniverse
1663 Liberty Drive
Bloomington, IN 47403
www.iuniverse.com
1-800-Authors (1-800-288-4677)

Because of the dynamic nature of the Internet, any web addresses or links contained in this book may have changed since publication and may no longer be valid. The views expressed in this work are solely those of the author and do not necessarily reflect the views of the publisher, and the publisher hereby disclaims any responsibility for them.

Any people depicted in stock imagery provided by Thinkstock are models, and such images are being used for illustrative purposes only.
Certain stock imagery © Thinkstock.

Photography by Trevor James Samborski.

ISBN: 978-1-4917-9775-4 (sc)
ISBN: 978-1-4917-9776-1 (hc)
ISBN: 978-1-4917-9774-7 (e)

Library of Congress Control Number: 2016909072

Print information available on the last page.

iUniverse rev. date: 6/28/2016

STEP OUT OF THE ILLUSION OF
DIS-EASE, SAY NO TO SICKNESS AND
PAIN AND RECLAIM YOUR HEALTH!

YOU ARE WORTH IT!

Dear reader.

This book is dedicated to you,
to every single one of you that are struggling.
You are the ones to whom this book is written,
and the ones that Inspired me to keep going.
My love and compassion lies
between these covers,
and I thank you for reading.
My greatest wish is that you will
find Inspiration and remedy to walk
towards your greatest potentials.

This dedication goes to every single soul that is
looking for health, feeling lost and in despair.

You are worthy.

Hilde

CONTENTS

ACKNOWLEDGEMENTS

This might sound strange, but without my so called dis-ease, my pain and suffering, this book would not exist. I would have never found the truth about health and healing. I would have never awakened to my true self and calling, my life would not be this full and rewarding. I thank the Creator and this path for every single step and experience. I am grateful for my journey and the knowledge that has been revealed to me. From the deepest place within me, I can see how this book has been a part of me for many years and it is now ready to fly. By finding all of you that are ready for true health, it is fulfilling my journey *from HELL to Inspired*.

My dear family, who always knew that I was on to something. That always stood by my unconventional decisions and had faith in my choices. Thank you for your faith and support. My husband Helge, my daughter Therese, and my son Thomas, *you* are why I am breathing.

My best friend May, thank you for being sound minded during the toughest of times. This book is absolutely a product of my perseverance, and you are one tough cookie, like me.

Thank you Elena, who jumped in, ready to polish and support my writing. The world welcomed us at the same date, though some years apart. Not a coincidence. You're such a lovely spirit.

Without all the great healers that have walked before me, I would not be able to share this truth. They are many, and have changed and *are* changing this world. Thank you Dr. Robert Morse ND, Dr. Wayne Dyer, Bruce H. Lipton, Dr. Colin Campbell, Arnold Ehret, Bernard Jensen DC, PhD, Paul Twitchell, Jay Kordich, Norman W. Walker, Dr. Douglas Graham, Dr. Sebi, Paul Nison, Dan McDonald, Dr. Hulda Clark, Dr. Ann Wigmore, Dr. Joel Fuhrman, Dr. Max Gerson, Herbert M. Shelton, Dr. Masaru Emoto, Louise L. Hays, Andreas Moritz, Dr. Kenneth Sutter, Deepak Chopra, Echart Tolle, Neal Donald Walch and Tony Robbins.

Thank you Angela Rose at *IUniverse* for being a great support through this process of publishing two books back to back. Your on-point and speedy handling of my demands were fantastic.

Thank you Nature for blessing us with everything that we need to thrive. I am humble to have been shown the way.

To all that have given me the opportunity to guide and support them on their journey back to health. Thank you! *You* are who inspires me! *You* who are willing and eager to take charge of your own destiny.

Again, thank you!

ABOUT THE AUTHOR

Hilde Larsen, known as the one that Inspires, is the owner and founder of http://inspiredbyhilde.com/. She is a certified Health and Wellness Coach, from IIN, a raw food teacher, an author and a certified Detox Specialist. Her interest for healing and spiritual growth also led her to become a Reiki Healer. She is highly intuitive, and has a strong connection to Mother Earth and the spiritual world.

Her glowing enthusiasm for health and vitality, has the leading role in her work. She is an Inspirational media speaker, a blogger, and has her own YouTube channel. She creates online video programs, and is publishing a series of books on health and natural living. Born and raised in Stavanger, Norway, she and her husband of 28 years have a second home in Florida, USA. She is a proud mother and grandmother, and a tree hugger at heart. Called by nature and spirit, she is Inspiring many to take back their power.

Her career started as an interior architect, designing cruise ships and hotels. Being athletic all her life, she was the co-owner of an aerobics and spinning studio for many years. She closed her interior design and building company *Kolage*, in 2004, due to her severe illness. She then went on to studying journalism, and was guided to the path of healing and regeneration.

In her first book "From HELL to Inspired", Hilde shares her full story. A heartfelt gripping journey about her struggles from bedridden to living her dreams.

Hilde now spends her time travelling between Norway and Florida, exploring health, healing and the human connection to nature. She also values her quality time with her close family and friends.

To request to work with Hilde, visit the website www. inspiredbyhilde.com.

PREFACE

The one thing that never left me, was the willingness to fight for what I believed was possible. I knew that being sick was not who I really was. From being bedridden, and sick as a dog for years and years, I was tired, yes. I was sick and tired of being sick and tired, but I was never ready to quit. I was so worn down by drugs and hospital treatments, and I had no idea what to do, or where to start. Still, I was ready to be guided, to be shown the way.

There is no glory in giving up, and there is no glory in staying sick. Life is about living the very best way that we know how, and to realize that suffering does not have to be a part of it. Pain is inevitable, but suffering is a choice. In my first book, "From HELL to inspired", I take you with me on my own journey from feeling completely lost and sick, to living the life that I love. I have shared my experience on living with a so-called chronic illness, and my encounters with our so-called health care system. I am happy and honored to be able to share my path and my knowledge, and I am confident that if you are in the need of healing, on any level, you will find truth between these covers.

"I needed a break. I knew my time at the University was done. I knew I could not continue with what I was doing. I knew I had to change bigtime, but how? My husband and I decided to take a weekend trip to Barcelona, to try to get away from everything. As if I could get away from me! I remember I so wanted to be able to feel happy and healthy. I had only one wish at this time, and that was to be able to wake up and not feel pain. To be able to live for just one day, without the discomfort and the despair that I was experiencing.

The trip was the furthest from fulfilling those wishes imaginable. I spent ours in the hotel bed in pain, and I had to realize, this was not me anymore. I was done travelling, and I was done having fun. I was done.

The night we arrived home after our trip, I had the dream that changed everything.

I had an experience that changed the course of my whole life. This dream was the first of many guided dreams and messages. It was the turning point. One dream or vision, would wake me up to change the course of my life. It was time.

"I am looking at this enormous barrel, the metal kind that some use to burn garden leaves in. I remember it being red, and all my needles, all the syringes, they are all in that barrel. They are sticking up, every shot I ever did, all put into that one barrel. It is filled to the rim! I keep staring at it as it explodes. The whole thing blows up, and I wake up in a state of shock! It was scary real, I could smell the fire, the smoke."

That whole day I felt overwhelmed. I kept throwing up between classes, but it was like it did not matter anymore. Nothing mattered. Not me, not what I was doing, not my body, and not my life. I drove home early. I laid down on the living room sofa, and that was that. I just laid there. I was done. This was it. I had made up my mind. This had to stop, right now, right this very minute. I was done.

No more.
No more anything.
No more feeling like I was going to die, and not knowing how to get help.
No more medications, that only kept making me worse.
No more doing what I did not want to do.
No more acting like I was fine, when I was not.
No more trying to look great, when I felt like crap.
No more being afraid of anything.
No more not listening to me and my body
No more bullshit.
I was done!

My husband found me on the sofa after work. I was still lying in the same position. When I sat up, this is what I told him:

"I am lying down now, and I will lie here until one of two things happen. Either I get healthy, or I die. I do not care which, as long as it is one of them. No more medications, I am done! This, I cannot do anymore. This *is not living. I am done!*"

At 42, my body did not want to keep signaling me anymore. My whole being went on strike to save my life. I had been called. ""
-   *"From HELL to Inspired"*

By reading this book, *you* have been called. The rest of your amazing life is in front of you, and you are about to change the course of it. The power is in your hands, and the truth is out. From walking my walk and my talk for many years, I am eager to share with you what I have experienced. Truth is simple, change is not. Health is there for us, if we let it.

We are all in this together, and you are never alone. Your spirit, your soul, who you *really* are, is always healthy and strong. The real you, is never in despair or pain, only our bodies are. Know that the body is a self-healing mechanism, and that *you* deserve to feel amazing!

Thank you for being a part of my tribe and my life.
Thank you for blessing me by reading this book.
Thank you.

MEDICAL ADVICE/DISCLAIMER

This book, with its opinions, suggestions and references, are based on the author's personal experience and is for personal study and research purposes only. This book is about health and vitality, not disease. The author makes no medical claims. Information in this book is not meant to treat or diagnose any disease. This is not medical advice, but a sharing of personal experiences.

The information, ideas, and suggestions in this book are not intended as a substitute for professional medical advice. Before following any suggestions contained in this book, consult your physician. Neither the author nor the publisher shall be liable or responsible for any loss or damage allegedly arising as a consequence of your use or application of any information or suggestions in this book.

Taking responsibility for oneself is a great message to take from reading this book. This is for educational and inspirational use only. Self-empowering is a great asset to any health regime, and it is of great value for every aspect of life. Seek freedom from disease, seek healing.

PART ONE
TRUTH REVEALED

Chapter 1

Be ready and Inspired!

Our modern world, the medical industry and our quest for health through a pill and quick fixes, has left us in less than optimal health. We are sick, and we are confused. I know I was, and my awakening to the truth about health and healing took many years of searching. From the day that I decided I was done, that there was no way that I could live my life in pain and despair, I started searching for solutions. My life was dedicated to researching and experimenting. I was being led to change the way that I saw the world completely. Everything that I had been told about health was being questioned. I found that even scientists were disagreeing, and that the community of researchers were contradicting themselves. What was going on?

I had touched upon a new paradigm. A shift in perception and a completely new way of thinking. From reading everything that I could find on the subject of health and regeneration, slowly, I could see what has been suppressed and buried. Truth became simpler and simpler to me, and the longer I kept digging, the more amazed I got. There was no scientific proof of anything, we were not studying health. We were studying chemicals and the suppression of symptoms. That was not what I was searching for. I was not going to find my remedy in any medical journal or study. I was going to find it in nature. The truth is not patented or has a study behind it. It simply is.

By realizing that being sick and tired is not at all natural, the road to a better way of living reveals itself. The road less travelled is always open, though often very well hidden. By this I mean that no matter if we see the solution or not, it is always there. The road to freedom and healthy living is not a main street, it is far less traveled. One of the greatest obstacles I find when presenting my experience and thoughts on true health is that it is not *mainstream*. Being open to new ideas and non-scientific truths can be a real challenge. I was desperate in my quest for remedy, so my old beliefs were easily shredded. I was in too much pain to care.

Luckily it is hard to turn our back on the truth once it has been revealed to us. Once we know, we know, and it becomes a part of us. We carry it with us without even knowing it. It is like a seed has been planted. Every time I read something that resonated with my cells, it stuck. The more I read, the more determined I got, and the more faith I grew in nature, God and the amazing body that I live in. I found that I was not searching for something new, I was revealing something old. Our inner being knows. For example, when we are told that that sickness and so-called dis-ease is something we need to live with, we will feel resistance. Our spirit is speaking to us, poking us, saying; "Hey, this is not true." When my doctor told me I would never walk regularly again and that I would be medicated for the rest of my life, never being pain free or fit, my entire population of cells shrank. My whole body went into "falseness- alert". The body knows its ability to heal. It knows that chemicals are toxic.

I wish we were not driven by our intellect. While a great surgeon can be invaluable, the medical industry is in my opinion promoting pills and toxic substances that leaves us sicker than ever. The body is a self-healing mechanism, and it needs and wants to be treated as such.

The road less travelled and experienced includes some unturned stones. It can look like a dark and unsafe place to walk. When the authority of science and the commonly accepted beliefs are left behind, I know for a fact that fear will arise. I felt lost and scared at times. I was going against everything that I had been taught and everything my doctor was telling me. Who wouldn't be scared. Breaking new ground is never a ride in the park. It is hard work, and I honor all those who've walked before me, writing their books, telling the world about their findings. When I read Dr. Arnold Ehret's book "Mucusless Diet healing System", I remember my whole being wanting to read more. I felt so aligned with what he was talking about, and how the body will regenerate if we just get out of the way. I had my cabinets filled with supplements and remedies at the time. All so-called natural. Luckily my determination and perseverance never stopped until I saw the simplicity of it all. I had to stop everything and continue my research. The more I studied, the less remedies and supplements I found that I needed. I was seeing true freedom ahead, and I still do!

This freedom is very deep and it includes the freedom of not having to be able to prove what works and what doesn't. No one could prove to me that healing was going to be my experience, I had to live it. Health can never be proven, only measured through blood tests and other procedures. In Western medicine we study tests to find something "off", without looking at the whole being. I have that found we are so much more than that. We are energetic beings, souls, travelers. We are the generation who is awakening to the new paradigm of healing, nature. Simplicity is coming forth, and as I see it, proof is in the pudding.

The old paradigm of illusion.

The statement; "chronic illness is an illusion" will either empower you, or make you angry and sad. The truth is that once we realize that *we* ourselves, truly hold the key to changing our health and life, inner strength will come forth. The illusion is not that the illness/ imbalance or dis-ease that is being experienced and lived is not real. It simply means that it does not have to be chronic. Chronic simply means long standing, and the medical community is using it as a label for what they see as incurable. Nothing is stagnant, as the body can and will heal anything, when given a chance.

Your health is in your own hands, and that can feel like a burden, or it can feel like the true freedom that it is.

The illusion that keeps us stuck in our old ways is the one of misplaced authority. We simply are not conditioned to think for ourselves. We are led to believe that someone else should think for us, as they have studied and know better. Well, let me tell you, that illusion nearly killed me, and is killing people every single day. Some things in life are for all of us, and it is free, no study or textbooks needed. Life is a journey, and from exploring and trusting in your own ability to learn and grow, you will set yourself free.

Change must arise before change happens.

Embarking on any journey that requires change, will require a dose of inspiration and eagerness. It will require that you are ready, so to speak. Together with being open to new things and ideas, having the true deep-rooted desire for health is crucial. It is vital for the level of success that you will accomplish. You might not believe that you are ready, but you might feel called or spoken to, through a book, an article, or a video. Follow the lead, always. One thing will lead to another, always showing you the next step.

When you are ready to change, events and occurrences might seem as if they are happening out of the blue, but they never are. Nothing is random, and nothing is shown to us by accident. You are right here, reading this book, because this is where you are supposed to be. We are all in this together, and the reason that our paths have crossed is a part of your journey, and mine. Even when we are not ready to change, to take the leap of faith and dive right in to freedom, once we see truth, that seed has been planted. Once we have seen that opening, the way home, once we have felt that hope, and heard that whisper, it is hard to ignore. Impossible I might even say. Looking the other way, and holding on to what is already there, is easy. Change is hard. Still, it does not matter, as it was never about easy. Easy is overrated and anyone can do it. This is why so few will step up and take charge of their own lives, it takes some balls and a dose of determination and trust.

The uncertainty, and the seemingly lonely part of the trail, can be overwhelming and challenging, but when YOU are ready, it does not matter. Where you are going is calling you so beautifully, and the closer you get, the more beautiful the calling will be. Trust me.

When we want something to change, we need to change something. We cannot keep doing what has created the problem, the issue, the imbalances and the sickness, and expect something to change. Change requires change, pure and simple. On the other hand, change is inevitable, and nothing ever stays the same. Think about this. We are resisting the inevitable by resisting change, and yet we have to actually take the leap for it to manifest in the direction we want it to. I know, this is something to ponder.

By holding on to what is, we are resisting the natural flow of life. That flow, that inevitable change, is a natural part of us. By getting in the way, poisoning a perfect healing system with chemical compounds, we are creating suffering. The change that is needed to take back the self-power, might take a lot of courage. It will seem overwhelming and frustrating at times, but do not worry. *You* can do this, and *you* hold the power to reclaim your health.

Be Inspired!

This is *the time, and you are the one you have been waiting for. Get your gear together, and get ready for the ride of your life. Get ready to hang on the corner of Healthy and Happy, and let any sorrow or pain just walk on by.*

My greatest wish is that you, from reading all this information, will feel a spark of hope and inner knowing. This step by step plan is made so that health will be able to find its way back to you. I hope that by knowing that you can do this, you will be inspired to start your own path, and to get your game-plan on! The freedom that comes from having a plan is truly fantastic, and now you have one! Get ready to do what it takes, and get ready to reap what you sow. We make our beds, and *we* lie in them. The true freedom, or a fearful scenario. Make a choice and go for it. Make a plan and stick with it. Make a commitment to yourself, and remember that *you* are worth it! I *know* that if you are not quite there yet, not ready to fully commit, you *will* be.

I know all about pain and illness, and I am here to tell you that *you* can do anything you put your focus and attention towards. I will be your biggest fan and support, so don't you ever believe, not for a second, that you are alone. You are not, not ever. Together we've got this, one step at the time. My deepest wish is for you to find what you are searching for from the tips and guidelines found in this book. It was written to make sure that everything that I have seen do wonderful things for my own and many others' health, is there for you. I wanted to make sure that you were able to tap into this information between the covers of one book. A book that offers some bold truths about health and healing – not at all limited to a diet plan or a simple healing technique. This is what I have been studying and living, a collection of what I have found will transform your health and life. This is a new paradigm, and it is naturally amazing!

I want you to understand that significant parts of this book will have a theoretical approach. These parts are very important to your understanding of the various detoxes, recipes, etc. A step by step guide when it comes to true healing, is not simply how to do recipes, but how to change your entire life. Healing is a reflection of everything that you do, say, feel and ingest. By reading this book cover to cover, you will be guided through physical recipes, and emotional inner work for the soul. There is no one way to put together a healing plan that fits all, but simply a teaching of what is needed for real health to come forth, and the tools one can use to get there.

Cause and effect, what a true blessing it is! When we know better, we can do better, always!

Chapter 2

Why are we sick?

I found that looking for health became much easier once I understood why I was sick. When I realized what I had been doing to myself, it became crystal clear to me why I was suffering. While everything is perfect in nature, what we have become by moving away from it is not. It has created suffering, and we see it all around us. Being sick is not natural, being healthy is! It is what we are designed to be. There is nothing natural about having a body that is imbalanced, tired, sick and in pain.

There are no so-called dis-eases in nature. There are no animals with rheumatoid arthritis, diabetes, multiple sclerosis or asthma. I have never read or heard of any wild animal suffering with any so-called chronic disease. They are not allergic to the foods that they eat, and they do not get fat and tired. When they get sick, from a bacteria or a trauma, they lie down and rest, drinking only water, so that their body can heal and restore. Regeneration is therefore supported, and nature can take its course. The first time I read this, I "knew" it was important. You see, in nature, every species lives in harmony with Mother Earth. From living in harmony with sunrise and sundown, the seasons are honored, and food is gathered and killed for survival. Eating is not linked to suppressing emotions or feeding different types of addictions. Nature has a perfectly harmonic way of existing, and the further away from that harmony that we stray, the more trouble we are in. The further from truth that we wander, the more despair we will experience. As a species, we as humans keep drifting away from our natural path. This is where healing got lost, and dis-ease manifested.

Our path has been lost to us in many different ways, and we are now living the sum of our actions and ignorance. We are experiencing cause and effect, pure and simple. The cause being not honoring creation, and the effects being illness, stress, pain and depression. Violence, anxiety, fear and frustration, are all part of the same manifestation. The one we as humans created, and we as individuals can change one step, one bite, one thought and emotion at a time.

From once living barefoot in nature, we are now living in high-rises, surrounded by wireless electromagnetic radiation. This is a huge deal for our cells. The electromagnetic noise is hitting us from many different sources. Our wireless communication devices, including wireless power meters, cell phones, cell towers, wireless routers and cordless phones, expose us to both electric and magnetic fields (EMF). Anything that has a cord or a plug emanates an electric field. That includes all appliances, electric wiring, power outlets and extension cords. On top of this we are also exposed to power lines. Some are above the ground where you can see them, but many are below.

But what makes this such a health hazard? Why is this not something that our cells and vibration thrive from being around? Why are we suffering from living in this environment? I believe the key word is vibration. Our cells will get distorted from being exposed to a vibration that causes stress and dissonance. The frequencies are distorting the natural vibration of our cells, also inducing oxidative stress.

Oxidative stress is simply defined as a disturbance in the natural balance between the production of free radicals and the antioxidant defenses. It is an imbalance between the production of free radicals and the ability of the body to detoxify their harmful effects through neutralization by antioxidants.

Free radicals are atoms or groups of atoms with an odd (unpaired) number of electrons. They can be formed when oxygen interacts with certain molecules. Once formed, these highly reactive radicals can start a chain reaction, like dominos. They can then create real danger, even at the DNA level! Now the cells get sick and die, but this is where nature has a solution, the antioxidants. They are our defense system against free radicals, found in abundance in any living natural food. What we see as colors in living fruits are antioxidants.

So you see, all we need to do is to look around, and we will realize how far we have drifted. From being a tropical species, born without any clothes or shoes, we are walking on rubber soles, covered from head to toe to keep warm and fashionable. We even need the shoes to be comfortable, for support. Our body was not made for walking without shoes, so we need support and padding, really? We are now disconnected from the vibrations of the Earth, from the negative ions that nurture our cells. All this EMF disturbance, the electromagnetic smog, is subjecting us to positive ions, disturbing our cells in their natural healing and regeneration. We are experiencing decay and cell mutation, instead of natural vitality and strength.

I will keep this simple, as that is all we need to know; simplicity. When we spend time surrounded by cell-phones, computers and power lines, we are out of calm. We are in a space of stress and degeneration. When we are in nature, we are in a healing space of harmony for all our cells. Simple, yet hard to live by in this modern world.

Our lives even include travelling by airplanes, walking around in high-tech airports, driving cars and busses, underground and over ground. We are constantly bombarded with the frequencies and energies of instruments and vibration. The artificial lighting and the recirculated air are contributing to more cellular and mental stress. This might all sound very depressing, and in a sense it is.

We are sick as an effect of our lifestyles, as a direct and honest effect. Together with the genes handed down from our parents, and those before them, we are living the life that we created.

We even made food our enemy, so to speak. We made food something that is no longer nurturing and healing. What we eat affects every single cell in our body, positively or negatively. We are being presented with what looks like food and is perceived as food, but in truth is not. Supermarkets are filled with boxes and cans, bags and plastic bottles, all filled with substances that are a burden to the human body. Processed and altered, filled with anything from plastic to wood pulp. Our food is even genetically modified (GMOs), which means they have been manipulated using recombinant DNA techniques. It is not possible nor desirable in nature to transfer genetic material between organisms. The concept of genetic modification brings about alterations in genetic composition, and in the properties of the organism developed. The technique is highly mutagenic, and leads to changes in the DNA and the proteins produced by the GMO. Is this what we want to serve our children? Even seeds are being altered today. We are tampering with nature, creating mutation of cells, and a body that does not even recognize what we eat, as food. It's all poisons rather, and that is serious business. The DNA being altered and the tampering with our food also leads to toxic and allergic reactions. Nature is perfect as it is, and by altering any part of it we create trouble, big trouble.

GMO (Genetically Modified Organisms) is presented within about 70 percent of processed foods: Our corn, soy, cottonseed, canola, and sugar beet-based ingredients. According to "Seeds of deception", GMOs may cause organ damage, gastrointestinal and immune disorders, accelerated aging, and infertility.

We are really just scratching the surface of understanding what altering and tampering with our foods are doing to us. We are accepting the most dangerous paths of them all, the road of starvation and self-poisoning. Yes, starvation. Unless we are eating fresh produce, we are not serving the body the nutrients that it needs. Instead, we are eating what will keep us malnourished by clogging up our system. We are consuming nutrient-lacking food that has been altered to the point of complete unrecognition, and the body will react to it as poison. It makes us constipated, as the body is trying to hold on to it, to store it away. Also, the lack of fiber and natural enzymes will leave the body unable to get rid of the waste created. Mostly we are not aware that the intestines are where most of the absorption happens, through the villi of the small intestines. Foods like pizza, bread, hotdogs, hamburgers, processed, powdered, canned, fried and baked are all a burden to our perfect machinery. Our bodies are not meant to be hit with such massive amounts of poisons.

We are suffering, and being sick has become something normal. How could it not? We are feeding ourselves sickness, and that is what we are experiencing. Cause and effect, simple.

Visiting the fresh produce department can be very deceiving. The organic, naturally grown food, now has to be labeled for us to be able to find what used to be just food, it has to be labeled organic. Only a few see the benefits of paying extra money for clean food, but the number is constantly rising. The pesticides, herbicides, insecticides and fungicides are not adding health to the table, so be aware. The amounts of poison served on our plates are over the top, and we are living the effects. We are on toxic overload. Our deli foods, like processed meat, are filled with Sodium Nitrite/ Nitrate, linked to what has been labeled as cancer, which means it's damaged cells. So, in reality, everything that we have talked about, the EMF′s, what is being sprayed on our produce, the GMO, are all making the body react in the same way, damaging cells.

We are damaging our cells by leaving out real foods, poisoning the body, but also by hindering elimination. Our great grandparents would have had a hard time recognizing 80% of what is today sold in a typical supermarket as food. The health of a cell, therefore the whole body, is mainly about elimination. The cells can't be healthy if they are bathing in waste and acids. The environment, the internal terrain, needs to be supportive of healthy cell formation and regeneration. Look at it this way; if you leave a diaper on a child without changing it, a very sore little behind will manifest. The acids will burn. Waste is acids, and when left inside the body, it will burn our cells. The waste is created in many ways, and I will get back to that, but the simple explanation is this; The lymphatic system is our sewer system. It is where our metabolic waste and the waste in form of any bacteria, toxins, acids and damaged cells, goes to be eliminated. The kidneys are then filtering out this acidic waste, and this is where we've gotten into big trouble. By our consumption of a high protein diet, our poor genetic composition and stress, our kidneys are getting weaker by the generation. The stress that we put ourselves under has slammed our adrenals to the point of fatigue, and as they sit on top of the kidneys, controlling them, we are heading for a fall. Our precious adrenals, those little glands that have such an impact on our elimination of waste, are such an important key to our lost health. They fire up the kidneys, and by being impaired from stress, it is easy to see where things are heading. When the kidneys become weak, they stop filtering, and we are left holding on to that acidic waste. The acids are burning our cells, and we are living the result. Day by day, meal by meal, hectic day by stressful job, we are living and experiencing the result of our sick lifestyle.

This stressful lifestyle of the modern society is detrimental to the body. More so than we have been able to imagine. Through our food-choices and stressful jobs, we are headed down that same old road of dis-ease and so-called age-related discomforts. The whole scenario of chasing life itself has become an obstacle that needs to be overcome. We are eating what is not perceived as food, and we are living a life that is not in harmony with who we really are.

Do you get the picture yet? Can you see how many factors are impacting our health? And now that we are not feeling well, we go searching for what is missing. In all the wrong places. The search for happiness, the constant eagerness to perform and do good, is also stripping us of our natural calm and defense. The balance is lost between meetings and duties, house chores and social engagements. From being so conditioned into a life of doing, constantly striving for recognition and feeling good enough, we suffer from the lack of ever getting there. The chase becomes the life, and the suffering represents the lost path. Being happy is natural, and being healthy is too.

It is clear as day, the burden we have created for our body and soul, and it is dark as night, the consequence that we suffer.

It is no longer natural to spend the day outside, and a great part of the world is living without being exposed to sunshine for months at the time. Too many have an indoor job, leaving them completely depleted of the life-giving sunshine we all need so much. Nature is perfect in creation, and we are a part of that perfection. Our houses are getting larger, and we go to health clubs to exercise. Instead of being outside where we would gain healing, restoration and fresh air, we stuff ourselves in these health clubs and fitness centers.

Our God given fresh air has also been polluted by chemtrails and most people are not even aware of this fact. Long-lasting trails left in the sky by high-flying aircrafts are called chemtrails, and are believed to be chemical or biological agents deliberately sprayed into our skies. This is a topic of much interest and controversy. You see, normal contrails dissipate relatively quickly, chemtrails do not. They leave a veil and then clouds, blocking sunlight. Fresh air is our lifeline. We are dependent on it.

Another topic of great concern for our health is vaccines. We are being bombarded with vaccine options and scare tactics, leaving us lost and in fear of living in a pure and natural way. We have been lead to believe that we need living viruses and bacteria, formaldehyde, mercury, human albumin, toxic levels of aluminum and much more, to protect our health. Instead, now we are looking at autism and neurological damage as a very possible effect of our acceptance of these shots. We are submitting our children to pure poison, and nature was never about us having to do anything to poison ourselves, never. This is how far we have strayed, and this is how numbed down we have gotten. This has become our normal, in this world where true health no longer seems to be on the agenda. I am not for one moment hesitant to say that vaccines are a hazard to our health. There are countless books written on the topic. And the helpless parents of children that change and never regain their health after their vaccinations are heartbreaking to read about. I honor Jenny McCarthy for being a spokesperson and a role model for vaccinated autistic children. She healed her son from vaccine induced autism. Yes, you heard me, autism! [1]

Our so-called health system is based on chemicals and surgery, on poisons, taking out what is not working, and repairing by instruments. Always looking at the symptom, finding remedy by suppressing the symptoms, not true healing. A good surgeon is a true blessing, and

---

[1] "Louder than words: A Mother's Journey in Healing Autism", Jenny McCarthy 2008

the Emergency rooms save lives every single minute of the day. There is a place for all trauma and acute life-saving procedures, but the suppressing of symptoms we can do without. When you or anyone is labeled chronic, trouble is ahead. The body is in the need of healing, and the truth is now going to be hidden and buried.

Always looking for the magic pill, keeps us in the dark. It keeps us away from true health. We are sick because we stopped listening to our bodies, and fell for the marketed easy-fix-pill.

So, you see, we need not wonder why we are sick, but rather spend our time and energy looking towards health and vitality. It is right under our noses, as it always was. We were never meant to be sick, it is not natural. When we are hurt, and we know that accidents *do* happen, we can still do our very best to live in harmony with nature and the Creation.

We need to look towards restoring our health, not the masking of symptoms. We are standing in line, holding out our hands for a pill. The pill that locks you in its prison, wanting and needing more. What we do not know can hurt us big time. The Health Food field has continued down this road of fixing symptoms, by producing isolates in form of chemically made vitamins and minerals. The body does not do isolates. Nature is perfect, and there are no isolates in nature. Our minds are affecting our ability to think, one might say, or our ability to reason. Health has become the largest industry in the world, and sadly Mr. Money is the captain of the ship. The ship is sinking, and we are all watching it go under.

> *We are sick because we gave away our authority,*
> *We are sick because we forgot that we are sovereign beings,*
> *We are sick because we lost our quest for true health,*
> *We are sick because we accepted the labels of dis-ease,*
> *We are sick from not daring to step out of the norm, and*
> *we are sick because we lost our faith in God and nature.*

As we have been misled and misguided, confusion and lack of self-love has also become a great obstacle to overcome when it comes to true health. By that I mean that not loving ourselves is why we are not treating ourselves with the best care that there is. This lack of self-love is what allows us to keep hurting and punishing ourselves. We need to realize that we are all worth it. We are all worth having healthy, amazing lives. It's natural to be healthy, and happiness is a choice. *You* are worth it, every single bit of it. Every day, walking towards the life that you desire, you will realize that you are worthy. You just need to know that you want it, to start walking. And you just need to keep putting one foot in front of the other to get there. That is how we accomplish anything. One day at the time. One step, one bite, one thought and one spoken word at the time.

There was never anything wrong with who we were, or the way that we were meant to live. We became too smart, too greedy and too caught up in our minds to see where we were heading. *Now* we see, and now we know. When we know better, we can do better!

Chapter 3

Health is simple

Health was never complicated, and to understand how the body works, in general, is not hard. To be able to see the larger picture and to understand the basics of what makes or breaks our health, is not rocket-science. Not if we don`t want it to be. To be able to support the body in healing and regeneration, we need to understand the basic principles of healing. Let us look at the body using some simple analogies: The body consists of two major fluids, blood and lymph. There are some great ways to easily explain how this more than fantastic and perfect organism, our body, functions. Always doing its best to heal and regenerate, the body will do what is needed to do just that.

I like to look at the body as a built-for-success and regenerating fish tank. A truly smart ecosystem fish tank. It has everything it needs for everything in it to be healthy and happy. Each little fish represents a cell in the body, all 100 trillion of them, give or take. The reason we use this analogy is that the fish have to do what every cell in the body does.

They have to:

- *Eat*
- *Poop*
- *Perform their tasks*

Look at the water in our fish tank. For the fish to be happy and up for their everyday tasks and chores, the water they live and swim in needs to be in perfect condition. It needs to be slightly alkaline, it needs to have the perfect pH for the fish to be healthy and strong.[2]

Our interstitial fluids, being lymph and blood, needs to be this perfect water for our cells/fish to live in. See the water in the tank as our interstitial fluids, the water our cells have to live in. Let us imagine what happens when the fish ingest too much acids, and have to eliminate more than the tank is capable of cleaning up. The waste starts to accumulate in the tank, and the fish are left swimming around in their own poop. This is acidic burning hot poop, and it's burning everything within the tank. When our eliminative organs cannot handle the amount of waste produced from our cells and our toxic accumulation, they are left, like the fish, swimming in extremely dangerous and corrosive waters. Happiness has left the tank, and the gassy stench is unbearable. When we are ingesting to many hurtful foods and chemicals, our cells are left bathing in a hostile environment.

The tank itself will try to protect the fish the best way it can. By retaining more water, it can dilute the acids. In the body, we call this edema. Next the inflammation, bloating and gas comes in to play. Unfortunately, this first attempt to protect the fish will not be enough if the fish keep on eating more acids, pooping more and excreting more toxic burning

---

[2] pH is a measure of the hydrogen ion concentration of a solution. Solutions with a high concentration of hydrogen ions have a low pH and solutions with a low concentrations of H+ ions have a high pH. We measure from 1 to 13 in general, 7pH being neutral. Anything below being acidic, and above being alkaline.

Hilde Larsen

waste. The tank becomes a host for bacteria, viruses and fungus. They all love this new acidic water. Our body would not have a problem with any of these if the water was clean.

The fungus, parasites and bacteria are now having a party, making a real mess and disturbance. The fish need to find livable water, so they go after the calming alkaline minerals. This is a life and death situation, as fish are starting to suffocate, burn, and see some real damage to their health. The soothing base minerals are what they crave. These minerals are our building blocks, and they are now being pulled from wherever the cells can find them. The popular and easy to access calcium, is now being pulled from the structure of the tank itself. To save our cells, and to keep our blood alkaline, in the perfect pH balance, calcium is being drawn from our bones and tissue. As you can imagine, this will really hurt the structure of the tank, our bodies. The building-blocks of the tank are now fewer, and it becomes fragile and weak. Now, we are seeing brittle bones, osteoporosis, varicose veins and more. We are experiencing symptoms of systemic acidosis. This whole process is as hard on the filtering system of this tank, as it is on our physical filtering system. The whole sewer system is impaired, and the waste is no longer carried out as it should be.

As the quality of the water keeps deteriorating, the fish keep suffering, and the tank itself is falling apart. This is not a happy fish tank anymore. A lot of pain and suffering is present, and the tank needs to be even more creative to save its fish and it`s structure. Cholesterol is created to buffer and absorb all the acids that are floating around. More and more cholesterol is put out, but it is still not enough. This is not a solid plan, as this cholesterol is also very disturbing to all of the important functions in the tank/the organs of the body. They are not able to function as they should, and that is creating a whole new problem in our fish tank. The sewer system is now totally backed up. The main filtering unit, called the kidneys, are suffering and can't do their job. They're inflamed and eroded from all the acids, and more trouble lies ahead. What will happen to all that waste?

Everywhere, slime is building up, hardening, creating mucus. The smell and the gasses are creating a tank ready to explode! The fish are in fish hell. They are suffering and dying. No happiness to be found, and something really has to give. The tank is out of ideas, and needs serious help. It has a massive amount of unhappy fish floating around, not able to do their job. Water retention has been tried, inflammation is present, cholesterol is there, and still, not enough. The tank is shutting down. The fish are usually very strong, operating at an amazing level of efficiency and speed. Always eager and happy, so this is a sad scenario. Entire fish generations are suffering. As they give birth to baby fish they are seeing mutation, as they are handing down their genetics to their little ones.

No matter what chemicals are being thrown in to the tank to fix the symptoms, the malfunctioning processes, the problem, stays the same. The fish are still pooping, and the waste is still building. More chemicals added, means more acids in the tank, and the environment is not getting any better. Not until the caregiver of the tank realizes that the problem is in the water, can remedy be on its way. By simply cleaning out the filtering system, and at the same time giving the fish non-toxic food, creating less waste, the tank starts to clean itself like it was designed to do. During the cleaning process, the water retention, the inflammation and the cholesterol, all go away. The fish are all helping to put the calcium back to strengthen the structure, and life is good in Fish-tank Village.

Clean water, happy fish. Clean body, happy cells.

In other words, by simplifying we can easily understand what we need to address when we are dealing with less than optimal health. We have two major fluids in the body, blood and lymph. We can see the blood as being the kitchen in the body. It is the supplier of nutrients to all the cells. So, you can imagine how important it is to have clean blood. We need a clean kitchen. The blood also needs to stay alkaline, it needs to stay at a perfect pH of 7.34. When that changes, we lose. To keep us up and running, alive and well, the body will do anything in its power to make sure the blood stays balanced. When too many acids are present, it will still make sure that the blood stays within its perfect pH. It will do so by drawing alkaline minerals from the bone and tissue. The blood needs to stay in balance, so the rest of the body will have to suffer. This is when we see the loss of the alkaline minerals from bone and tissue. When acids take over, cells are not happy, and when cells are not happy, *we* are not happy.

The body is a perfectly designed self-healing mechanism. Like the fish tank, it is also self-cleansing and therefore has a sewer system, the lymphatic system. Every cell in the human body needs to eat and poop. Yes, like you and me, and the fish, they are no different. The waste is carried from the cells via the lymphatic system, to the eliminative organs. The waste needs to come out, all of it. If the acids stay in, we are in pain, and if acids win, we lose. This is what we are all experiencing when we are feeling loss of health. All so-called dis-ease, comes from not eliminating waste. The internal terrain is everything, and no waste-building stagnant lymphatic system will have happy, thriving, regenerating cells. This stagnant lymph, the acids, the toxins, are all directly linked to a downhill spiral of ill health. There are thousands of small septic tanks called lymph nodes throughout the body. They are little holding tanks, or "septic tanks," that are used by the lymph system to filter and destroy pathogens, toxins, antigens, etc. You might have experienced them being full and hardened, a sign of stagnant lymph and the body working hard to move the waste along. The lymphatic system dumps its waste in its septic tanks, to be processed for further elimination. Acidosis comes from acid forming food, anger, fear and stress.[3]

Let us take this a little further, without complicating everything. Let's keep it really simple, as we only need to know the basics of

---

[3] "The Detox Miracle Sourcebook", Dr. Robert Morse ND 2004

how we are holding on to sickness, and how to set the stage for a successful healing mission. There are four major processes that needs to take place for a body to be able to thrive;

First of all, we need to digest the food that we are eating to be able to absorb its nutrients. A good digestion needs enzymes and the proper digestive acids, and we know that digestion starts in the mouth. We chew and swallow, then absorb through the villi of the small and large intestines. This means that we need a clean GI tract (gastrointestinal tract) to absorb our nutrients. Now we need to utilize what we have absorbed. This is where the blood comes in. After involving the liver and glands for hormones, the blood carries the nutrition to every cell. Now, we are getting to the elimination. Most of what we put in, must come out. Again, the main problem that we see is lack of proper elimination. We are clogged up, congested and overly acidic. The main eliminative organs are the skin, the lungs, the kidneys and the colon.

Digestion, absorption, utilization, and elimination.

Here is another analogy that I like to use. The body is like a city we might also say. The immune and lymphatic systems act like a police force and a sanitation department. They pick up the trash from each house/cell in the city. Depending on the lifestyle within each household, the type of waste and the amount of it will vary. The lymph system, along with its immune cells, has the job of protecting and keeping the body clean. Many foods that people routinely eat, clog up this system, and we know what happens then. The waste is not being picked up, and it becomes smelly, burning, gassy and painful to be around. So, there you go, we need to take the waste from the house to the dumping ground. We need to clean the septic tanks, and we need every part of the process to flow on a daily basis.

The glands are the government, and they control almost everything. This is why gland health is so important, and why so many of our symptoms arise from weakened glands. What will weaken a gland? Acids, mucus, stagnant lymph around the gland. So again, when waste is not carried out, everything hurts. The whole village, the tank, the body, it hurts. We can look at the nervous system as the electricians of the body, keeping everything fired up. Without any power, everything shuts down. Any weak organ or gland most often also has a weak state from birth, but it does not matter. The body will regenerate anything, when it is given a chance.

The kidneys are supposed to filter out the lymphatic waste, and sadly, for most of us, that is not what they are able to do. When the kidneys suffer, we suffer. I tell people to pee in a jar. If you are seeing urine clear as day, and no sediments floating around, you are not filtering.

We can see that without proper elimination we are in big trouble. The adrenals are a major key to our health, as they sit on top of the kidneys, which again, filter out lymphatic waste. This function is crucial to a healthy body, yet we hear very little about these little glands. We know the lymphatic system is the sewer system of the body, and if we do not get the cellular and the metabolic waste out, we will burn from the acids. This is called dis-ease, or an acidic body. Any kind of stress, emotional or physical, will put a strain on the adrenal glands. When eating meat, we are consuming the animals' stored adrenalin, which will of course stress our adrenals. We have all heard of adrenal fatigue, but did you know that another sign of weak and tired adrenals is anxiety? Adrenal and kidney "failure" is the root-cause of most dis-eases, as they are the key to carrying out the lymphatic waste.

We are made of about a hundred trillion cells and two major fluids, blood and lymph. The blood feeds, the lymph cleans. Feeding the cells will not create optimal health, without cleaning out the sewage.

The bottom line is this; The majority of lymphatic waste should be filtered out by our kidneys. This is mostly visible waste, and we can see it with the naked eye. Wait a minute, are we not told that a clear urine is a healthy one? Well, the truth is that the urine should contain particles, strings, or be cloudy from lymphatic waste. This is very simple to check by peeing in a jar. Not the typical thing to do, but very effective and revealing. We are not looking at the color, as that will simply change by how much liquid we have consumed, we are looking for what we refer to as sediment. Sediment will look like stringy mucus strains, floating snow-globe particles or just general cloudiness. Most likely, when you are not of great health, the kidneys are not filtering and there is serious work to be done. The skin being the third kidney, will often let you know how your kidneys are doing also. It has to eliminate lymphatic waste on behalf of the un-filtering kidneys. The tube is closed, so the skin must eliminate. As long as we keep creating and ingesting more waste, we are building and holding on to more dis-ease creating acids.

The answer to any health concern is always alkalization, detoxification and regeneration!

Detoxification is an art, and a way of letting the body get rid of the waste that is burning and damaging the cells. I have found through my studying that the more simply I looked at the body, the more I was able to see what it needed to heal. It was never about the symptoms - it was always about a system.

When looking at health and healing, the food we consume will play a major role. There is no getting around it. We have a species specific diet, like every other creature on this planet. We are primates. What we are witnessing is what happens when we really, I mean *really* move away from that, and feed our bodies dead and altered chemistry. All animals that are taken off their natural diet get sick. Animals in the care of humans often get dis-eased, just like we do. Wild animals don't, how could they? Something to think about? What we are eating is killing us. Period! When we look around, and start counting those over 50 not taking any pills, having a happy, positive, strong, athletic, healthy, glowing, natural body, they are few and far between. We could even start counting those over 30, and have a hard time finding someone with no glasses, no digestive issues, skin issues, weight issues or emotional imbalances. I used to view this as normal. I bought into the idea that it is natural to get old and sick, that it is natural to have aches and pain. I tell you, the truth is very far from it.

Children are now being diagnosed with what used to be old peoples dis-eases. That in itself should get the big red light to go on for all of us. Their weakened handed-down glands and organs, together with a poor diet, contributes to ill-health and depression. Un-clean water, lack of movement, sunshine, lack of sleep and rest, are all factors that rob the body of health. Every generation is getting weaker. We are the ones passing those weak genes onto our children, so let us take responsibility by healing our bodies and strengthening our organs and glands. Through detoxification, alkalization, hydration and regeneration, we can restore what nature has so perfectly created. What we put in our mouths, what we feed our cells, what vibration we choose to reside in, will lead us to the rest of our choices.

What we do not eliminate we accumulate.

By changing what we are putting in our mouths, we are changing the whole chemistry of the body. We are setting the stage for our cells' health. And together with making sure our eliminating organs are happy, with a strong functioning filtering system and sewer system, we are all set! We are only as healthy as our ability to eliminate waste, and once what we don`t need is able to come out, health will come in. The key to health and longevity is not the diet, not in itself, and not in the sense that most people think. It was never about the food, it is about the detoxification, alkalization, absorption, elimination and regeneration. It is about the healing that takes place when the body is functioning as it should. We know the body is a self-healer. We experience that every time we cut ourselves with a knife. The body will rush to stop the bleeding and to heal the wound. When we take out the garbage even old scars heal. Seriously, old scars fade and heal.

Every part of the body is ready to do the same, to heal and to regenerate. It is only obstructed and set back by weakened organs and glands, poor diet choices and stress. This leads to the only condition there really is, and that is over-acidity, all from the lack of elimination of molds, parasites, sulfur, viruses, chemicals, damaged cells, and other toxins. We are so full of shit, and we are living it. Once we are clean, the body will naturally start to regenerate weakened and damaged tissue, even inherited weaknesses will be taken care of. How amazing is that? By letting go of the urge to chase symptoms, and further weakening the system with nasty chemical drugs, we are on the same team as our bodies. The winning team of health and rejuvenation. Suppressing anything will never lead to anything good. Believe me, I have been there, done that, and almost died in the process. We need to break free from the treatment-based thinking. It was *never* about the germs or the bacteria. It is about the culturing medium, the terrain. Truth is simple, and *health* is simple!

Yes, we need nutrition, and yes many other factors come into play, but once we get this simple key covered, the rest will follow. Once we realize that our lymphatic system, the carrier of waste, holds such a power when it comes to our health, we are on our way. We need to get out of the way and let the body do what it was designed to do.

Nature is perfect, and we need to deal with it! *We* are meant to be healthy, and we need to deal with that also by taking charge of our whole being and life. How well we heal depends on how well we are ready to take full charge and responsibility. That includes letting go and letting flow.

Are you ready?

Chapter 4

Self sabotage

Now that we know why we are sick, we are ready to get to work. All we need is a plan, and we are all set for success, right? It sounds easy, and it really would be, if we had no brain. Our wonderful, amazing, sabotaging, remembering brain is often holding us back. So, before we get to the more practical part, let's make sure you are not sabotaging your own ability to move forward. I know this sounds strange, but bear with me.

I believe that everyone wants to be healthy and happy. No one chooses ill health and pain consciously. I have never met anyone who will state that they would like to stay sick, yet I have met many that are not willing to, or are reluctant to do what is needed for positive change to occur. Two different things in a sense, but not really. First of all, the conscious mind is only the tip of the iceberg when it comes to what we are thinking and telling ourselves. Our programming, our understanding of life, old memories and conditions, are all present in this enormous databank - the subconscious mind. It has it all recorded, and it knows more about what you believe than your awakened state ever will. Only through our actions and our experiences can we truly see what our beliefs are. We act and live according to what we have been conditioned to believe, and that might not always be as it seems. We might have beliefs we did not even know we had. How interesting is that?

So, what does this have to do with health and healing you might ask? Well, look at it this way; Here you are, eager and willing to do what it takes to reclaim your health, yet still, you keep slipping, falling off the protocol. It simply feels like even though you really want to do this, you keep messing it up. You keep getting in your own way, so to speak. That is what we call self-sabotage. It might be your subconscious mind playing a trick or two on you, and being aware of this scenario can be of enormous help moving forward. Self-sabotage simply means standing in your own way.

Our subconscious belief system might show up as a false identity, and our lives are sabotaged by our own inner thought-forms. By exploring how we live and act, we might find that we are living a typical pattern of self-sabotage.

The not-being-worthy identity:

A very common subconscious belief that I have seen surfacing for many, is the "I do not deserve to get well"-pattern. It emanates from the lack of self-love. While deep down, you do not believe that you deserve to get well, you will keep doing things that will make that manifest as a truth. That way, you were right. Even though this is a subconscious belief pattern, it might be so strong, that it shows up in your conscious thinking as well. The feeling of unworthiness comes from holding on to old hurts. As a child, you might have been scolded and abused, physically or mentally. A child will believe that it does not deserve any better than what is, and this will be imprinted as a truth until the spell is broken. As the child grows, every time the same pattern of abuse or critique appears, it validates the already known inner truth.

31

A true longing for change, for healing and freedom is still there, even though the subconscious mind is playing the same old song on constant repeat. This constant underlying repetition is what manifests as frustration and the feeling of being a failure. Your soul and your spirit knows that you are worthy, and that health and abundance is for you, me, and all of us to live and breathe. What you know, and what you are programmed to believe, is not in balance, and inner chaos will arise. Even though your inner belief system is telling you that you are not worthy of this amazing health that you so long for, you consciously might want it more than anything.

A very typical way for this self-sabotage to manifest is as a self-created, very valid-looking obstacle. You will not reach your goal because you found that this was not the right time for you. Your husband lost his job, your children are too young, and they need you to do what is expected for them. This really is not the best time to take care of *you – "It did not work out, because I did not have a car at the time, and could not get what I needed for my juicing".* The stories are endless, and all valid. They make sense as something the conscious mind can sort of believe, as the subconscious mind keeps playing the story of your life. The truth is though, that nothing, and I mean nothing will stand in your way once you are ready. No-thing. Once that tape is turned off and replaced, none of these reasons will feel valid anymore.

Make this the time to forgive everything. Make this the now *that you have been waiting for. No matter what you have experienced, now is the time to let it all go. You are worthy, and only by forgiving are you showing yourself that. Forgiveness is an act of self-love. It is recognizing that we are soul-beings.*

Absolutely every single thing that you think, becomes truth to your cells, meaning they listen and they believe. What we are telling our cells, that we do not know we are telling our cells, is the tricky part. More on that later.

The fear of the new identity:

Another aspect to have in mind when we are dealing with self-sabotage is the "fear of losing what we know"-pattern. It is the flip side to change, so to speak. It is the direct opposite of inviting in the change that is needed, this fear of losing what we already have.

Once we have made the decision that we are ready to go, to move forward, and to walk towards health, we know that change will be ahead. We know that we will have to change something. That is logical. The intellect knows that the protocol of eating and living will be different, and the conscious mind is ready.

Then, even if what we have been experiencing is not good for us, it's hurting us even, it is still what we know. Even if we are in an abusive relationship, and we *know* that we are, it is what we are familiar with. Breaking free means uncertainty, and insecurity. The obvious scenario is that we would rather stay in pain, in fear of the unknown. I know, it really does not make sense, but for those that are living by their inner-beliefs of not being strong enough, or smart enough to be on their own, this is very real. This pattern arises from the understanding of not being able to take care for ourselves. This is a very typical one, and is also why we see so many relationships built on dependency. We are all sovereign beings, and it is absolutely natural to take care of oneself. Together we stand, yet we are all alone. All together in support and compassion for each other, yet still as separate beings.

Out of fear of losing that familiarity, we can self-sabotage any real progress that will make us leave the old. We might feel we are heading for major life changes like breaking out of a relationship or a walking away from a job. Every aspect of our life affects our health. A typical scenario might be that you decide you are fine as you are. There was no need for any major change after all. You are fine. Your health is so much better now, it was all just a false alarm. Nothing to worry about, you are fine. No change needed.

Although fear is never a constructive energy, nor is it a healing one, it can show us a lot about what our belief system is all about. If you sense that there is any fear at all connected with doing what you *know* you need to do to get better, you are ready to work on your freedom.

The attention identity:

Being sick, might have given you more attention, that has led to the feeling of being loved. This pattern is most definitely imprinted in our early childhood. The experience of getting more attention and love, will stay with us, and we will continue to use the same patterns into our adult lives. A child will do what it feels it needs to do, to feel loved and accepted, and if a need was fulfilled when health was impaired, the pattern will stick for life. This does not mean that to get attention you are making yourself sick, not at all, but not being healthy will be associated with something that feels familiar and safe. That way, once you change your health for the better, you might feel unsafe, and fall back to the old comfort zone. Some relationships are built on this energy. The pattern of one being the needy and one being the servant, the caregiver. The partner who is in need of care, might feel extra important or seen, while the caregiver feels there is need for them.

The fear of loss is also present in this pattern and belief-system. *"If I get well, he will no longer need to be here, and he will leave me."* The fear of not being loved for who you are, has made you, through your experience as a child, holding on to pain and dis-ease, so that someone will care for you, and therefore love you. The self-sabotage might sound like this: *"Nothing works for me. I have tried everything, and nothing works"*. This will draw in even more of the compassionate attention that you believe that you need. The truth is that you do not need any bodily dis-function, or anything else for that matter, to get the attention that you need. By being the radiant, healthy, shiny you that you were meant to be, there will be no need for anything else. You are it. You are what will attract to you what you believe that *you* are.

The dis-ease identity:

Without even knowing it, you might be holding on to a dis-ease as an identity. For example, that you feel like your chronic diagnosis is serving you in some way. How in the world would being sick serve anybody, you might ask? *"All I want is to get well, and there is no way being sick would serve me or anyone."* Well, I am afraid there could be. A number of things might be lingering as a subconscious belief and understanding. These are beliefs that will keep you locked in your current situation, clinging to what is, even if it is suffering and pain. Remember, these are most often unconscious patterns, not something you are choosing in the awake state. Unconscious meaning hidden to us, but often we can still feel the pattern when awareness is brought to the situation.

This very common pattern will manifest as a need to talk about the dis-ease, and about the body in general. You will notice that some people have the desire to keep telling their story. They have an eagerness to talk about their suffering. It has become their identity. They might be the head of a diagnosis organization or a chronic dis-ease forum. They might be on dis-ability and are feeling locked into the lifestyle. Their friends and colleagues are of the same mindset and understanding, and getting healthy will feel like a loss. Getting healthy might even feel as a deceit. It might feel like they are turning their back on their friends and followers, their tribe and their family.

This programming comes from the need to belong. We all need to feel that we belong, and when we have not had that feeling growing up, we will search for it in any community or situation. Once we find it, as it is one of the basic humans needs, it is very hard to let it go. We tend to want to stand by our tribe no matter what. They are the ones that have stuck by us, and have taken us in. We've felt welcomed and loved. The dis-ease might even be our livelihood now, our business. A very good and sane reason to hold on to it, now that it is "working" for us. Our perceived identity is worth holding onto for our dear lives, and the true and devastating story is that that is exactly what we do.

Every single one of us will have one or several of these patterns lingering within our great mind. I am sorry to say that none of us are very special for recognizing these belief systems. I am sure that you recognize a part of you in some of the above situations. To be aware is always the first step, and I want to inspire you to take a good look at your attachment to your current health situation.

This is but a brief introduction, but for me a very important topic to introduce, as mind is always over matter. I am sure you have heard the expression, *mind over matter.* It means that our mind is powerful beyond our cells, and that by using its power we can change almost anything. The mind will win every single time, although it is not quite that black and white. Be aware of your reactions to a new, amazing, healing, regenerating and soul-loving journey, and the self-sabotage will not be an issue. *You* are the one in charge, and you can absolutely override any old record. As long as you know that it's there, you are the boss of the playlist.

Here are some hidden benefits you might perceive from being so-called chronically sick:

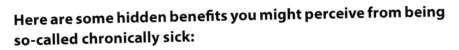

- You are getting more attention from your partner.
- You are finally getting the rest that you need.
- You can say no to any event that you would rather not attend.
- You do not have to do the job you did not enjoy.
- People are more compassionate towards you.
- You have found community with people that are suffering the same way that you are.

- You love all the help that people are offering you.
- Finally, you do not have to "perform".

For anyone that is ready to take full charge of their life and health, addressing the self-sabotage, this is a great place to start. Take a good look at your inner beliefs and self-talk. If you are sensing that you might have a reason to hold on to your current situation, work on letting that go. You no longer need to be, do, or say anything to be loved and appreciated. Just by being you, the Universe is celebrating. It is doing the happy dance just because you are being right here. The fact that you are here, right now, breathing and living, is worth a celebration. You deserve great health, we all do. There is no reason what so ever, that would validate any suffering or pain. This is the time to let go of those old patterns, and you will.

Stand in front of the mirror every day, look into your beautiful face and say:

- I deserve health
- Being healthy is what is best for me
- I will never need to be sick again
- I love myself
- I love getting healthy and free
- I can choose what to do with my life
- Being healthy is true freedom
- It is safe to be strong and fit
- I am always loved, no matter what

All self-sabotage is born from the misbelief that we are less-than, not good enough, do not deserve and are not worthy of love and abundance. We carry with us the pattern that reflects back to us what we believe. All depending on which types of situations we have experienced from the early part of our lives, those same patterns are still ruling. Here is another example:

You never seem to be able to stick with a diet plan, or an exercise regime for that matter. Every time, you fall back on the old habits, and you never seem to be able to stick with it and to follow through. You are used to "failing" and you even tell others this – "*I do not have the same willpower that you do. I am never able to stay on such strict diets. I have no idea how you do it*". Every time when it seems like you are going to make it, something happens that gives you a valid reason to stop. It can be a stressful event, an invitation, or the likes. Anything that will make falling off the wagon okay, for you, and for those around you. The truth is that it will make what you believe about yourself true. What you believe will be true, you *always* fail, and you *knew* it would happen. These patterns are hard to fully see, because the one living with the pattern, has a trustworthy story, and the self-sabotage is covered by a true struggle. The magic in realizing we are in fact sabotaging ourselves by holding on to old belief-systems, is the freedom that comes from letting go. When we know, we can change something. We can start to let go of the imprints that false and destructive thoughts create, and open up a whole new pathway of supporting beliefs. We can harvest the fruits of self-love and self-care, and experience that doing what is best for us is easy. It is natural and joyful.

It does not matter if you believe you can, or you believe you cannot, either way you will be right.

We can't change the past. Yet, as adults we can identify the self-sabotaging thoughts and actions that we've internalized. We can consciously choose to act against them. When we fall victim to our critical inner voice, and get sucked in by its deceiving directives, self-sabotaging is a fact. The actions we then take are always self-limiting and not of our highest potential. Every day we need to collect our thoughts, and to do so carefully. We are our own protectors of thought, and will always live what we believe. Cause and effect. We can control our thoughts, and by learning how we really think, how we are subconsciously thinking, we can dive into changing the destructive patterns.

The subconscious mind can be reprogrammed, and every single day, it is. By the way that we live and think, we are telling our inner being what we really believe in. By walking in the direction of change, and at the same time changing our conscious thoughts, we are slowly but steadily changing from within. This is the only way true change will ever happen. I will talk more about this in a later chapter, so get ready to hit the reset button!

You are worthy and you are ready. This is the time to fearlessly let it all go, all of what has been holding you back. It does not matter if it's the fear of change, the fear of not being able to have pizza or coffee, or if it's the fear of getting well itself. You better get ready, because you have officially been poked. You have been called, this is your time to roll. Go get it!

> **"Never let the fear of change stop you from doing anything. Change is inevitable, and only when we become fearless, life becomes limitless." - Hilde**

Chapter 5

Taking full responsibility

To be the one who is making all the decisions, and who is in charge and on top of everything must be fantastic! We all want that, right? Well, yes and no. Most of us, the vast majority of people out there will answer; *"Yes, of course, not only do I want to be in charge of my own life, but I am!"* Oh, really?

First of all, what does it mean to take full responsibility, and why would I boldly state that most of us are *not*? I mean, you *will* be, as you will certainly get there by taking back your health and power. You see, what we perceive as being in charge, might not be, not really. From simply living in the Western world, having been born and raised in a society that breeds followers, we are conditioned to follow. We are conditioned to give away our power to an outside authority. When we are not feeling good, we go to the doctor. We want someone to take charge and to make us feel better. Sometimes calling on those that have an expertize is absolutely necessary, but that is a different scenario. To take responsibility does not mean to never seek help or guidance. No man is an island, and together we are stronger. We stand together, yet alone. What I am getting at is the *power* that we give to someone, while stepping back in ignorance and lack of interest. When your body is not functioning optimally, or any other part of your life is not running smoothly, it is *your* business. Everything concerning our lives is *our* business. There is never anyone to blame for our experiences, and even if we try, over and over, we are the ones living with our choices.

I believed that I was in charge of me my whole adult life, until I realized that I could not have been more wrong. I had given my power away to doctors, friends, my partner and everything that was holding me back. I had given it away to old hurts and anger, to frustration and sickness.

I was driven by what I believed I was supposed to do, and how I was supposed to act. I believed what I was told by "authorities", about what was good for me and what was not. I am sure you know what I mean when I say: I cared what others thought of me, and I tried to fit in and to be accepted by the crowd. I wanted to please and to be acknowledged by others, and I lost my power in doing so.

When everything fell apart, and my body was too sick to function, truth revealed itself to me. A long process of letting go of old conditioning started. I could see clearly that I had been giving away my inner power, and that I had not been true to myself. My wanting to please and perform had kept me from living an authentic heart-felt life in peace with me and the Creation.

"We are who we choose to become, and every second of every day holds the potential to take charge of our own destiny." Hilde

Taking charge and full responsibility for *you* and your life, means that you are now being true to yourself and your life-purpose. It also means that you are taking charge of everything about your life, and you can see that there never was or is anyone but yourself to blame for anything that you experience. It means that no matter what you are living right now, you know it is up to you to change it. It is always up to you.

> **Self-empowerment is about taking charge and responsibility. Through feeling powerful one becomes fearless. When one becomes fearless, life becomes limitless.**

Taking charge of your life is the single most important shift of perception towards living a life free from suffering and despair. Yes, a shift of perception. Giving away your power is a mindset. Every time we feel disempowered, we have freely given away our own power. That means that every time you feel frustrated or angry about something that anyone else said or did, you have given it away. What others say or do, has nothing to do with you. You hold the key to your own emotions. You are the boss of your inner terrain, physically, mentally and emotionally. Everything you do, say, think or feel is 100% your own responsibility. Now *that* is true freedom!

When we change and take charge, we are owning our whole life; past, present and future. To change the future, we have to change our perception of the past. By realizing that even our past is for us to embrace and take responsibility for, a shift happens. You have become the authority instead of giving that power to someone else. Every time we give someone the opportunity to change our emotions and our feelings, we are giving them power, making them the boss. It does not matter what the situation is, if it has been, or if it is what you believe it is going to be. It's all about you, about your readiness to own it all. You *are* the most powerful being in your life, and the one that holds the key to change everything.

Taking charge means *taking full responsibility. We have been led to believe that others are responsible, and that they know better. We have been taken off the job as the one who knows what is best for us, and we are disconnected from our inner knowing.*

Think of it this way. If you are the one that knows what is best for you, and no one else could ever be to blame for anything that you experience, wouldn`t you like yourself to be in charge? I would most certainly like to be the one that was on top of my game, if I was the one living my life. I realized that I was the one that had created the situation, and only I could choose to change it.

Signs that you are in charge of your life:

You know that it is you that has to change, to change anything in your life.

Your health becomes your own responsibility.

Educating yourself and thinking for yourself becomes a priority.

Being true to yourself first becomes natural.

You make choices based on your own inner guidance and research.

What other people think, is no longer of importance.

You have a strong sense of who you are and where you are going.

Fear is no longer the driving-force of your life.

You are taking action towards your goals.

You have no need to follow anyone, blame anyone or point fingers at anyone.

Being the boss of your own life, feels like true freedom.

You never feel like a victim.

You realize how amazing you are just being you.

Life is so much better when you *know* that you are the one in charge of your life. Even when I was at my sickest, in pain and despair, knowing that I held the power to change, changed everything.

Becoming one`s own authority is freeing and liberating. It sets the stage for a whole different story. It comes with limitless opportunities and no strings attached. There are no hidden agendas and there is no one to impress or seek approval from.

Being one`s own authority simply means to be the one that is responsible for everything. Absolutely everything.

The true freedom that follows is the key to true healing. When we no longer seek validation from anyone but ourselves, we leave the need to perform. We leave the stage that has kept us preforming for acceptance and acknowledgement. What a big word that is, acknowledgement. When you are truly the boss of your own life and health, you will never seek that big word again. You will never seek validation, or have the need to follow the crowd. The eagerness to live from the heart, in sync with your own truth, will leave no room for interference.

Taking full responsibility means that you acknowledge that it is up to *you* to take care of you, and no matter where you are right now, *you* hold the power to change that.

A few tips on how to take charge of your life:

1. **Make a choice.** Decide that you are the boss of your life, and that only you can do what is needed to live the life you want and need. Once you make a decision, stick with it, and keep your focus. Give yourself time, and realize that everything is going to be ok.

2. **Be the authority.** We are so used to listening to others, that hearing our own voice can be hard. Let go of needing

everybody's opinion and validation, and listen more to *you*. This does not mean that you will not need advice and guidance, but never give the power away, and always follow your own intuition. Make your own decisions, no matter what others might think or say.

3. **Get educated.** It is important to do your own research about any topic that involves your life. There are so many opinions out there, and so much information, only you can find what resonates with you. You are the one that will live the outcome of every decision you make, so make sure you are in charge of it.

4. **Take action.** Every transformation requires action. We can think all the positive thoughts we want, but without action there is no progress. Get going, and once you take a stand, once you know what you want, walk towards it, and do not be afraid of failure. Act like you mean it.

5. **Be your own cheerleader.** Be your own best friend and support. Speak highly of yourself, and think empowering thoughts. Try to eliminate any complaining, and be proud that you are taking charge and being the boss of your life. Once you see how valuable you are, you also see the same in others. This means you can be a great support for others as well.

6. **Let go of the past.** Letting go of anything that is holding you back will make a huge shift in your ability to move forward. The past has no bearing on the future or the now, if we do not carry it with us. The past can be obstructing to the flow and it's like carrying a heavy luggage filled with something you do not want to own. Once you are free from any burden of past experiences, the freedom will empower you to make better decisions in the now.

7. **Start today!** The only time and the best time is always now. Procrastination takes you nowhere, it is merely a resistance to change. Analyze why you would resist doing what needs to be done, and work on setting goals for your life and your health today.

You are the one that is living your life, and giving away any form of authority is like saying you do not really care. I know you care, so make sure that is what you are living.

"When you feel the enthusiasm, the eagerness and the inspiration, stop, and listen. This is your zone. This is where your calling is. Your soul is calling you.
When we are in alignment with our true calling, our passion, and what we love, life becomes fluid, and every cell in the body is dancing. That is the dance worth dancing, and there is music played, if you listen.

Let your heart guide you, and your feet lead you, and do not be afraid to follow that tune. Don`t wait until tomorrow, there is only today. Do not skip a single beat, as this life is happening right now. This is the time to let all fears and hurts go, and let yourself express all that you are.

You are the amazing artist, the empowered lead performer in your life. When your heart sings, listen to the music and dance!"

Hilde

PART TWO:
TRUE HEALTH,
STEP BY STEP

Chapter 6

Detoxification

This chapter is going to change the way you look at health and regeneration. This is where everything starts and ends, with the only healer there is, your own body. From understanding how the body works, why you are sick, and how you can get better, comes the confidence and the inspiration to hit that pedal. You are ready to move forward, the step by step plan is here.

My personal experience with detoxification has been long standing and educating. It has at times been more than scary, painful and emotionally devastating. I have been experiencing symptoms I did not even know existed. It has also been completely life-changing and life-saving, as without the knowing and understanding of true detoxification, I would not have gotten my life back. My book "From HELL to Inspired", is a complete story of my journey back to living. I invite you to read it, as it will give you some additional inspiration and insight, I am sure.

I had been asking for complete healing and I was going to get it on a cellular level. As we embark on this journey of restoring our health, the body will know exactly what to do. It will start the process of cleaning out every cell that is not of the highest quality, every toxin stored, and every uninvited guest that might be hanging around. We have no idea how toxic we are, really, we have no clue at all. Now that I know, I am even more in awe of what the body can actually endure and do. My body was going to get rid of every weak cell, no matter where it was in the body, and it was going to push out every toxin stored, in any way that it could. The body that I had been abusing for so many years, the body with the weak kidneys and adrenals, the weak skin and stomach, was going to take out the garbage.

What is detoxification?

This is the most important chapter in the book of life, as our lives are dependent on this knowledge. Detoxification is as natural as breathing, and yet we are holding our breath by obstructing this process, which is meant to be effortless. It has become an art, as we have let ourselves down for so long. The more toxic we are, meaning the more acidic we are, the more impaired our eliminating organs will be. Now, the cleaning job is becoming more of a challenge, and the experience a tougher ride. What was meant to be a constant sweep, has become a life-saving task. My dear friend and a true healer, Dr. Robert Morse, calls it the art of detoxification. This is the true understanding of health and healing.

Detoxification simply means cleansing, and the body does that around the clock. It needs to cleanse to live, and by obstructing that flow, we are slowly dying.

We know there is no magic bullet to great health. There is no quick fix, no pill or supplement that will take you from suffering to thriving. There is no product of any kind that will restore health in an un-balanced, diseased body. *Only* the body can do any healing, any balancing, and any regeneration. Only the body has the intelligence and the ability to heal itself, it is what it does. It is a self-healing mechanism. It will do anything in its power to stay healthy, and to regenerate. The truth is that what we are seeing as symptoms of ill health, is the body doing its best to save our butts. Every snotty nose, cough, fever and inflammation, is the body doing its healing and cleansing job. The symptoms are reflecting the effort made to push out bacteria and acids.

Detoxification is the process that the body undergoes to get rid of what is obstructing health, on top of any everyday created waste. Most likely there would not be such a word, had we not engaged in the exposure of so many toxins and destructive eating habits.

If we cut ourselves, we heal. The body rushes to stop the bleeding, and to regenerate. We tend to confuse symptom-suppression with true healing. Detoxification is a word we use when we talk about self-cleansing, and it has many meanings and connotations. To regain health, to strengthen the whole body, to thrive and live free of pain and suffering, the body needs to be clean. It needs to be running smoothly in every way. It needs to get rid of what is obstructing the flow of life. When we talk about detoxification, we are talking about letting the body do what it was designed to do. We are simply talking about getting out of the way, about stopping what is hurting it. We are stopping what is creating more waste, so that the body can use its energy to cleanse.

Why does the body need to cleanse?

We already talked about the 100 trillion cells, that all "eat" and "poop". The "poop" is what we call cellular waste. Every cell generates waste, and on top of that, what we eat, breathe and live, generates waste. In the same way that we are brushing our teeth and taking a shower, ever cell and every organ needs to cleanse and clean itself on an ongoing basis. When we are experiencing symptoms of less than optimal health, the body is showing us that our elimination of waste is not functioning as it should. The lymphatic system is now stagnant, and the acidic waste is burning our cells. Again, look at the lymph system as the sewer system of the body. It is where all the waste is dumped to be carried to the different elimination organs. The blood needs to be clean, as it is the kitchen, the carrier of nutrition, oxygen and all vital components for a healthy cell. All we are is cells, more than a hundred trillion of them. That is a lot of "poop"!

If you are not living in great health, you are full of waste. You are backed up with acids, poop and sewage. This is what is making you sick. The longer it sits, the sicker you get. It is burning, corrosive and damaging to the cells. It is in short making you sick, and by feeling the symptoms you are feeling the systems that are down. We are all making ourselves sick by ignoring the laws of nature, and by resorting to more poisons to feel better, by taking drugs and stimulants.

So - the blood is the kitchen, bringing in the food to feed the cells. More to eat, and more waste is created. This simple idea is to awaken us to the fact that it's only through proper detoxification, by moving the lymph, eliminating cellular and metabolic waste, that true regeneration, alkalization and hydration can happen. On top of waste naturally created in the body every minute, just from living, the diet of the modern world includes more waste. Food is not supposed to be waste, but sadly it is. Chemicals, GMO, cooked and altered, filled with more damaging substances than I even care to focus on, are poisoning the body every day.

Not only have we been conditioned to believe that processed foods are ok to eat, we have also been handed down weakened organs from our parents. Every generation seems to get weaker, and time is of the essence. We moved away from the tropics, and we started to cook our food. We thought we got smarter than nature, and are suffering the consequences. Technology and greed, power and mind-games, they all contributed to our suffering today. To think that we could feed the body substances not from this earth, and bombard ourselves with toxins and not have to pay for it, just shows that we might not be as smart as we thought we were.

The kidneys are especially impaired by the ingestion of animal protein. So much metabolic waste comes from trying to break down the protein, that the kidneys get really tired and weak. Through the weakening of our most important elimination organ, the kidneys, the lymph system is unable to properly filter out the acidic, metabolic and dietary waste. Along with the intestines, the liver, the lungs, and the skin, the kidneys are on a mission to keep you healthy in every way possible.

We are created so perfectly, and through honoring that creation, we will heal and thrive. It is natural to be healthy, and the body is working in that direction every single minute!

The longer we wait, and the longer we stay in pain and ill-health, the harder it is to get back to a clean house. Our house, or body, will feel less and less livable, as clutter and garbage will be obstructing the energies and the peace. The air will be hard to breathe, so to speak, and the different equipment within will no longer function optimally. Our body is our temple, and where we spend all our time in this lifetime. It is a permanent residency, and that is an absolute. The lymph system is the body's sewer system, and to carry out the waste, it needs to be moving and disposing of the garbage.

How do we detoxify for regeneration and healing?

Detoxification is about letting everything that is not serving us be processed and leave. A true healing regime or program will include emotional and mental work as well as a physical cleansing regime. It will be impossible not to include all aspects of the being. The mind-body-soul connection again. Never the less, changing what we eat most often is the simplest and most potent way to start. The body will detoxify all our bodies at the same time; The physical, the mental and the emotional body. That means that once we start to eat what the body is designed to eat, it will also let us know which emotional waste we have been holding on to. By giving it a break from having to digest and eliminate more waste, it now has the ability to use the energy to clear everything from old emotions, to mucus in our intestines.

We need to look to nature, get back to the basics, and trust in our own bodies and their ability to heal. We will heal by eating fresh living organic foods, like we were meant to. That way, we are constantly letting our body take care of business. In this lifetime, in this world, the challenges are many for most of us. It seems the non-foods presented to us, alongside the stress, the polluted air, the negative programming and the fear of change, is holding us captive in our polluted houses.

All you have to do is to let go of everything that is not serving you, be it foods, emotions or actions. There is nothing to figure out, or to speculate in, really. The body will do the rest. Simplicity is a challenge for the educated mind, and this very fact is important to acknowledge. Our intellect and our craving for intellectual growth, has contributed to the state that we are in. It is time to hit the shift button and think again. Less is more.

The simplicity of detoxification:

- **Stop bringing in more garbage:** This means, no more altered chemistry, chemicals or toxins. Not in form of hurtful drugs, or supplements as isolates or pesticides. Do not eat anything that requires a label, as no real food does. Stay away from salt, oils and stimulants, and keep the standard high on a preferably organic, high fruits diet. Stop using harmful chemicals in your home, as anything you eat, breathe and smell, you in fact eat. It is all absorbed into your blood and tissues, creating a toxic overload in your body. Look for ways to make your own lotions and detergents, and be inspired by the many tips and recipes found in this book. You've got this.

- **Move the lymph:** Through eating raw living foods only, the lymph will start moving. By also being active, adopting the suggestions in the upcoming chapters, you will move to heal. Make sure that your kidneys are filtering, or you will have some extra work to do. More tips to come on how to restore kidney filtration.

- **Open all eliminating organs:** Clean out the intestines, and do some liver flushes. Use a sauna to open up the skin, and look to herbs for extra strength and organ support. Sometimes working with a practitioner that is also a detoxification specialist, as myself, will help determine your weaknesses and how to address them with herbs and essential oils.

- **Let the acidic waste and toxins out**: Allow yourself to live through the detoxification process. It can be a long process, all depending on your age, your current state of health, how long you have been out of health, and how your organs and glands are conditioned from birth.

- **Watch health be restored:** Enjoy the ride back to your inspired state of perfect health, and keep your focus on your path. Do not let anyone or anything discourage you or make you lose your focus. This is your time to shine, and you are so worth it!

The deepness of cleansing being done, and the pace it will happen in, depends on many different factors. If you are diagnosed as terminal, long standing so-called chronic and degenerative, you know that you have some serious work to do. You know that your body means business, and that there is no time to go slow and easy. We need to do what we need to do – it is that simple.

When time is of the essence:

Not everyone has time to transition into a healthier lifestyle. Some are barely hanging on, trying to save their lives. For everyone who is in the situation of long standing, chronic, painful and degenerative disease, I say there is no time to lose. Even though the change can be hard and challenging, the decision has to be made. A diet of fruits, berries and melons are on the menu, and that is that. The top-of-the-mountain, acute healing diet is a grape fast, and nothing will allow the acids to move like the grapes do. No one knows how deep you will have to dig, or how long it will take, but the body will do its very best every single day. Know that *you* hold the power, one step at the time. Get support and a close follow up, to ensure that you are allowing your body to heal safely.

When you are tired of feeling sick:

You might be low in energy, and have many different hurts and pains. You might even be on some sort of chemical medication. You are functioning and need to keep going to work. You really want to get healthy, and will do whatever it takes, little by little. I say to you, *do not* wait any longer. I waited and waited, until one day I was almost out cold. I had done my best not to listen to my body's signals for years. If you are where I was, I recommend you start by reading my book "From HELL to Inspired". My hope is that it will inspire you to wait no more. Be done. Step into the raw right away, and include some greens and raw food recipes if you like. Your house is on fire, even though it might not look that way.

When you know what you are doing is not optimal, but:

You are the lucky one, the one that is doing what we should all be doing. Educating yourself, with the intent to change before the symptoms of ill health set in. You are the one that has the opportunity to walk healthy through this lifetime, by simply changing what will create a problem down the road. When you transition to the raw food diet, and change the way you live and think. You will feel what feeling good feels like. If you believe you are feeling great right now, wait for the real buzz. Do not wait until later, go get it!

Healthy is the typical norm, what we are designed to be. The smallest indication that we are not, is a cry for change.

Detoxification, the art:

Dr. Robert Morse once said it to me so wisely; "You need to know when to hold them, and when to fold them". The process which is so simple, yet so complex, is absolutely an art. It is an individual journey that requires faith, knowledge, diligence and patience. It also needs a firm and sound mind, to ensure that the process is running smoothly. Sometimes slow and steady is the way, and sometimes we need to really dig in deep. The body might tell you to back off a little bit at times, to slow down, and that can be an important part of your journey. Sometimes the body simply needs to recap and rebuild some energy. It will cleanse in its own timely manner, and cannot be forced. Sometimes though, if we are using herbs and very astringent foods, the body will have a reaction to that. This is where the art comes in again. When you are working with herbs, these amazing God given healers, you are working with powerful substances. They are potent and strong, yet gentle on your system. I strongly recommend to get an herbal protocol to go with your regime, to support and sooth, as you are moving on up.

Some of you, like me, might want to keep going, even though the body is saying "not so fast, missy", so take it from me - *listen*. At other times, it will be more beneficial to keep on going. To walk through the tunnel, and not stop until you are through. The symptoms of cleansing can be many, and scary. Make sure that you are informed, and that you know what to expect. For some, the journey is simply fun from the get go. For others, it is not. The body might beg to differ, as it is cheering and clapping, saying: "Finally, this shit is leaving me!"

Educate yourself on the topic, and find your inner guidance. If you need support, find it. As you keep reading, you will know what to do.

Look for kidney filtration:

At the base of most severe symptoms is a non-filtering set of kidneys. This is one of the most important keys to great health. Look for filtration by peeing in a clear glass jar. Hold it to the light and look for sediment. You are looking for anything that floats around in your urine. It might look like small particles, like small snowflakes, or a stringier mucus looking sediment. If the urine is cloudy, you can let it sit overnight, and watch if any sediment will settle at the bottom. You want the sediment in your urine. It is telling you that your kidneys are filtering out the lymphatic waste. If it is, the body will able to detoxify at a more rapid pace. This has nothing to do with the color of the urine. In general, the color simply indicates how much you have been drinking. If your urine is clear, you know that this has to be your main focus moving forward, to get your kidneys to filter.

Step by step we will look at what has to be done to let your body cleanse and restore. We will look at the physical tasks at hand, as well as the mental and emotional work that needs to be done. Gift yourself a few beautiful notebooks and some new pens. Taking notes can be very helpful, and you might have your own revelations come up along the way.

Bottom line is this: Before the body has gotten rid of that which is making it weak and sick, it has no capacity or means to regenerate. Once it is able to clean, it will do so, and once the majority of the cleaning is done, regeneration will take place and symptoms will disappear.

Chapter 7

Parasite cleansing

We might as well hit perhaps the most un-easy chapter to deal with, right away. Now that you are ready to go, you need to be ready to let *them* go. I would love to say that we should simply love them all, but the truth is that when our bodies are imbalanced and sick, when our inner terrain is acidic and toxic, the parasites will thrive. They multiply by laying eggs and by secreting toxic waste, and therefore they are adding to the burden of an already sick body. Not a fun scenario, so this is where we have to start. We let these uninvited guests have a grand party inside of us when we keep the terrain to their liking. In any so-called chronic stage of a disease, parasites will be present. Why? Because they have been invited! They will not miss the offering of free room and board, and most likely they will invite their friends to join the party.

We all have them, the parasites, so the topic is nothing to freak out about. Yes, I saw them come out, and yes, you might too. They are a part of any living being. Microbes, cells, parasites, viruses, all living and vibrating. Parasites are any type of creature that feeds off of another host. Their intention is not to destroy the host, because if the host dies, they will be forced to die as well. Although they can feed off of just about any kind of nutrient and food substance, there are certain foods in particular they thrive on. These are foods high in complex sugar/ starches, unhealthy fats, and any man-made ingredient such as food-preservatives, food-colorants and many other food-additives. They are also attracted to heavy metals and other toxic substances. The more the merrier.

You do not have to look for them, or even wonder if they are there. If you are sick they are there, period. As long as your house is that of imbalance and over-acidity, you have work to do. This takes us back to the inner terrain, the cultivating medium. For a parasite to thrive, it needs to live in an environment that feeds its needs. It needs to eat, and it needs to have a comfortable place to reside. Mucus is perfect, as they love a good conglomeration of bacteria and microbes. They lay their eggs, they eat, they secrete, and they reproduce quickly. Sounds pretty simple, doesn't it? Some of them are very attracted to the complex sugars and will let you know that they are there, through your cravings. Depending on the kind, the parasites will eat different things. One thing that is certain is that they will feed off of you, and leave you depleted and more toxic. They also love your nutrition, and will take the best for themselves, leaving you with the leftovers.

So, what do you need to do, do you change the environment, or kill the parasites? Sometimes, when sickness has arrived, the big guns are needed, and I say you need to do both. Absolutely, the terrain needs to be changed, and it will, but a parasitic overload is a large burden on all the bodily systems and organs, so a good parasite cleanse is a must. No living being will die without a fight, and the parasites are no different. They will kick and scream, try to manipulate and hide, all to be able to save themselves and their family. By using some specific herbs and foods, you'll simply be inviting them to leave, together with making your house no longer desirable as a breeding ground. You are changing our home to that of health and vitality, leaving toxic waste and sickness behind.

Let us look very shortly at some interesting facts before we let them be on their way:

There's said to be over 1.000 types of parasites that can reside in the human body, but we identify only a fraction of these. We are mostly physically aware of the larger worms in the intestines, but they do in fact spread throughout the body. Only about 30% of them camp out in the intestines. These are the ones that we most easily identify, and they have been invited through eating meat, drinking un-pure water and by being in contact with animal carriers. If you have a pet, there is a great carrier host right there.

Here is a story to illustrate the longevity of parasites in the human body: In 1979, a British study was reported on 600 former prisoners from World War II. These had all been stationed in the Far East. As long as thirty years after the war, as many as 15% of them, were still infected with a parasite called Strongyloides. This infection is caused by a roundworm that resides in the intestinal tract. They had contracted the parasite during the war. This means you could have eaten meat and gotten infected more than 10-20 years ago, and still be hosting the tapeworms or other types of parasites that you ingested.

Parasites are divided into two main groups, worms and small parasites. The small ones are mainly microscopic in size, including what are called protozoa and amoebae. Despite them being almost invisible, small parasites can be dangerous. Microscopic parasites are said to be able to get into our joints and eat the calcium linings of our bones. They can also eat the protein coating on our nerves (the myelin sheath). Not a fun scenario.

Large parasites, which are the worm type, are usually large enough to be seen by the naked eye. I know this to be very true. Some can even be up to 12, or even 15 inches long, but luckily they do not travel to other parts of the body. They mostly stay in the digestive tract. It *can* happen, but it's very rare, so nothing to worry about.

The larger parasites are worms which reproduce by laying eggs. Eggs are deposited in the intestinal tract, where they stick to the walls of the intestines. Here, they will hide in the mucus-lining. When the eggs hatch, the youngsters feed on the food that we eat, and eventually grow into strong adults. What we have to note is that their cycle of life can be many months long. That means that we need to do a cleanse that lasts for at least 3 months to make sure we get the full cycle, eggs and all.

The smaller organisms are the protozoas and amoebas. They function almost like bacteria, by travelling through the bloodstream to any part of the body. They reproduce without laying eggs and are behaving more like an infection in the body.

70% of all parasites that can live in the human body are microscopic - only 30% are visible to the naked eye.

I have shared some very brief information about the most common parasites below. I have consciously left out the main symptoms for each of them, and any visual explanation of their behavior etc. This is to not take the eye off the ball. We need to know about them, it is truth, but we also have to focus on where the main problem is, and that is never the parasites, it's our environment.

> The most common human parasites are: Ringworm, tapeworms, pinworms, candida albicans (yeast infections) and plasmodia (which is the malaria causing parasite). Roundworms including ascaris, hookworms, whipworms, flukes including the blood fluke the anisakid worm, and microscopic parasites and all parasitic larvae and eggs.[4]

---

[4] «Cure for all Cancers», Hulda Clark

Roundworms:

The Roundworms are what most people think of when it comes to human parasites. They are the pinworms, the whipworms, and the hookworms. They are much larger than the one-celled protozoa, the microscopic ones. They are all round and small, and can cause a large amount of damage. We do not eat the worm itself to be infected, we ingest the microscopic eggs, which then hatch in our bodies.

- **Pinworms:** This is the most widely spread parasite in North America and Europe. They are the most frequently seen of all of the species of parasites because they live in the colon. They come out at night to lay their eggs in the anus and on bedclothes. The adults are white and ½ inch long. The eggs can become airborne and are able to live without a host for 2 days. If you have children, you might be familiar with this one. You might even remember having them as a child. School age children have the highest infestation rate, and if one member of a family has pinworms, it is highly likely that all members are infected.

- **Hookworms:** They come from contaminated food and water. These are busy ones. The eggs hatch in the intestines, and then they migrate to the lungs through the bloodstream. They are then coughed up and swallowed right back to the small intestine to reproduce. In the lungs they can cause pneumonia. In the intestines they hook themselves into the intestinal walls, (hereby the inviting name), where each one drinks up to 1cc of blood per day. We get these from pets licking us, or us petting or grooming them.

- **Whipworms:** These will attach themselves to the intestinal wall. They inject their digestive fluid into the tissue, and this fluid turns into a liquid. They then suck up this liquid, which can cause many different symptoms. Each female can lay 10,000 eggs per day, and each adult can live for several years. When the eggs are passed out through your feces, without even being seen, they are able to live for three weeks without a host. This tells us how important it is to not be an inviting host for these parasites.

- **Ascaris:** This is a round worm that lives in the small intestine. Adult female worms can grow to over 12 inches in length - adult males are smaller. Ascariasis is the most common human worm infection, and I was heavily infected. Children are said to be more infected than adults. The immature worms can migrate through the lungs, and you may cough up an ascaris larvae or pass an adult worm in your stool. Ascaris eggs are found in human feces. Infection occurs when a person accidentally swallows infectious microscopic Ascaris eggs. Once in the stomach, immature worms hatch from the eggs. The larvae are carried through the lungs to the throat where they are swallowed. Once swallowed, they reach the intestines and develop into adult worms. Adult female worms lay eggs that are then passed in feces. This cycle takes between 2-3 months.

Flukes:

The flukes are the hardest parasites to get rid of, as they can stay in the human body for up to 20 years! Each adult fluke will live for one year. Flukes come from raw fish, undercooked water plants, such as watercress, and are also carried by dogs, cats and other fish-eating animals. They are also found in beef, chicken, pork and unwashed vegetables.

- **Liver flukes:** These will infect the bile ducts of the liver and the gall bladder. They start out as small white flattish worms, being wider on one end and more narrow on the other. The young adults are various shades of pink while the older adults are bright red to almost black in color. These are easy to see when you do a liver flush. They are often referred to as tomato skins, as that is what they look like. The longer they live in the liver, the darker in color they become. The blood from the liver stains their skin.

- **Lung flukes:** Obviously found in the lungs, and sometimes mistaken for lung cancer on x-rays.

- **Blood flukes:** They travel all over the human body and into all organs including the brain and spinal cord.

Tapeworms:

The head of the tapeworm hooks into the intestinal wall. Most tapeworms are ½ inch long and are a grayish white color. There are however some species that can grow up to 33 feet long and can lay over 1 million eggs per day. The tapeworm bodies are mostly reproductive organs. The length of their body is made up of sections that are nothing but ovaries and testes for reproduction. Their tails release these eggs. The eggs then hatch into larvae that can migrate to other parts of the human body and can form cysts. Even if the sections are broken off, the tapeworm can regenerate itself from only it's head. Some tapeworms can live for over 25 years.

- **Pork tapeworms:** They are carried by undercooked pork, and by the anus, hand, mouth route. They can incubate in the human body for up to 30 years before reproducing. They can affect the eyes and the brain. Once inside the body, the tapeworm egg hatches, penetrates the intestine, travels through the bloodstream to the brain and nerves.

- **Fish tapeworm:** This is the largest of the species. It can grow to 33 feet in length.

- **Dog tapeworm:** They are passed along to us from cats and dogs through petting and grooming. I know, not a fun thing to think about. The adult tapeworm is made up of many small segments, and the tapeworm itself can measure 4-28 inches long. Each segment is about the size of a grain of rice. As the adult tapeworm matures inside the intestines, these segments break off and pass in the stool They look almost like grains of rice or corn. These are the tapeworm eggs.

Now that this is noted, we know that the parasites are a real concern. I could write up pages and pages of parasite symptoms, but like I said, that would throw us off focus. I want us to keep our attention on the health of the body, on the task at hand. We do not need more lists of symptoms to run to for validation. It really doesn`t matter what symptom is present at this time. The solution is pretty much the same, to get healthy. To do that, there are some simple steps and guidelines, and we are ready to do a parasite cleanse.

The Parasite cleanses:

There are many great herbal blends out there that will invite them to leave your body. The ones I have seen work really well are:

- **The Humaworm** is a very powerful cleanse. It consists of dried and capsulated herbs, taken every day for 30 days. You are then advised to wait for 90 days, before you take the next round. Several rounds might be needed. There are in-between herbs that can be taken during those 90 days. Humaworm started as a family business, and has grown tremendously into a modern, full-scale operation. Each order of Humaworm is still hand-grounded, weighed, and hand-packed in the production department, the same day it ships to the customer.[5]

---

[5] https://www.humaworm.com

- **Natures Botanical's** Parasite G and Parasite M are also amazing products. These are designed by Dr. Robert Morse, an herbalist and Iridologist from Port Charlotte, Florida. His wisdom and over 40 years of experience has led him to make these two slightly different formulas. The Parasite G is made to target the worms in the intestinal track, and are sold as dried, capsulated herbs. The Parasite M formula is made to target the smaller microbes, mold and fungi. This blend can also be found as a tincture.[6]

I know there are several other products on the market. If you cannot get a good product, these herbs all have anti-parasitic properties.

- Wormwood herb
- Betel nut
- Male fern root
- Wormseed
- Parsley root & leaf
- Cascara Sagrada bark
- Cloves
- Pink root
- Tansy herb & flower
- Pau d'Arco bark
- Black walnut hull
- Garlic
- Chinese Goldthread
- Cat's Claw bark
- Goldenseal root
- Olive leaf extract
- Usnea Lichen
- Thyme leaf
- Butternut bark

---

[6] https://www.drmorsesherbalhealthclub.com/collections

- Barberry root
- Black walnut.

> Always use caution when using herbs. They are very potent, and not all of them might be for you, and not all mix well together. Always seek help from an educated herbalist before starting any herbal protocol.

Foods with anti-parasitic properties:

- **Papaya seeds**: The seeds from the papaya fruit have anthelmintic and anti-amoebic properties. This means that they kill intestinal worms and other parasitic organisms in your digestive system. Using papaya seeds for parasites has proven to be very effective. The seeds have a distinct slightly peppery flavor. They can of course be eaten as they are, or you can simply sprinkle them over salads and other dishes.

- **Extra Virgin Coconut oil:** This well-known oil consists of medium-chain triglycerides, which help to strengthen and build the immune system. Furthermore, this oil is also high in both lauric acid and caprylic acid, which possess antiviral, antimicrobial and antifungal properties.

- **Garlic:** This common household spice is also a potent herb for medicinal benefits. It is especially useful for flushing out parasites such as giardia and roundworms.

- **Cayenne pepper:** Increases circulation, boosts the immune system, and fights parasites.

- **Pineapple:** This much loved fruit contains the digestive enzyme bromelain that helps to clear certain parasitic infections, such as tapeworms.

- **Pumpkin seeds:** Pumpkin seeds contain "toxic, tetracyclic triterpenes" within the seeds, which are released upon chewing- or by grinding them. This substance is known to intoxicate and paralyze the worms, causing them to release their grip on the intestinal wall. They will need help being expelled, so be sure to move the bowels.

- **Aloe Vera:** Aloe Vera helps to eliminate parasites, and it also helps to heal the body from the damage that might have been done. It is very effective at restoring the body at a deep cellular level by promoting new and healthy cell growth. A great alkalizer and intestinal healer.

Remember to always make sure that you are moving your bowels while cleaning out the parasites. We want the bowel to move, and during a cleanse it is even more important. Use an enema bag if you need to. I used one every single day during my heaviest cleanses. That way you are sure that what you are killing off is coming out. You can use a regular enema bag that you buy online, with room temperature water.

Using Essential oils for anti-parasitic properties:

The Essential oils are natures treasures, they are our helpers and our blessings. Together with our wild botanicals, they are our gifts from God. Essential oils are created from plants, stems, and botanicals. They are used in many ways, and have many benefits. There is a whole chapter dedicated to these amazing healers, and here's some information that relates to the topic of parasites.

- **Frankincense:** This is the king of all oils. Although mostly known for its anti-tumor properties and all-round healing abilities, I include it in any regimen. It is such a powerful restorative helper, that is will enhance the property of any other oil. You can inhale it, diffuse it, use it topically or put a drop under your tongue.

- **Myrrh:** A very powerful antioxidant, and antiviral, anti-parasitic and analgesic/anesthetic. The oil can be taken orally, a few drops in a small glass of water, in a capsule, inhaled or diffused.

- **Oil of oregano:** This has also been used for its powerful antiviral, antibacterial, antifungal, and anti-parasitic properties. It can be diffused, used topically with a carrier oil (1part oil, 4 parts carrier oil). It can also be ingested, but it is very strong, so do not put it directly into the mouth.

- **Peppermint:** Great anti-parasitic properties, used against intestinal worms. Also antibacterial, antiviral, and antifungal. You can place a few drops under the tongue, use it topically, a few drops in a glass of water, or inhaled.

- **Tea Tree (Melaleuca):** A truly powerful antibacterial, antifungal, antiviral and anti-parasitic oil, used in many cultures. Mix a few drops in a glass of water, or put it in your diffuser.

- **Clove:** This is one of the most antimicrobial and antiseptic of all essential oils. It is also an anti-fungal, antiviral and anti-infectious. Rub it on your skin or diffuse it.

- **Lemon:** Such a great all-round oil. Inexpensive and very potent. A great alkalizer, and no parasite likes an alkaline environment. Use it internally, topically, diffuse it and smell it.

- **Cinnamon Bark:** one of the most powerful antiseptics known, strongly antibacterial, antiviral, and antifungal.

- **Eucalyptus (radiata):** Great for topical use. It is anti-infectious, antibacterial and antiviral.

- **Rosemary:** This oil has great antiseptic and antimicrobial properties. Diffuse or use topically.

An old recipe says that mixing 3-5 drops each of oregano, peppermint, and tea tree essential oils in a glass of water, 3 times a day will kill off candida overgrowth.

Parasites and frequencies:

During my search for a better life, I came across what is called a Rife machine. I was searching for ways to clean out my parasites, and I discovered how frequencies affect everything, as everything has a vibration. Royal Raymond Rife was a brilliant scientist born in 1888. After studying at Johns Hopkins, Rife developed a technology which is still commonly used today in the fields of optics, electronics, radiochemistry, biochemistry, ballistics, and aviation. The frequency machine that he built, holds his name today.

Dr. Royal Rife's study of frequencies raises an important question concerning the frequencies of substances we eat, breathe, and absorb. Many pollutants lower healthy frequency. Processed/canned food has a frequency of zero. Fresh produce has up to 15 Hz, dried herbs from 12 to 22 Hz, and fresh herbs from 20 to 27 Hz.[7]

According to Dr. Gary Young, essential oils start at 52 Hz and go as high as 320 Hz, which is the frequency of rose oil. Clinical research shows that therapeutic grade essential oils have the highest frequency of any natural substance known to man, creating an environment in which disease, bacteria, virus, fungus, etc., cannot live.

I used my Rife machine for some years, and I will say it was a valid experience. It is not the route that I promote or recommend today, as I have seen that there are gentler and more natural ways of balancing the body's vibration. Every essential oil has a frequency, and each of our organs and body parts have a frequency. The frequency of an essential oil will attract a like-frequency in the

---

[7] www.rife.org

body. Lower frequencies become a sponge for negative energy. The frequency is what stays in the body to maintain the longer lasting effects of the oil.

"Low frequencies make physical changes in the body. Middle frequencies make emotional changes in the body. High frequencies make spiritual changes in the body. Spiritual frequencies range from 92 to 360 Hz. Bone frequency is 38-43; neck and down frequency is 62-68." -Dr. Gary Young[8].

The parasites will fight for their lives, and simply resist to leave. They might play with your emotions and your cravings, leaving you with symptoms you never had before. They will beg you to stop, to self-sabotage and to go back to feeding them. I call it *die off*, the toxic waste that they secrete when dying. It is toxic, and therefore a new burden to all of the elimination organs. This is why making sure that your bowels are moving is very important. You want that waste to move. This whole journey towards health and truth, this whole book, is connected as one, and one piece cannot stand alone. The whole picture must be seen as one, as no part of our bodies can be separated. Not the organs, not our systems, not even the symptoms stand alone. Read the chapter "Cleansing reactions and remedy" over and over again, until you are confident and clear on what is happening inside the body.

Send the parasites on their way in love and peace, as you do not need them anymore.

---

[8] «The missing link», Dr. Gary Young, «Chemistry of essential oils made simple», David Stewart

Chapter 8

Raw living food

Now I want us to dive into one of the single most important topics on the journey back to health - what we eat. You've now learned that the parasites are feeding off you, and that they are having a party - let us get to changing the guest list. We are what we eat, think and feel, and what we eat, is affecting everything about our experience.

First of all, what *is* raw food?

Raw food is simply put food that has not been cooked or in any other way altered from its natural raw state. That means it cannot be heated past 47 degrees Celsius, or 115 degrees Fahrenheit, and still be considered raw. This way the fruits and vegetables will keep their enzymes and nutritional value intact. On top of that, they will keep their energy, their God given, life-giving energy. Furthermore – the enzymes help us digest our food. The body can also create them, but that is a process which takes a lot of energy. This is the process that can make us feel tired and heavy after a cooked meal. The unaltered food will also have its organic minerals intact, which are easy to absorb. The inorganic minerals are not easy for us to absorb, and will therefore deposit in our bodies. It is further believed that your body has a limited amount of enzymes that it can produce. If the supply is finished, our bodily organs will function less and less. The lack of enzymes is also said to accelerate aging.

Raw food has all its vitamins intact, and is therefore a nutritional powerhouse. Cooking anything will destroy the nutritional value, alter the food chemically and strip it of its life-force. Living food has living energy. Think about this – a raw seed will grow, a cooked seed won't.

Life promotes life, and death promotes death. No other species on this planet will eat anything that has been cooked, fried, boiled or steamed. It is not natural, pure and simple. Most scientists seem to believe that our physiological composition tells us we are made to digest living foods, and this makes perfect sense to me. Not that eating is a science, or that we need to study what to eat. It is a natural thing, and by following our intuition we *know* what is best for us. We are designed to pick, chew and digest ripe fruits and vegetables, some nuts and seeds, period. In our society we most often wait until we get unwell and unhealthy to look at what we are eating. I know I did. I was lost in the programming that food was everything and anything that tasted good to me. I was not brought up, like most of us, to see food and health as connected, and boy was I wrong!

Whenever you are feeling heavy and tired after eating, the body is simply saying it has too much to do, and that it is too much to handle. It has to use all its energy on the digestive process. Further, the enzymes our body makes are not as efficient and effective as the ones that were destroyed in our food when we cooked it. Consequently, our food is not broken down as well it should be, and is therefore harder to digest. This also results in food starting to rot in our digestive tract, our intestines, and our uninvited guests, the parasites, are happy as can be. Raw food is the sweeping, cleaning, vibrating, regenerating food from nature. Cooked and altered food is what breeds and feeds what we do not want. It feeds the parasites, leaves us lacking energy, diseased and in a state of physical degeneration.

We've learned that everything has a vibration, a frequency, and that every cell in our body will feel the frequency of what we put into it. We will therefore be affected energetically by everything we eat. We can connect with nature, or stray from it. We can honor it, or alter it. Raw food is simply food. It is simply food as nature intended, being everything we need, period. That is all. No list of ingredients, and nothing added that we do not need. All pure, perfectly put together food, vibration, nutrition, and love. Like every other species on this planet, we have been blessed with foods that will nourish and heal. Foods that will cleanse and hydrate, strengthen and regenerate. We have been given the perfect food, and we do not need to add anything to it. It is all perfect just the way it is.

The most important aspect of raw food, when it comes to our health, is not what it is, but rather what it is not.

Are we designed to eat raw food?

We are all human beings, born with identical chemistry, the same organs, glands and systems. Our glands and bodily functions are all the same. On the inside we do not differ at all. Every human baby will drink their mother's milk if available, and if not, they will still be given the same formula to drink. If we look at nature, all species eat the same within their kind, their species. Every lion has the same diet, and every gorilla does too. This is because what we thrive on eating, is what we have been designed to eat.

We are designed to eat raw fruits and vegetables, and this truly is our natural diet. We are tropical species, yes, we are primates.

We can easily define the difference between *carnivores, omnivores, herbivores*, and *frugivores*. They all have different teeth, intestines and stomach, saliva production, stomach acids, general physique, and much more. These differences are indicating what they eat, and how they are able to gather and hunt their food. It also indicates how they are able to break down the food to utilize and eliminate it. This food will leave them lacking and missing nothing - thriving, and functioning optimally. No animal will wonder if they got enough nutrition, or if they are eating what is good for them. It is a natural process. They eat what makes them feel good, and they eat until they are full.

- **Carnivores** kill other animals with their claws and tear them apart, eating primarily their organs and drinking their blood. The word carnivore is derived from Latin and means "meat eater." Obligate carnivores are those that rely entirely on animal flesh to obtain their nutrients. Examples of obligate carnivores are members of the cat family, so know to feed your cat animal food only. Facultative carnivores are those that also eat non-animal food in addition to animal food. There is no clear line that differentiates facultative carnivores from omnivores though, but a dog is considered a facultative carnivore. This is why we see dogs healing on a diet high in raw vegetables. The wild cats, such as lions and tigers, are examples of carnivores.

- **Omnivores** will eat from the plant *and* the animal kingdom. The Latin term omnivore literally means "eater of everything". This is not quite the case though, as omnivores cannot really eat everything that other animals eat. They can only eat things that are moderately easy to acquire while being moderately nutritious. For example, most omnivores cannot live by grazing alone, and they are not able to eat some hard-shelled animals, or successfully hunt large or fast prey. The omnivores have a long and complex digestive track. This is to allow enough space and time for microbial fermentation to occur. They have great sharp fangs, walk on paws/cloves, have a strong stomach acid and small salvia glands. A bear is an omnivore.

- **Herbivores** eat only green plants and herbs. Some of them are also grazers, like the cows. Herbivores are animals whose primary food source is plant-based. They have evolved digestive systems capable of digesting large amounts of plant material. The plants are high in fiber and starch, and this is what provides the main energy source in their diet. Some parts of plant materials, such as cellulose, are hard to digest, therefore the digestive tract of herbivores is adapted so that food may be digested properly. That means that many large herbivores have symbiotic bacteria within their guts to assist with the breakdown of cellulose. A giraffe is an herbivore.

- **Frugivores** eat primarily fruits, berries, and some tender leafy greens. They can easily grab ripe fruits off the trees. They have "hands" to pick, and teeth that can easily rip open a ripe fruit. The length of the intestines and the pH of the stomach acid, shows that they are designed to digest fruits. Chimpanzees and other primates are frugivores.

When we take the time to examine the human body, we will easily recognize the signs of a frugivore. No education needed, nothing but logical common sense. We would have a very difficult time ripping apart skin and flesh. Our nails are not claws, and our hands are like those of a fruigivore - designed to pick and peel. Most of the animals that we are conditioned to eat, we would not even be able to run down, let alone kill with our bare hands. We have primarily flat molars, not designed to rip, but for mashing and grinding. Our jaws move from side to side, not like a carnivore's only vertical movement. Our convoluted colons are quite different in design from the smooth colons of carnivorous animals. We are, like other primates designed to eat fruits that will digest very easily, and need to be held in a long digestive track for optimal absorption.

Carnivores are made to thrive on a high fat diet, we are not. Our intestinal tracts measure about 30 feet. That is about twelve times longer than our torso. This is what allows the slow absorption of sugars from our food. The digestive tract of a carnivore is only three times the length of its torso, and it has ten times the amount of acid. This way it will be able to digest blood and muscle very easily. If a primate ate that same thing, it would sit inside and rot, and that is what it does, in humans. We, you and me, we sleep around 8 hours every night, while a carnivore will sleep around 18 to 20 hours per day. If you own a cat, you know this to be true. Your cat is not lazy. It needs its sleep to be able to digest all the animal proteins. So you see, plant eaters thrive on alkaline foods, while carnivores thrive on acidic food. This is not a taste preference, but nature speaking.

By all the criteria mentioned, in my opinion we fall into this last category. We are frugivores. We also love animals. We naturally have compassion for all of them, and if you leave a baby with a rabbit and a carrot, I will assure you, the rabbit will not be looked at as food. We are drawn to the produce market by the smell and the colors. These are the living foods, the source of our sustenance. When we see road-kill or even a slaughter house, we are revolted. Our mouths do not water from seeing a cow walk by, or a rabbit for that sake. I mean, there is nothing about a live animal that makes us hungry. We are simply not designed to look at them as food.

Mostly we have to have someone else kill for us, then we cook and season to taste. Nature is smarter than that, and we are living the consequences. You will never see an elephant eat a cat, or a lion eat a banana, not unless something was very, very off balance.

The natural diet of a primate is primarily fruits with some tender leafy greens, seeds, blossoms, some bark, pith and an occasional insect. This is an important realization to us, because by eating what we are designed to eat, our body will be able to heal and restore.

If you pass a monkey in a tree holding a banana, will you look at the monkey or the banana as food?

We are only as different as our weaknesses. That means that we are created equal, but have been passed down weaknesses from our parents. Animals do not typically have our lifestyle generated weaknesses, and therefore they all thrive on the same species-specific diet.

We cannot improve nature, and when we try, we suffer. By eating what we were designed to eat, we can find our way back to our natural heathy state.

What most humans are consuming today is very far from being foods from nature. We were not made to consume pesticides, fungicides, additives, carcinogens etc. We were made to eat *food*. All this poison is making us acidic. It is creating so many imbalances within our system that we think we are different from each other. We think we need chemical medicine to function. An animal will only get a human dis-ease when it starts eating human foods. Think about that, the food and health connection is huge! No matter how spiritual we get, it is all energy, and foods are energy also.

Cause and effect is one of the laws of nature, and that means that what you eat affects your body. It is all energy, as everything holds a vibration. That is nature at its best. It is a natural part of this amazing creation that we are all a part of. So, how different are we? Not at all, not really.

Why is eating raw so important to our health?

We now know that we have a species-specific diet, like every other creature on this planet. We are primates. What we are witnessing is what happens when we really, I mean *really* move away from that, and feed our bodies dead altered chemistry. All animals that are taken off their diet gets sick. Animals in the care of humans often get dis-eased. Wild animals do not, and how could they? Nature is perfect and no species will get sick, fat, and unhealthy from eating the foods intended for them. We, the humans, tend to believe we can outsmart nature. That we are more intelligent, and that our will can override the simple laws of the Universe. It is not so, and we are being told this and shown this, every single day, symptom by symptom. What we are eating is killing us, and it is about time we knew it, and really owned it.

Raw food is pure and natural food, and the simple sugars will feed our cells, not our parasites. The body will not create mucus in the need to get rid of the food, or because we have irritated the mucosa. The parasites will have no more playgrounds to play on. To see and experience the terror that the body is experiencing from being exposed to dairy, gluten, meats and processed food, is soul wrenching. The simple, yet so hard to grasp fact, that the body is in fact made in the same manner as any other mammal or primate, to be fueled on raw living food is a deal breaker for many. The social conditioning is so strong, that breaking free from the eating complex is harder than the will of healing. The parasites and the underlying emotional hurts are too strong to conquer.

Truth is truth, and there is nothing that an empowered mind and being cannot do. One step at the time, as I did - anyone can.

When we do not eat up to our potential, we will know it. I know it, and you know it. Food is supposed to be fuel, and not a burden. Most of what we eat today in the Western world is actually a burden to the human body. Every time we eat something that is outside of our natural diet, it becomes a burden. I remember heavy dinners as well as you do. You know, when you just wanted to lie down afterwards, completely drained of energy. Food is supposed to be fuel, not drain your energy. This only shows that the body has a hard time with what it has been fed. There is no way we can eat what is not good for us and not know it on one level or another. The problem is that we are surrounded with so much toxic waste that our pineal gland is clouded. Because of this, it is hard for us to see truth. When we detoxify our bodies, this changes. We regain our awareness and our natural instincts.

Eating raw is important for our vitality and rejuvenation, and to live at the level of health that we were designed to do. Most importantly though, as we have fallen into the trap of social conditioning and programming, we need to go back to raw to be able to detoxify our bodies. Detoxification simply means cleansing, something that the body does naturally when given a chance. Every day it works to clean and restore, but because of what we are feeding this amazing organism, it is working to survive, not to thrive. So, in that sense, you might say that without raw living foods there will be no real health, because only when introducing the vibrancy and the healing effect of our natural food, will the body be able to clean and restore.

We need to let go of the burdens, to give our body the break that it needs. When we want something to change, we need to change something, and when in any way off balance, look to nature, always.

The body does not only need a break from the cooked damaged foods and the animal putrefying decaying matters, it also needs to be able to clean out what has been stored from years of consuming these poisons. The whole digestive tract is impacted with mucus plaque, but that does not appear overnight. It builds up over time. I will be bold and say that most of our everyday diet consists mainly of so-called mucus forming food. I am talking about dairy products, soy and eggs, bread, pasta, processed meat like burgers, and any processed food, drink and product that contains additives and preservatives.

These foods lack fiber, and cannot move by themselves. They stay in your digestive tract and simply petrify and lead to constipation. The colon becomes sluggish from the lack of exercise, from mucus forming foods, and from the lack of fiber in the diet. Fresh fruits and vegetables are all very high in fiber. Made to move, as movement is lifesaving. Not only do the intestines carry out a major part of our waste, the small intestine is also where we absorb most of our nutrients. This hardened mucus is now hindering absorption, and we are in real trouble. A congested bowel may not absorb nutrients effectively, or be able to eliminate metabolic waste and toxins from within the organism. Now, even though you might be getting your nutrients from your food, you are not absorbing them. We have mal-nourishment at our hands, or mal-absorption rather.

We have wandered off from our natural diet since leaving our natural environment, the tropics. By migrating to the Northern climates we have been forced to eat what nature could provide. It is hard to live in a cold climate and eat raw living foods all year round. It is a challenge for anyone who has tried. It is still very doable, and when really sick, you have to do what you have to do. When there is a crisis, we need to step up and take charge, no matter what. It does no matter where you live, you need to ingest what is going to promote healing within the body.

By switching to a raw food diet, we simply stop what is hurting us, and let the body start its own cleansing project. Mucus plaque provides the ideal conditions for harmful yeast, parasites and bacteria to grow, and this results in an imbalanced gut flora, and deeper troubles. By cleaning out the entire intestinal tract, we are opening for healing on all levels, as this is the trunk of the tree. The intestinal tract is the trunk and where we absorb life-force and nutritional energy. We can clearly see that eating the wrong food is detrimental to our health. It is obstructing everything from elimination to absorption.

83

I was led to raw foods, as I was seeking truth. I was seeking true health and vitality. I was asking "show me the way", and I was shown. I was shown the simple way, the easy way, and the natural way. Still it was not easy to do, but it need not have to be, health was more important to me than eating any type of food. I was finding my way back home, through re-connecting with nature and creation. Health is simple, change is hard.

Raw food is simply natural foods, straight from nature. There is no labeling or ingredients list necessary. There is no complicated list of additives of fillers. The body will be able to digest it with ease, and not be harmed or intoxicated. It is the real fast-food, pure and simple. The foods we eat are secondary to all the other things that feed us; our relationships, career, spirituality, and exercise routine. At the same time, they are the key to everything, as you will no longer harm what you now love. Raw living foods will raise the vibration and the awareness, and also magnify the feeling of love and compassion.

You can eat for health, for sickness, for spirituality, for the environment and for the animals. It is always your choice. *It all is*!

On a raw food diet, you will always get what you need, and nothing that you don`t. You might still believe that you need milk from an animal, mostly from a cow, to get the calcium that you need. Think about it, do we really need to drink breast milk made for a calf, to get the calcium that the mother cow made from grass? Do we need to keep drinking it, to stay healthy? No other species will drink any form of milk past the infant stage. Have you ever seen a cow drink milk? Of course not! They get their calcium from the greens, like we were also intended to. We are made to eat fruits and greens. We thrive on what we were designed to eat, and we will never lack any nutrients. It is obvious to me that animals eat to live, while humans most often live to eat. Eating can be a spiritual experience, and what we eat can kill us.

Be willing to let go of the old, and the truth shall set you free.

Chapter 9

Simple healing recipes

want to share with you some simple raw living recipes. These are simple to make, and will help you to transition into a raw healing diet. Transitioning can be different for everyone. If you are really sick, with a degenerative diagnosis, there might not be time for transitioning, and you will have to dive right in. If you are in a lot of pain, you might want to do the same thing. Sometimes there is no time left to waste, and today is the best day to start. Well, today is always the best day to start, but sometimes we need to start slower, to let our body adjust to the new diet.

I know that changing the diet can be a great challenge for many. For some it seems to be very easy, and for some, very far from it. I believe that several factors come in to play. When you are overloaded with parasites, they will give you strong false cravings towards the foods that feed them. This is typically anything that will turn into complex sugars, the carbohydrates and the starches. These are breads, pasta, potatoes and anything made with flour and sugars. The pale brown and beige foods. You need to be prepared to crave these foods, and that it is not really you that is craving them. The low adrenals, which also leads to fungus overgrowth by the way, will nominate these foods as their comfort foods. Another typical craving is salt. When our adrenals are sloppy, we will crave salt. We will crave anything salty, as salt is a stimulant. It will stimulate the adrenals, and we will feel better for a short while, when in truth we are hurting ourselves even more.

Inorganic salt is poisonous and unassimilable to the human body. They are salts from rocks, not absorbable and therefore will accumulate in the body. It does not matter what salt it is. Table salt or Celtic sea-salt. It is all inorganic salt. We absolutely need our salts, all the minerals, and also the sodium, but we thrive on real, natural organic plant salt. The plants turn the salt from dead rock salt into living organic life giving salts. The photosynthesis is all about transforming. Photo, meaning photon, and synthesis meaning combining two things together, to form something new. So actually photosynthesis means combining photons with dead, inorganic matter, to create something new, the organic, living vibrant plants. True magical transformation, all for us to enjoy and thrive on. The plants contain all the salts that we need, all in organic perfectly absorbable form. Nature is perfect, and know that when you are craving salt on this new healing lifestyle, it is only your adrenals that are looking for their "fix", their false sense of energy. We will include celery in our diet, to make sure we are getting all the sodium and other mineral salts that we need.

We cannot keep doing the same thing that created the problem, we must look towards the other side, towards health and vitality. What creates health, we must ask?

What is a transition diet?

If your health is deteriorating fast, if you are in a state of degeneration, transitioning might not be what you need. You might need to jump right in to save your life, your limbs, your eyesight or your digestion. In that case it is very doable to change overnight. Make sure that you read the chapter about detoxification many times, to ensure that you are ready for the ride. There *will* be symptoms of cleansing when we stop what is hurting us, as the body will start to cleanse the first chance that it gets. Be prepared, be smart and be educated. Being in charge requires that you are on top of your game. Either if you are helping someone else, helping yourself, or simply educating yourself on true health, *you've* got this!

When we transition from a typical standard Western diet, we start by letting go of what is obstructing our bodies the most, and that is the food that is creating the most mucus. On the top of that list, we find dairy. Yes, absolutely *all* dairy, even the kefir, the yogurt and the goat milk. Anything that comes from animal milk will produce enormous amounts of mucus in our bodies, and we know what that means. It means hello parasites, an impacted intestine, congestion all over the body, and general acidity. We are simply not made to digest the proteins in the milk, and we suffer bigtime from trying to. So there we have it, first thing to go has to be the dairy - all of it.

All acid forming foods are mucus forming, so we are moving towards the alkaline side of chemistry. We want to slowly move to the alkaline side of eating, meaning more alkalizing fruits and vegetables, and less acid forming foods like animal meats and processed foods. Here is a short and very basic list of acid forming and alkaline forming foods, to give you a general idea. You will see that the most important thing to do is to move towards the plant based diet:

Acid forming food:

- **Meat:** Bacon, beef, clams, corned beef, lamb, lobster, mussels, organ meats, venison, all fish, oyster, pork, rabbit, sausage, scallops, shellfish, shrimp, tuna, turkey, veal, and any processed meat.

- **Dairy and eggs:** Milk, yogurt, kefir, all cheeses, butter, all eggs, ice-cream, soy cheese, sour-cream, mayonnaise and all other dairy foods.

- **All processed foods:** Soups, cooked food, fried and baked food, bread, pasta, candy, pizza, chips, biscuits, canned food, ketchup and the likes.

- **Others:** Rice, noodles, alcohol, cigarettes, artificial sweeteners, soy sauce, vinegar, tamari and salt.

- **Beverages:** Alcohol, soda, energy drinks, black tea, flavored water.

- **Oils:** Any cooked oil, like olive oil, palm oil, flax oil.

Alkaline forming foods:

- **Fruits & Berries:** Apple, pear, prune, grapes, apricot, dates, mango, banana, peach, all melons, orange, lemon, grapefruit, lime, pineapple, cucumber, avocado, tomato, peppers, strawberries, raspberries, currants, aronia berries, blackberries, lingonberries and any fruits you desire.

- **Vegetables:** Tender leafy greens, asparagus, broccoli, zucchini, kelp, collards, chives, onion, carrot, spinach, kale, cabbage, beets, cauliflower, brussel sprouts, celery, sprouted seeds, pumpkin and radish.

- **Fresh herbs:** Parsley, dandelion, plantain, garlic, fresh turmeric, basil, oregano, coriander, and many more.

- **Nuts and seeds:** In moderation and always soaked or sprouted, almonds, coconut, flax seeds, pumpkin seeds, hemp seeds, chia seeds, sunflower seeds, brazil nuts, hazel nuts, macadamia nuts, pistachios, pecans and cashews.

*Nuts and seeds are very high in fats and are not a detoxification food. All beans and lentils, are very high in protein, and somewhat mucus-forming and acidic to the body. They can be used as a short term transition food.

Dietary transition short list:

1. Remove all dairy products.
2. Remove all animal protein.
3. Remove all gluten containing products.

When you have **left the dairy**, you are ready to let go of everything that comes from the animal kingdom. You are ready to eat a vegan diet. This is very important for anyone who wants to get well, or live well. **The animal proteins** are detrimental to our kidney health, and that also means, the whole body's health. Nothing puts a toll on the kidneys, like having to break down those animal proteins;

Look at a full animal protein as a brick wall. It is a finished product, so to speak. It is made out of bricks, which are the amino acids in our body. They are the building blocks which are found in all fruits and vegetables, in all living plant foods. So, the body needs those amino acids/building blocks to build its protein, to make muscle and tissue. When we eat that animal protein, the body first has to tear it apart, using a lot of energy. Then it has to get rid of the waste, the mortar. This is where the kidneys come in, as they have to get rid of and get bothered with all this metabolic waste.

Very simply put, all proteins that we ingest are a burden to our kidneys, but nothing slams them like a steak does. So be aware. If you are hurting, or in any form of pain, stop eating animals this very minute, and feel the difference.

The next step when transitioning is to **stop all gluten containing products**, and also move to a whole foods diet. This means we are now at a vegan whole food, no gluten diet. This whole transition period should take you no more than a month, and then you are ready to hit the mostly raw diet. Some will feel better doing 80% raw, adding some steamed vegetables to their salad at night, to ease into the healing lifestyle even more. Then, there is no turning back. The time is now right, and going 100% raw on a healing, regenerating, alkalizing, hydrating diet will be a piece of cake, or a piece of melon rather. You are good to go!

Change starts with awareness, and by what we are putting in our mouths. When we eat to live, we go from surviving to thriving!

Remember, if you are feeling sick, have a painful experience, degenerative and in desperate need of regeneration, start right now, and do not spend another day eating anything that is not optimal for your amazing, beautiful, perfectly ready to heal body. No dis-ease will be treated, and no diagnosis will be given, only true health will be promoted here, and you are worth it!

This is a typical diet for detoxification and healing. I want to give you an idea of what a day and a week on life-giving foods looks like. Play with it and have fun. Experiment with the tastes and choices that you have where you live. Always use organic when you can, and as locally grown as possible.

Monday:

Breakfast: Optimal D-tox juice consisting of 1 cucumber, 2 lemons, 1 grapefruit, 1 green apple, 5 stalks of celery, a 2-inch piece of fresh ginger, a pinch of cayenne pepper. (This juice will be your everyday cleansing juice). A bowl of ½ large watermelon.

Lunch: A delicious smoothie consisting of 2 mangoes, 1 cup parsley, 2 pears, 2 cups berries of choice and clean water.

Dinner: A large salad consisting of a whole green salad of choice, or a large box of mixed greens, 1 cup of spinach, 1 chopped red

pepper, 1 cup cherry tomatoes, 2 spring onions, and ½ cucumber and 2 stalks of celery finely chopped. Dressing of choice.
Dressing choices below.
Snack: between meals, and never closer than 1.5 hours to the dinner salad, eat as much fresh fruits as you like.

Tuesday:

Breakfast: Optimal D-tox juice, 2 large mangos, topped with fresh raspberries and blackberries.
Lunch: A large bag of grapes (about 500gr/1,1 pounds), and 2 pears.
Dinner: A large salad consisting of a whole salad green of choice, or a large box of mixed greens, ½ cup of parsley, 5 chopped tomatoes, ½ finely chopped red onion, 2 grated carrots and 1 grated beet.
Dressing choices below.
Snack: between meals, and never closer than 1.5 hours to the dinner salad, eat as much fresh fruits as you like.

Wednesday:

Breakfast: Optimal D-tox juice, and 1 large bag of grapes.
Lunch: 16 0z, or ½ liter of freshly squeezed orange juice. A large fruit salad consisting of 2 large mangos, 2 bananas, 3 apples and 2 cups of berries.
Dinner: A large smoothie consisting of 5 bananas, 1 cup spinach, 1 mango, 2 cups of berries of choice, 5 dates and clean water.
Snack: between meals, and never closer than 1.5 hours to the dinner salad, eat as much fresh fruits as you like.

Thursday:

Breakfast: Optimal D-tox juice, 1 Large cantaloupe.
Lunch: A delicious smoothie consisting of 2 mangoes, 1 cup spinach, 4 kiwis, 2 cups grapes, 1 cup berries of choice.

Dinner: Zucchini noodles (very easy to make with a spiralizer) of 2 large or 4 small zucchinis, ½ cup arugula, 1 chopped yellow pepper, 1 cup cherry tomatoes, 2 spring onions, and ½ cucumber finely chopped, ½ avocado, dressing of choice, the tomato dressing is amazing.
Dressing choices below.
Snack: between meals, and never closer than 1.5 hours to the dinner salad, eat as much fresh fruits as you like.

Friday:

Breakfast: Optimal D-tox juice, and a tasty smoothie of 4 bananas, 4 kiwis, 2 cups of berries and clean water.
Lunch: The juice of 1 cucumber, 2 apples and 1 lemon. A large bowl of ½ watermelon, ½ cantaloupe and ½ honeydew melon, or melons of your choice.
Dinner: Wraps using large collard greens, filled with grated carrots, grated beets, tender leafy greens, chopped celery and cucumber slices. As a spread, use one of the dressings. The tahini lemon is great for this one.
Snack: between meals, and never closer than 1.5 hours to the dinner salad, eat as much fresh fruits as you like.

Saturday:

Breakfast: Optimal D-tox juice, a bowl of 4 chopped bananas and 3 chopped apples, with cinnamon sprinkled on top.
Lunch: The juice of 3 oranges, 1 grapefruit and 2 lemons. A filling large smoothie of 2 mangoes, 2 pears, 3 kiwis, 1 cup of parsley, 1 cup of fresh blackberries, and clean water.
Dinner: Noodles made from 2 large European cucumbers, noodles made from 3 large carrots. 2 stalks of celery finely minced, 5 sundried tomatoes finely minced, and 4 chopped large heirloom tomatoes.
Dressing choices below.

Snack: between meals, and never closer than 1.5 hours to the dinner salad, eat as much fresh fruits as you like.

Sunday:

Breakfast: Optimal D-tox juice, and a wonderful smoothie of ½ pineapple, 2 pears, 4 kiwis, and clean water.

Lunch: The juice of 2 cucumbers, 1 beet and 2 lemons. A large bowl consisting of ½ watermelon, ½ cantaloupe and ½ honeydew melon, or melons of your choice.

Dinner: A large salad consisting of a whole green salad of choice, or a large box of mixed greens, ½ cup of coriander, 5 chopped heirloom tomatoes, 2 stalks of celery finely chopped, ½ chopped large cucumber, 1 chopped red pepper, 4 sliced radishes, and 1 cup grated cabbage.

Dressing choices below.

Snack: between meals, and never closer than 1.5 hours to the dinner salad, eat as much fresh fruits as you like.

Salad dressing options:

The Tomato-love dressing: Blend 4 Large ripe sweet tomatoes, ½ cup sundried tomatoes with no oil or salt, 1 red pepper, 1 clove of garlic, 1 stalk of celery, ½ cup fresh basil, 1 teaspoon dried oregano, 2 pitted dates, and 1 tablespoon of lemon juice. Add some finely chopped red onion and tomatoes and blend in with a spoon.

The Tahini-blast dressing: Blend the juice of 1 large lemon, 1 tablespoon of tahini with no oil or salt, 1 cup of water, 1 tablespoon of kelp if you have a fresh good brand, if not use a stalk of celery, 1 teaspoon of cumin, and 1 clove of garlic. You can spice this up with cayenne pepper, and any other spice you fancy.

The Creamy Italian-dream dressing: Blend ½ avocado with ½ small white onion, 1 tomato, 2 tablespoons of Italian salt free seasoning, 1 stalk of celery, the juice of half a lemon, add water if needed.

The Mango fresh-delight dressing: Blend 1 large mango, 2 pitted dates,1 stalk celery, 2 tablespoons of lime juice, 1 spring onion, and one jalapeno.

Use the recipes as a guideline, and feel free to experiment. There are a few simple rules when mixing together foods, even the raw. The general rule is to not mix vegetables and fruits too much, as they are in need of different digestive juices. I do however see and experience that mangoes do good with salads, and that citruses, the acidic fruits do well with vegetables and fats. Note that tender leafy greens are not considered vegetables. Fats is the other issue, and I would not bend on that rule. First of all, we keep the fat uptake very low during a detoxification and healing journey, and we never mix them with fruits. This is why you will not see any fats blended in any of the fruit meals, only with the greens, in the dressings. Also, the fruit dressing does not have any fats. The fat will inhibit the cell from absorbing the simple sugars, and both digestion and blood sugar will eventually suffer.

When you are eating a diet consisting of fresh fruits and vegetables, no oils and no salt, there are no limitations to the amount of food that you can eat. Eat until full, and never overeat. Food is not about the amount of calories, but the amount of energy that you need to thrive. It will differ throughout your life, depending on the phase that your body is in. This is a cleansing phase, not a building phase. When we have cleaned out our bodies, it is time to rebuild. The body cannot cleanse and rebuild at the same time. The cleaner we get, the more the body is able to absorb, the less food we will also need.

Basic food combining rules:

- **Acidic fruits** go with all other fruits, and can be used in salad dressings, even with fats. These are the citruses mainly. Pineapple is also an acidic fruit. The acidic fruits are the most astringent, the most lymph-pulling, aggressive detoxing fruits.

- **Sub-acidic** fruits go with acidic fruits and sweet fruits. The sub-acidic fruits are the apples, pears, grapes, mangoes, kiwi, berries and the peaches. These are the medium astringent fruits.

- **The sweet** fruits go together with the sub-acidic fruits also, but not with the acidic fruits. The sweet fruits are the bananas, the dates, the papayas and the figs. These are the least detoxifying fruits.

- **The melons** have a separate set of rules. It says to eat them alone, or leave them alone. They do not digest well with other fruits, and are best eaten alone.

NOTE: Unripe fruits are very acidic, so make sure your fruits are ripe. The banana is the only fruit that will ripen after it has been picked. This is a challenge, I know, as so many fruits are being picked unripe, but be aware and do the best that you can. When the fruit is ripe, it has all the sweet sugars that your cells need. An unripe fruit will sit and ferment, and not be optimal as food.

"When we love ourselves just the way we are, we start to treat ourselves like a loved one, the best way we know how." -Hilde

When you have a challenge with foods, it is a combined physical and emotional problem. Weak glands, candida and parasites will send the body signals to keep feeding the cause. It is often also a lack of self-love problem, an "I am never good enough", problem. A stressful job and a dysfunctional relationship can also easily determine how we eat.

We are in charge of all that we do, say, and certainly what we eat. I was aware that I had a choice, yet I was not aware that I was not making a conscious one. I was waking up to the responsibility and the logic behind life and health, but I could also see the wall of misinformation and social conditioning that was present.

The sugars that are present in so-called foods today are very addictive. They give us a false craving for more, and to connect with what our body really needs is next to impossible. Most often when we are hungry, it is not real hunger. We are feeding our parasites and our addictions. The complex sugars are feeding the fungus and the parasites. The adrenalin in meat, the salt and the coffee, are all boosting our adrenals, while at the same time destroying them, declining our health and vitality. Our supermarkets are filled up with sparkling labels and addictive foods to keep us coming back, and to keep us from waking up to the true masters that we are.

A master is not a follower, and a follower is what makes the profit. With ingredients that our grandparents would not be able to pronounce and nothing that nature intended us to eat, the body will shut down its most precious life-force. Sickness is taking a hold, and medications are next. A grim truth that I know only too well.

This is the time to break the cycle, to get back to basics. It is simple, it is natural, it is logical and it is truth. Nature is perfect!

Chapter 10

Wild food and medicine

Wild food is the original true food. At one point all food was wild food, and all food was medicine. In nature, there is no obstruction, constipation, or bad choices. We can state that no matter what we live or do, it is ok, and that every journey is the right one. Yet, cause and effect is still present. By choosing a path, any path, we will have to wear the robe, to walk our talk. Cause and effect. We are seeing the effect of not following the laws of nature, and we are paying the bill. Through sickness and stress, the lack of feeling loved and safe, we are experiencing the panic of not having or being enough. We are always enough, always. Our basic needs are simple and few in numbers. There is no solution in complication, and there is no large puzzle to solve. There is only life, the simple exercise of breathing, loving and being. We can complicate it if we want, with but`s and reasons for hanging on to stuff, but it will not set us free.

True freedom is seeing the simplicity in everything, and knowing that it is perfect the way it is. Nature is effortless in its growth and manifestations. We are not meant to struggle.

The wild herbs are natures medicine, and by ingesting them, we are ingesting the healing vibration that comes with it. The nutritional composition is out of comparison with our farm grown produce. The wild food is very dense in nutrients, and will go a long way. Spending time in nature, picking and eating what nature has provided for us, is a calm connecting practice in itself. By embracing true wisdom from nature, we will be nourished on all levels.

The wild greens, the medicinal herbs, the flowers - they are all there for us to explore and to use. I have seen profound effects on all my bodies from taking the herbal blends, and also from using them fresh from the forest. During the season, I pick herbs fresh every single day, and blend them up in my smoothie. Some of the most potential all-round healing herbs are willingly growing right in our back yard. Many of them, we categorize as weed. Not only have we forgotten how to use them, how to appreciate the gift that they are, we also look at them mostly as a nuisance, as weeds. The most common ones are dandelions, plantain, ground elder and stinging nettles. I am sure that most of you know about some of them, if not all of them. I pick them, rinse them, and eat them fresh, yes, even the stinging nettle. I also use birch leaves, clover, fire weed, chickweed and thistle.

I have a way of making sure that I get that magic into my body all year round, so I pick more than I need all summer, then I dry the herbs, powder them, and use them during winter. I gift the powder to others, and I am empowered by this free, easily available, powerful food and medicine being there for us all. I am in awe that I am able to grow into more freedom through nature. The process is very easy. Simply pick the wild greens, and dry them. If you do not have a dehydrator, put it on your wish list, and in the meantime you can hang the herbs in a dry doom, or spread them on a table on top of some newspapers. I then use a nutria bullet to powder the greens, but you can use a regular high speed blender. Store in dark grass containers, in a dry cool place, and use all winter long.

Let me get you on your way to foraging your own wild food. I hope to inspire you to use them as a part of your healing regime. They will most certainly give you the upper hand on health.

NB! Before you forage and ingest any wild edible, make absolutely sure that you are picking the right one. Talk to someone who has experience, and have them show you. Google for pictures, and look for my next book about nature, healing and wild food, and always make sure you are safe.

The most general wild herbs that I use and love:

Dandelion is great for the liver. While the antioxidants like vitamin-c and Luteolin keep the liver functioning in optimal gear and protect it from aging, other compounds in dandelions help treat hemorrhaging in the liver. Furthermore, dandelions aid in maintaining the proper flow of bile, while also stimulating the liver and promoting digestion. Proper digestion can reduce the chances of constipation, and is a very big deal for maintaining a healthy functioning body. It is seen as a liver detoxifier, and a kidney cleanser. It is also believed to cleanse the blood, and help build new blood cells. Its nutritional benefits are a powerhouse compared to other greens. It is a survivor, and will never quit. It can grow almost anywhere, even straight through asphalt. Dandelion, which literally translates into "lion's tooth" in French, is rich in vitamin-A, C, iron and calcium, which explains its common inclusion in medicines. It grows in your back yard, on any open field, in the forest and on the sidewalks. It is not leaving us alone, saying: "Hey, I am your free food and medicine, *use* me!"

You can use the dandelion fresh in your everyday smoothie, dry it for your tea, or make powder for later. You can use the younger leaves in your salad, as the older ones might be too bitter. It is also fantastic for juicing, and has a great place in any healing green juice. The root can be dried and used for tea also, and some even ground the roots to make coffee substitutes. The flower, yellow and bright is also very potent and edible. Use it in your salad, dry it for your tea, or ground into powder together with the leaves. Anything goes.

Plantain leaf has a natural anti-inflammatory and antibacterial benefit. This makes it great for wound healing. Medicinally, Native Americans used plantain leaves to relieve the pain of bee stings and insect bites, to stop the itching of poison ivy and other allergic rashes. It was also known to promote healing in sores and bruises. It is diuretic and great for kidney and health. Many of its active constituents show antibacterial and antimicrobial properties, as well as being anti-inflammatory and antitoxic. The young leaves are the mildest and tastiest, but you can dry them all season and make tea or powder. Plantain is very high in vitamins A, C and in calcium. Plantain tea can be used as a mouthwash to help heal and prevent sores in the mouth, and as an expectorant. I have seen plantain being marketed as a stop-smoking aid, adding one more use to the list of ways that this versatile herb can be used. It grows in your lawn, on any forest trail, and on the side of the road. If you have a driveway that is not paved, you might find it there.

You can make tea from plantain and spray it on insect bites. The leaves are edible, and you can use them raw in salads, or cooked as greens. They are great for blending in your healing and detoxifying smoothie. Older leaves have a stronger, sometimes objectionable flavor, and can be tough and stringy. This goes for most of the wild herbs. The leaves, shredded or chewed, are a traditional treatment for insect and animal bites. The antibacterial action helps prevent infection and the anti-inflammatory helps to relieve pain, burning, and itching.

Stinging nettles are great as both medicine and food. They're highly nutritious, and is believed to stop any internal or external bleeding. It will clear mucus from the body, and is great for diarrhea and water retention. It also stimulates the organ glands. For thousands of years, people around the world have used stinging nettles to treat a wide variety of health conditions. The leaves and stems in some of the subspecies have long stinging hairs that inject an array of chemicals when touched, including histamine, formic acid, serotonin, and acetylcholine. This produces an irritating, uncomfortable sensation in the skin, which is why some of the other common names for stinging nettles are *burn weed* and *burn nettle*.

It's a natural cleanser that removes metabolic wastes and is both gentle and stimulating on the lymph system, promoting easy excretion through the kidneys. As a diuretic substance, stinging nettles can also ensure that those toxins being neutralized in the body are then eliminated quickly. Stinging nettles are also known to be alterative, meaning that it can improve the nutrient uptake efficiency of the gut and ensure that the digestive processes run smoothly. This is, as you can see, quite an amazing free plant! It also stimulates the lymphatic system, and helps to rid the body of excess toxins in the kidneys.

You can use all parts of the nettle plant. It is widely used in herbal tea, tinctures and ointments. During season, when you can find it fresh, use it in your smoothie. No, it will not sting your mouth or throat. The first time I used it fresh, I was a bit hesitant, but the stinging property stops once it gets moist. Therefore, you cannot use it in your salad, but dry it for powder or tea. The powerful array of nutrients makes it a great addition to any green powder. The herbal detoxifier that combined with the plantain and dandelion will rock your house!

Ground elder is the modern name for *goutweed* or *Herb Gerard*, and as its name suggests it was a specific remedy for gout and sciatica. Our grandparents will remember it being used to treat any form of rheumatism. It gets the name *ground elder* from the resemblance of the flowers to those of the elder tree. Most of those who have a garden and that has run across the ground elder, will know it as a pain in the garden. They seem like they are spreading as you watch, and never letting go of their territory. They are hard to get rid of, but maybe now you can look at them differently? It was used as a green vegetable in earlier times, and was used by monks and bishops to counteract the rich food they so often ate. It is also a diuretic and has a mild sedative effect. It is often referred to as the wild parsley. It has a very similar taste to parsley, and also some of the same properties and benefits. It will strengthen the kidneys and bladder. Overall it is said to activate our metabolism, help to detox our system, and it provides us with an abundance of chlorophyll and Vitamin C. All the green plants are loaded with chlorophyll, our blood-fuel and sunshine energy. Not bad for something known as an annoying weed, and quite interesting that these amazing plants are so wildly available to us.

> The ground elder is absolutely most beneficial during spring, in its growing phase. Before it blooms with its white flowers it is mild and palatable. After that, it becomes bitter and harder to digest. The wonderful thing about this plant though, is that it will grow new buds, young plants, all season long. This is why it is so hard to get rid of - it keeps shooting new leaves. You can make ground elder pesto. You can also put some in your smoothie and in your salad. It is food and medicine, and great for drying and powdering. A poultice of the leaves can also be employed to help heal burns, bites, and wounds.

Red clover is often used for respiratory and hormonal health. It is considered to be one of the richest sources of isoflavones, which are water-soluble chemicals that act like estrogens. Red clover is therefore used for hot flashes, PMS, breast health as well as lowering cholesterol. It is also said to improve urine production, improve circulation of the blood, and to help prevent osteoporosis.

Red clover leaf is a staple of herbal blood cleansing formulas. One of its common uses is to help with overall cardiovascular health. Red clover is an excellent blood purifier, and over time, it gradually cleanses the bloodstream. It is also said to correct deficiencies in the circulatory system. It has been shown to thin the blood and reduce the possibility of blood clots and arterial plaques. These are mighty statements, and gives the red clover a very special place in our tool box.

The flowers possess antispasmodic, estrogenic, and expectorant properties. Chinese medicine uses red clover in their teas as an expectorant. During the Middle Ages, the red clover was considered a charm of protection against witches. We are used to thinking about the regular four-leaf clover as lucky, but the same is true of the red four-leaf clover. Red clover is also a source of many valuable nutrients including calcium, chromium, magnesium, niacin, phosphorus, potassium, thiamine, and vitamin C.

Topically, it is used to accelerate wound healing and to treat psoriasis. The flowers are so beautiful and very potent, which makes them such a beautiful part of any salad. The leaves, together with the flowers, can be dried and used as a tea. Also, blend them up in your smoothie during season, and dry and powder them for the winter.

Fireweed has a long history of use as a medicinal plant. It is easy to spot in any terrain with its beautiful purple flowers and long leafy stems. The herb is antispasmodic, hypnotic, laxative and tonic, and has agents that cause tissue to contract, which will soften and soothe the skin when applied locally. Historically, medicinal use includes oral use of the plant extracts, often in the form of an infusion or tea, as a treatment for prostate and urinary problems including benign prostatic hyperplasia or enlarged prostate, and for various gastrointestinal disorders such as dysentery or diarrhea. The Blackfoot Indians used the powdered inner cortex rubbed on the hands and face to protect them from the cold during the winter. They also made tea of the roots and inner cortex which they gave to their babies as an enema for constipation. Chemically, the fireweed contains an abundance of phenolic compounds, tannins and flavonoids, many of which appear to have biological activity. It has been used to aid any digestion troubles, inflammation, and it has antispasmodic and astringent properties. They grow willingly on the side of the road, and in gardens and fields.

The shoots are tender and great to use in salads, and can be used as an alternative to asparagus. Very young leaves are also edible in salads and soups. Make tea of the young leaves for an upset stomach. Only use the leaves when they are young, and do not overdo it. If you ingest too many, you might experience some nausea. The mature leaves become tough and bitter, but by then the unopened flower-buds are tasty and beautiful for all types of raw food creations. Topically the plant has been used traditionally as a soothing, cleansing and healing agent to treat minor burns, skin rashes, ulcers, and numerous other skin irritations and afflictions. The root can be eaten raw, cooked or dried and ground into a powder. Used in spring, it has a sweet taste. Dry the young leaves for tea and powder, and use the flowers in your salad.

Chickweed is mild, delicious, and has a fresh taste which is great in any salad. It is one of the most common weeds out there. It has been used to calm inflammation and reduce stress. It is useful for people with stomach and duodenal ulcers to use regularly. Because chickweed is cooling and moistening, ingesting it reduces hot and dry conditions, such as fevers and dry, red, itchy, eczema and psoriasis. Its moistening properties help relieve constipation, and aid any digestive issues. The cooling and anti-inflammatory properties ease arthritis, joint and muscle pain. Chickweed helps the body absorb nutrients better, and is a safe and nourishing herb for a person of any age to take over several months. It will strengthen the body when weak, chronically tired from overwork and stress, traumatized, anemic or recovering from a long-term illness or surgery. Chickweed not only effects physical health, but is a psychic healer also. It opens us up to cosmic energies and gives us the inner strength we need to handle those energies. Chickweed has a delicious, fresh taste and is high in minerals and vitamins.

Pick them and put them straight into your salad all summer long. You can also use it in your smoothie and in your juices. A fresh chickweed poultice reduces swelling and inflammation from bruises, mosquito bites and bee stings. It helps heal skin ulcers and other inflamed or itchy skin conditions. A fresh poultice also draws out infections from abscesses, boils, cuts and pus-filled wounds very effectively. A chickweed salve can ease itching of eczema or psoriasis and assist in healing hemorrhoids, minor cuts, skin eruptions and inflamed skin rashes.

NOTE: Make sure that you are not picking anything that has been sprayed with weed killers, or has been growing on the side of a busy road.

My healing wild smoothie:

- 2 large mangoes
- 1 cup dandelion leaves
- ½ cup stinging nettle leaves
- 5 leaves of fireweed
- 5 leaves of plantain
- 5 red clover flower heads.
- 1/2 cup of ground elder leaves
- 1 cup of fresh or frozen berries.
- 1 cup of distilled water

My healing wild juice:

- 1 cucumber
- 1 lemon
- 1 green apple
- 1 hand-full of chickweed

- 1 hand-full of dandelion leaves
- 2 hand-full of ground elder leaves.

Note: The above information is for educational purposes only, and while you research the wild edibles further, you will find that the benefits that have been studied and experienced are far more extensive than what I have touched upon. These are true healers, and by using them as we heal, we are getting closer to nature, and to our natural environment.

The more I consume of the wild edibles, the more connected and aware I feel. I am a firm believer that what will feed us and nurture us with the highest potential, nutrition and energy is the wild edibles. The berries, the herbs, the greens, the flowers and the leaves. The roots and the sap, all magical and healing. Ever since I started my walk towards health and my re-connection to nature, I have gotten more and more connected to the plants. Through eating them, having dreams and visions, and through being around their energy - I have found true love for nature and all the life within it. The purity and the vibration is nurturing for every cell in your body. The herbs are intelligent and tissue specific, they are true healers. What started out as a quest for healing, *physical* healing, has ended up as a passion and a calling.

By letting go of what is no longer serving us, we are making room for what *is*. By re-connecting with nature, we are calling upon the highest form of healing.

Birch sap:

Nature has more wonders than the leafy greens and the obvious berries and nuts. If you have never had or heard about birch sap, there is something new for you to explore. This is a true elixir, and a healing drink for the entire body. The taste is like pure water, with just a hint of sweetness. Clear and cool, straight from the tree. This is a natural ready-to-drink liquid. I was gifted this elixir from a series of birch trees that are growing in my neck of the woods. I was amazed at how easy it was to tap the tree, and how invigorating the sap was to drink. The traditional virtues of birch and its efficient removal of toxic substances from the liver and kidneys, has been known and appreciated for ages. There are very few single substances that are capable of targeting the body's two major cleansing and purification systems at the same time. It is a fantastic detoxifying elixir!

Birch trees contain powerful diuretic properties that aid in flushing out harmful toxins, uric acid, and excess water from the body. Again, it helps in maintaining good kidney and liver health, which is a welcoming trait for all of us. There are numerous more benefits, one being its high nutritional value, another the living energy of this water. The unbeatable pure vibrating energy. *That* is what we want to ingest, the pure life-force of nature. Birch sap can help boost immunity, fight fatigue, treat arthritis and joint pain. It also acts as an energy booster and is believed to prevent migraines. It is claimed to help treat liver disease, flu, headaches, dandruff and eczema. It is also believed to flush out toxins and help reduce cellulite. Like coconut water, the sap is very good for rehydration due to the high content of electrolytes, macronutrients and potassium. Birch sap also contains saponin, which has been shown to control blood cholesterol levels and is good for the immune system. It is the essence, the life-blood, of the tree, carrying nutrients essential for growth. Birch sap is also a seasonal source of vitamins, minerals and sugars, mainly fructose and glucose.

The sap from the birch tree can be collected in the early spring, the perfect time to collect some rejuvenating elixir after a long winter. This is when the sap is travelling up the trunk of the tree. Just before the leaves open is the best time, and the window is short – the sap will only be available for us for about 30 days. After this point, the tree will need all its own juices, and we have to back off.

> Birch sap is amazingly high in macronutrients and micronutrients, including proteins and amino acids, as well as enzymes, electrolytes and potassium. This is a true gift from nature!

You can tap the tree the same way one would drain syrup from a maple tree. It can be collected by driving taps into the base of the trunk or by cutting off the end of one of the branches and attaching a bottle.

- Drill a 40-60mm hole with an 8-12mm sterile drill-bit at a slight upward angle, close to ground level but high enough to get your collection container underneath.

- Insert a desired length of sterile 'food grade' plastic tubing into the hole. It has to be the same diameter as the hole. You then put the other end into a sterile 'food grade' plastic container.

- Use some duct tape or plastic wrapping, to ensure that the plastic tube and the bottle has a closed connection. You are leaving this outside overnight and do not want bugs to get into your sap.

- Once tapping is complete, spray each hole with clean water and plug it with a slither of wood or sod of earth, like applying a band aid. This is very important. Never leave a tree bleeding, as it will get hurt, and we are walking lightly on this earth.

If you only want to collect a small amount of sap you can make an incision in the bark with a sharp knife, and use a piece of wood as a lead for the clear liquid. You can also leave a bottle at the end of a branch, if you only want a small amount of sap.

Birch water can be drunk fresh, but has a shelf life of just a few days, so be sure to use the sap for its intended purpose within a couple of days. You can store it in a tight glass bottle for no longer than a few days in the refrigerator. That's it.

If you want to try this for yourself, remember to ask the tree's permission. Never tap the same tree for more than 24 hours, and always tap when the sap is rising. After that, it needs it for its own leaves. Then, remember to plug the hole that you made to ensure that the tree will not be bleeding. A grand thank you will then be in order. We are welcome to harvest the gifts of nature, but we must always show our gratitude and tread lightly.

Kelp, the wild sea food:

Living in Norway by the coast of the North Sea, has a few great benefits. While the tropics have their ripe juicy fruits, we have the wild herbs and the kelp, the wild seaweed and sea vegetables. The kelp that I am harvesting is nothing like what I have been purchasing in any capsule or powder. This is fresh from the ocean, all pure living sea goodness. My love for the wild edibles include the seaweed, the sea vegetables, and on this cool coast, we have them in abundance. Kelp is a fantastic source of nutrition, and it is very high in iodine. This important mineral is a thyroid fuel, and a mineral generally lacking in a modern diet. I am not at all for counting levels of substances that we can analyze and categorize though. I believe the body will balance and take what it needs at all times, when we feed it what it needs, and not as much what it does not.

The kelp has a salty taste, and can be used on salads and in dressings, eaten as it is, raw, or dried and grounded into a powder. I have had periods when I have craved it bigtime, and I know that the kelp, the pure fresh ocean gold has helped my body in many ways. It is because of the kelp's support of the pituitary gland and the thyroid, that makes it the superhero of supplements for nail and hair health.

Harvesting kelp is very simple. I recommend to only harvest the fresh ones, still living, connected to their roots, so it will take a little bit of muscle to get the big fish, so to speak. There are many types of seaweed, but the one that I have found the most potent, and that I have been using for several years is the Laminaria digitata. It can vary in color from dark brown to olive green, but is more commonly a golden brown color. It can grow up to 2.5m long and 60 cm across the frond. It holds onto the rocks, so it can be hard to loosen. Use a garden rake, and bring a large container. To be able to catch the fresh kelp, still growing from their roots, calm seas and a low tide is often a must. This wonderful sea vegetable can be harvested by the lucky ones all year round. If you are ever able to harvest your own kelp, go get it!

Once the kelp is out of the ocean, I do not let it sit for more than a day, in a cool place, before I dry it. Use a dehydrator, or lay them outside in the sunshine. There is nothing wrong with eating kelp fresh, straight from the ocean, but they are great for powdering and using as a supplement or a seasoning. Sprinkle the salty powder over your salad, or use it in a dressing.

If you cannot get your own kelp, I would consider buying some from a reliable source. It really is a great addition to any healing regime. The minerals, especially the iodine is very much appreciated by the body.

Love everything that nature has to offer, and turn another stone to see what you have been missing. It has all been created to nurture and support, and is always one step ahead.

Chapter 11

Liver and gallbladder flushing

In the midst of healing, and in the zone of fire, the liver will most often be in the need of some very special care. From having been your friend and trusted power-organ through thick and thin, through health and less health, a heavy night on the town, drowned in drugs and medication toxins, the liver is an organ that needs love. It needs to be able to regenerate, and by letting it, and even helping it, the detoxification and healing journey will be shorter and more enjoyable. The liver is not an elimination organ, but it is absolutely a detoxifying one. It is taking a big hit from the toxins that the body is trying to eliminate, and it gets clogged up from cholesterol and bile, forming small stones to protect us from the toxins. Remember what you read in the chapter about detoxification. It is important and necessary that you fully understand the healing crisis and detoxification symptoms.

Look at the liver as a large filter, with bile ducts that get clogged up with stones. I was definitely clogged up from years of being medicated, from alcohol and less than optimal lifestyle choices.

When we have lived a toxic life, and our health has been impaired, the liver is always struggling. Sometimes so much so that we can feel the pressure under our left rib. The liver is an organ of transmutation. By this, I mean that it changes one substance into another. Some of the toxins that enters the liver, are broken down and passed out of the body as waste. Others are actually changed into substances that the body can use.

When we talk about gallstones, we usually think about them as being only in the gallbladder. This is a common false assumption. Most gallstones are actually formed in the liver. The cleanse that we are going to embrace here, is actually a liver and gallbladder flush, as it will cleanse the gallbladder as well. This is a very old remedy for gallstones, and many gallbladders have been saved by using this method. It does not matter if you do not have a gallbladder, the flush will still be of great benefit to you. Just wait and see, this will most certainly make you a believer in a clogged up liver. By taking full responsibility you are now about to do something that will change your health from one day to the other. By that I mean that by doing a liver and gallbladder flush, you will be on your way to a cleaner, better you. It will remove obstructions, and we know that any form of obstruction is hurting our physical and emotional bodies. Like the kidneys and the colon, the liver needs to be able to hold the energy of flow, for the body to let go of all that it does not need.

Practically everyone that is suffering from a so-called chronic disease will have a liver with stones. Some more than others, but all will have stones. This is because without toxicity and acidity there would only be true health. The formation of stones in the liver is merely the body trying to protect itself. It will encapsulate parasites and other toxins. The body will always do whatever it needs to do to save our butts. It will always try to stay healthy, for as long as it possibly can.

According to the mother of liver flushes and parasite cleansing, Dr. Hulda Clark, one should not do a liver flush with live parasites residing within the liver. This is why we have been on top of the parasite cleansing at such an early stage of the journey. Dr. Clark also found that one should keep on doing these liver flushes until there are no stones present for three flushes in a row. For some of us, that will take some time. For me, it took 52 flushes, and close to two years. I was sick and I needed to save my life. I was ready to do anything that needed to be done. It was my time, like this is *yours*.

When we are ready for change, the change that will rewrite our whole life-story, the power we need to do so will rise from within. When we take the first step, the road will reveal itself.

The most common recipe to use for this cleanse comes from Dr. Hulda Clark and Andreas Moritz. They have both done an amazing job by helping many people clean out their livers and gallbladders. I have made some modifications, but the basics are still the same. If you do not release any stones the first time around, don't worry. Sometimes the stones need to move further down the ducts, before they can be released. The liver is filled with these ducts, and they can be all clogged up by smaller and larger stones. Be prepared to release from none to 600 hundred stones. Yes, indeed, they can be many in numbers.

Preparing for the flush:

Eat a diet high in fresh fruits and vegetables, and very low in fats for 7 days prior to the flush. This goes for anyone who wants to do this procedure. It does not matter if the person is cleansing or not, the week before the flush, only very light fresh meals will do. This is very important. You also need to drink a few glasses of freshly made apple juice every day during this week. There are a few good store-bought ones, but as you are on your way with juicing anyway, you might as well make it fresh. The malic acids in the apples will help dissolve the stones. It will soften them, so that they can come out more easily. If you are taking any supplements, do not take them the day before the flush, and not on the day of the flush itself.

This is what you will need:

- Epsom salt (Magnesium sulfate). You can find it online, at the health food store or at your local pharmacy.
- 2 large grapefruits. You will need 125ml (1/2 cup) of freshly squeezed juice.
- Organic cold pressed olive oil.
- A large glass.
- A glass bottle.
- A tablespoon.
- A colander.

You are now ready to do the flush itself. Choose a day where you can rest the next day, like a Saturday. Remember to stay away from your supplements, and leave any medications that you feel you can do without. We do not want anything to interfere with the upcoming event. If you are on a parasite cleanse, or an herbal regime, stop that also on the flush day. Let us keep it as clean as possible. As with any program, following the guidelines is important to ensure success, so make sure that you stick to the outlined steps below.

The day of the flush:

Eat a fruity breakfast, or fruits and vegetables only. Drink fresh juices and water. No coffee or tea. Prepare the Epsom salt blend in a glass bottle, by mixing 3 small tablespoons of Epsom salt with 2 cups of water (500ml). This is to be divided into three different servings, so make markings on the bottle to see how much you should drink each time. Leave the bottle with the water and salt mix in the refrigerator. The Epsom salt will relax the bile-ducts, making it easy for the stones to travel through.

3:00 PM. Do not eat or drink after 3 o'clock. This is a very important point. You can be quite ill if you do not follow every step. Make sure that you have everything that you need. Leave the colander in the bathroom.

6:00 PM. Drink one serving of the mixture you've made (1/3 of the prepared mixture). If you forgot to do this ahead of time, mix a small tablespoon of the salt with a glass of water. Do not complicate it.

8:00 PM. Repeat by drinking another dose of the mixture. The timing here is very important, so get your chores for the evening done. After the oil drink that comes next, you will not be able to do anything, so make sure that you've done everything you need to do. You might notice that you have to go to the bathroom after this drink and that is very normal.

9:30 PM. Squeeze the juices from the grapefruits, and remove all the pulp and all the stones by hand. Get the large glass, and poor 1/2 cup (1,8dl) of the olive oil together with ½ cup (1,8dl) of the grapefruit juice in the same glass. Cover the glass, and do not drink yet! This is the actual flush-drink. Bring it with you to the bedroom, together with a spoon for stirring.

Do your bathroom before-sleep tasks, and try to be ready for bed by 10:00 PM. This is important.

10:00 PM. Make sure the lights are out, your door is locked, and that you do not need to get up after this point. Sit down on your bed and stir the mix until well blended. Drink the potion you have mixed. Bottoms up!

Lie down immediately. This is very important and why you need to make sure everything is ready for bed before you drink the mix. Do not break this rule, you might fail to get stones out if you do. Put down the glass on your night stand and lie down on your back.

Your head should be higher than your stomach. After about 20 minutes, lie on your right side, with your knees pulled up. You need to lie in this position for 20 minutes, so do not move. Focus on your liver, and try to visualize the stones moving. Do the same with the gallbladder. You might feel the stones travelling, and hear a rumbling sound. The bile ducts are very relaxed due to the Epsom salt, so you should feel no pain. Some nausea may occur. Try to go to sleep in this position.

If you need to get up during the night to go to the bathroom, that is fine. Go back to bed right after. The more sleep the better.

The following morning:

6AM or upon awakening: In the original protocols, several glasses of Epsom salts are to be ingested. I have found that it can be a bit too much, and that the one glass is sufficient. If you are thirsty after this, sip on some water. Keep resting if you like, but you can also start your day in a calm and quiet manner.

You might feel dehydrated and that is normal. You might also feel nauseated, and that is normal also. The liver has been forced to spasm, and to push the stones to move. A lot of bile has been released, and it takes a toll on the body. Many toxins have also been released, and the body just needs a little time. It will pass during mid-morning hours.

10AM: You can now drink your morning juice and eat your fruity breakfast. Only fruits and juices will do. To experience diarrhea is very normal, and it's mostly due to the Epsom -salts mix. Use the colander when you go to the bathroom and look for stones and parasites (if you have been parasite cleansing).

Follow up on your light meals all day, and let your body rest when it wants too. You have done a very hefty job on your liver, and the benefits will be many. Continue with your regular healing diet the next day.

The bowel movement sinks but the gallstones will float because of the cholesterol inside them, so even without the colander you will be able to spot them. It can be a fun thing to count them, roughly. Some say that after releasing a few thousand stones some real change in your health will happen. You might also see what we call "chaff". This is cholesterol crystals from the bile ducts that did not form into round stones. This will float on top of the water, and might be tanned, and is also a very important part of the cleanse. The stones will come in different shades of green, and this is from the green colored bile from the liver. They come in all sizes and shapes, and the light colored stones are the newest. The blackish stones are the oldest, and might have been with you for a very long time. The size will range from little mini pea size or smaller, to as big as an inch in diameter.

I recommend using an enema bag the next day, to make sure that every stone that has been released is removed from the colon. The same goes for all the toxins that have been dumped also. You can get an enema bag online or at your health food store. Simply fill it with lukewarm water, and hold it in as long as you can. If this is new to you, I recommend getting one ahead of time, and doing a few practice rounds. That way you are up for the task on a day that might not be the best to experiment.

Great job!

Congratulations! You did it! This was a great step, moving forward, and I hope the experience was a good one. Look forward to doing it again, because you will need too. I am suggesting that you keep going, approximately every 3-4 weeks until you see no more stones.

From doing this 52 times, I know this is safe. That being said, there will be those that will experience a hard time due to a very clogged up liver and a congested digestive track. Depending on your body's weaknesses and the level of toxicity, the experience will of course vary. The healthier, the less symptoms, in general. Get back on the parasite cleansing right away, and keep going. This might not be for the faint, but boy is it worth it! The procedure has saved many from having had their gallbladder removed, and it has been in use for many, many years.

The belief that the stones only reside in the gallbladder is not what this flush is showing at all. The truth is self-evident. People who have had their gallbladder surgically removed will also get plenty of green, bile-coated stones. If one were to dissect their stones, they would find that the stones were the same as those looked at as purely gallstones.

Here is something else to be aware of during a liver cleanse and a parasite cleanse. The liver represents anger, and the anger resides in the liver. We know that we cannot separate the emotions from the body, not really, so this might be something to keep in mind. To me, it was very revealing, and it gave me some deep self-realizations. The emotional releases, felt like volcanos bursting out of me. Lifetimes of anger, all wanting to leave. The parasites were trying to hang on, dumping toxic gasses and waist as they were dying, making my whole body feel like a warzone. The liver dumping its stones and "chaff", releasing a ton of emotional upheaval. The reactions will vary from flush to flush. On some flushes I felt an intense calm afterwards, like what had been clogging me up, had been released.

When we have been abusive and ignorant to our health and body for such an immense period of time, the heavier methods are necessary.

Know that your body knows what it is doing, and if you are unsure, read about the detoxification symptoms in a later chapter and be kind to yourself. *You* are on the right path, and you are on your way to a cleaner, healthier, happier *you.*

Chapter 12

Oral health

love to smile, and I am sure that you, like me, would love to have some strong healthy teeth to go with it. The mouth is a reflection of our general health, and most often it does not get the attention is should when it comes to health and wellbeing. Mercury fillings, root canals and acidic foods, are not healthy choices for our mouth *or* body in general. We need to see the mouth as a very important part of our body. Some will state one is only as healthy as ones` mouth.

When we get acidic in our body, from the wrong foods, stress and chemicals, the gums get acidic also. This will manifest itself as inflamed gums, the loosening of teeth, and residing gums. Loss of enamel is also a reflection of the inner health, of being acidic, losing your alkaline minerals like magnesium and calcium. We might tend to believe that if we are losing enamel and our teeth are weakening, we are lacking consumption of those important building minerals, but that is not quite so. It is all about the absorption and the utilization. When our parathyroid gland is weak, we will not be able to utilize our calcium, and our tissue and teeth will suffer. Only by addressing the cause will we see real healing of the issue. The thyroid and the parathyroid are always, *always,* involved in weak bones and teeth issues, and any other structure issue.

One of the most uplifting things about walking down a true healing path, is that there is nothing that will be left out by the body. When all the systems are in place, the symptoms will vanish. The solution is always the same. Move the lymph, and thereby the acids, giving the body the chance to rectify and regenerate. It does not matter if it is tooth-cells, heart-cells or skin-cells, the body will rejuvenate and regenerate.

Now, while you are doing what you need to do, your teeth and gums might be hurting, and we want to make sure that they suffer as little as possible. We know that during a detoxification period, any weakness will show itself, so even if you are doing everything right, your mouth might release extra acids for a shorter or longer period of time. This calls for a very strict and good oral regime. We are tapping into everything that we know about oral health, and you will be able to make sure that your teeth are staying with you for a long time.

When we are on a fruit, berries, melons and vegetable diet, the one for thriving, we have to make sure that we are not hurting our teeth. When we detoxify, we are pulling on acids, as that`s what the body will do. To make the body healthier, the acids will come to the surface to be released. Sadly, one might say, that is also true for the mouth. Our gums might be harboring an abundance of acids and bacteria. Once that surfaces, it will burn, and anything from inflamed gums to blisters in the mouth might occur. Stay calm and stay prepared. You are armed with some great detoxification remedies in a separate chapter, but for the mouth, here is a really great oral health protocol. This is what I have seen do wonders, and I am confident that you will love both doing this and feeling the results. We will reap what we sow, and boy are we heading for an amazing harvest!

I was diagnosed with chronic periodontitis, a disease of the gums, a chronic deep inflammation. After getting this news, I upped my oral hygiene and I came up with a killer protocol for healing my mouth. The next dentist appointment and check-up showed nothing but healthy gums! No plaque, no cavities, no inflammation, only a clean super healthy mouth!

People often ask me, what my oral hygiene protocol is, what do I do daily? Well, after being asked from my dentist what I do to keep my mouth so clean and healthy, I want to share it with you. Now I *know* this is good, and I know that it works!

For me, only 100% natural will do:

1. *I oil pull as often as I feel like, but when I had an acidic mouth I was diligent, doing it every single day. Being persistent is very important. I use 1 tablespoon of organic cold pressed coconut oil and half a teaspoon of organic turmeric powder. The coconut will clean and keep the bacteria out, and the turmeric will heal any inflammation and as a bonus keep your teeth really white. This is a great thing to do in the shower every morning. Try to oil pull for 15 minutes. (Read about oil-pulling and full regimen below).*

2. *I brush my teeth 3 times a day, morning, mid-day and at night. I love the really clean feeling. This also depends on your diet, as I have noticed that any fats will stick to the teeth. Fruits keeps them the cleanest by far. I use an electrical brush, and make my own toothpaste. I will share the recipe below for you.*

3. *I make my own mouth-water, and gargle twice a day after brushing my teeth. It helps the mouth stay fresh, and that way, we will always smell fresh also!*

4. *Flossing! So important. For me, once a day is enough. I make sure nothing is left in my mouth before going to bed at night.*

5. *I always keep toothpicks in my handbag, they can come in really handy.*

6. *The diet is very important, as I talked about above, an acidic mouth is an impaired mouth. Eating a raw high fruit diet, will help you stay alkaline, and also provide you with the minerals you need to keep healthy teeth. I have found that we need much less minerals than we are led to believe, and being clean and absorbing the nutrients is where the focus should be. I swear to my home made kelp powder for my minerals and strong teeth.*

What is oil pulling?

Looking back, brushing and flushing is not something that has been around for that long. I have been made aware that the nylon bristle toothbrush became a part of the Western society as late as the 1930's. Before the toothbrush we still had teeth and gums, and it is true that they did not all have rotten teeth. They of course ate a cleaner diet, there was nothing not organic back then. They also chewed on sticks and used oils to clean their mouth. So, in spite of them not having toothbrushes, they had strong, healthy teeth. Oil pulling is an age-old remedy that uses natural substances to clean and detoxify teeth and gums. It will not only clean your entire mouth, it will also whiten the teeth naturally. The benefits doesn't stop there, it will also draw bacteria from the gums, thus improving the health of the gums itself. Now, people from all around the World are oil pulling for their health and white shiny teeth, simply by swishing oil around in their mouth. Sounds simple? It is!

You might say that oil pulling or swishing is like using an oil as a mouthwash, to cleanse the whole mouth and teeth. You might even have heard the word before, as there is a lot of information about the procedure out there. You might want to look at the oil as a mouth soap, but it would not be an entirely correct picture. The oil will literally suck the toxins out of the gums and teeth, leaving a clean and antiseptic environment. This leaves the mouth free from cavities and inflammation. It will pull out any acid and bacteria, and yet it should not replace the brushing, flossing and rinsing. This is an addition, a tool for even brighter, whiter, healthier smiles!

The type of oil you use matters. It must be food grade and edible. It is not to be swallowed though, as it will be filled with bacteria and toxins. When oil pulling, the oils bind to the biofilm, or plaque on the teeth and reduce the number of bacteria in the mouth. Streptococcus mutans is one of the bacteria that is prominent in the mouth and it has been studied for its role in tooth decay and gum disease. For this reason, I recommend using coconut oil for the pulling session. It has natural amazing anti-bacterial and anti-septic properties. In the older traditional recipes, you will find sunflower oil, but now it is very common to use the great coconut oil. For me, it really makes the teeth so much whiter than any other oil that I have tried. I have another trick also for the whitening, all in the description below.

Coconut oil has also been shown to balance hormones, kill candida, moisturize skin, improve digestion reduce cellulite and so much more. It is a great oil to have on your shelf, as it has many great uses for health and vitality.

How to do the oil pulling:

- Make this your morning ritual. Do not eat anything before you oil pull. It is a great while-in-the-shower routine. Do not even brush your teeth before doing this.

- Now, mix a large tablespoon of organic cold pressed virgin coconut oil with half a teaspoon of turmeric powder. This is my extra whitening secret! Make sure that you do not spill the mixture, as it will stain most anything.

- If you wish, you can blend a drop of oregano, clove or myrrh essential oil, for some extra antibacterial properties

- Put the potion in your mouth, and swish it around between your teeth for 15-20 minutes. Make sure that you do not swallow any of it. This is very important.

- Make sure that you do not swish for more than the 20 minutes, as it is believed that the toxins then might be re-absorbed into your bloodstream.

- Spit the oil into the trash can. It can clog up your sewer system.

- Rinse the mouth with warm water, and you are good to brush your teeth!

You can do this every day, or you can do it 3-4 times a week. Try it and see, you might become hooked. I use about half a jar of coconut oil, and blend in about one large tablespoon of turmeric powder. This way I have it ready to go each morning. I also add my essential oils in the blend.

Toothpaste recipe:

- 3oz/100ml Bentonite clay
- Organic cold pressed coconut oil
- 5 drops peppermint essential oil
- 5 drops clove essential oil
- 5 drops Frankincense essential oil
- A glass jar with a tight lid

Put the Bentonite clay in your jar, and mix in some coconut oil. Use as much as you like to get your preferred consistency. Add 5 drops of each of the essential oils to the mix. If you wish, you can substitute Myrrh essential oil for the clove oil. Myrrh and clove are for bacteria/

antiseptic purposes, and the peppermint is for taste and cleansing. I use Frankincense for its all-round healing properties. Read the chapter on essential oils for more information on their ability help in healing and regeneration.

Mouth water recipe:

- 1oz/30ml water
- 1 drop peppermint essential oil
- 1 drop Myrrh essential oil

Mix everything in a glass, and gargle for a few minutes. Swoosh the blend around in your mouth and throat, and spit it out. You will feel the cleanness and freshness right away. Homemade beautiful creations like these, makes me happy. It is so freeing to know exactly what I am putting in my mouth, and to see that it works in healing and regenerating. Take back your power and take responsibility for *all* of your life and health. Forget about toxic mouthwashes and even more toxic toothpastes. Everything you put in your mouth, you eat. Everything you put on your *skin*, you eat.

Some simple tips to remember:

- *Always use a straw when drinking juices.*

- *Rinse your mouth in clean water after every meal.*

- *Do NOT use baking soda in your toothpaste, I have found it very corrosive. It can be handy as a mouthwash in very acidic cases. So if your mouth is burning with acids, put a little baking soda in some water, and swoosh it around. You can check the pH of your saliva with some simple litmus paper. The saliva should be slightly alkaline, so slightly above or around 7pH. It will fluctuate around your meals, so do the test in the morning before eating.*

This is just an indication of your mouths condition at that very time, so it is simply a guideline.

- The acidic fruits, the citruses are alkalizing to the body, but acidic to the teeth.

Taking care of *you* is an act of self-love, and every act of self-love is healing to the body. It does not matter what it is, as long as it is done with care and compassion. *You* are always worthy.

Chapter 13

Breathing

have yet to meet anyone that does not breathe. We all do it, is the essence of life itself. The breath is what connects us physically to all that is, and we take our first and last breath as our entrance and exit in this body. In the meantime, we are said to take about half a billion breaths, all of them to sustain life here on this planet. We can live for weeks without food, and for days without water, but we can only live for minutes without our breath. It is the first, the last, and the everything. The fact is that we take about 17,000 breaths a day, for our body to be saturated with oxygen. Breathing also triggers many physiological mechanisms.

In itself, breathing seems simple, we do not even have to think about doing it. This is keeping us alive, yet it can be hindering us from optimal health. The simple technique is that we draw the air through our nose and mouth, then the process of breathing is mostly a lung job. Together with the diaphragm and the ribs and the intercostal muscle, the whole process is automated and a no-brainer.

"As long as your path is that of your heart, it will always be the right one. The journey is yours alone, and only you are the one doing the walking."- Hilde

Being the connection to life, the breath is also the connection between all of our bodies. Our mental, emotional and physical bodies, all connected through our breathing. The thoughts that you think, and the emotions that you feel will automatically influence and alter your breath. Think about when you are fearful or anxious, the breathing becomes more rapid and even shallow. The calmer the mind, and the more secure our feelings are, the slower and deeper out breath is. This shows us that we can use our breath in the healing of our whole being. We can learn how to consciously use our breath to restore and to balance.

I myself used to be a very shallow breather, which is a quite typical scenario when you are living a stress-filled life. What shallow breath means is that one is only using the narrow top portion of the lung surface for oxygen exchange. Our breath literally stops at the diaphragm, therefore we call it shallow. A good breath for health will go all the way down, expanding your abdomen. It will take some work, but by being conscious about our breath, we can reprogram our automatic breathing to benefit our whole being. We can re-connect ourselves through the breath of life. When we mainly use shallow upper-chest breathing, we reduce the efficiency of our lungs and the respiratory system. It will result in less blood flow and less productive distribution of the vital lymph fluids than if deep-breathing. This is also an interesting fact about the shallow-breathing; it actually reduces the amount of digestive juices available for the digestive process! We know how important a functioning digestive system is, so let us be reminded that it is all very connected. Mind-soul-body *and* breath. All perfectly interwoven and created by God.

Changing how you breathe can foster the self-healing powers of your body.

Are you a shallow breather also? There are a few obvious ways that you can tell, so get to it and find out. Lie down and put one hand on your chest and the other one on your abdomen. Breathe like you usually do, and watch your hands. Breathe normally. If the hand on your chest raises first, you are a shallow-breather, if the one on your abdomen raises first, you are a deep-breather.

By spending time alone with our breathing, we will start to experience ourselves as more than this physical body. It is the simple way to start any meditation practice, to simply be aware of the breath. Once we become a part of our breath, or breathing, the mind loses its grip, and stillness can come forth. This way, even the subconscious mind will start to dissolve its thought patterns. This in itself is a major key to why conscious breathing is healing on all levels. The breathing might open a flow of emotions and feelings, as you are able to really connect with them. Keep breathing and know that it is all good. It is all as it should be, you, your breathing, your healing and your future life.

> On the physical level we know that breath moves lymph, and in the light of detoxification, we know how important this is. Our lungs are also one of our main eliminating organs, and we need them strong and working up to their potentials. Simply lying on your back while taking deep breaths will let your lymph move all through your body.

A regular daily practice of deep breathing techniques and conscious breathing practices will give long standing benefits. Any breathing exercise can also be used as a tool for calming a stressful situation, or for driving away anxiety and uneasiness. When you notice that your breathing is hectic, shallow or stressful, use one of the techniques below. This way, as you practice, you will slowly be able to stay in a place of calm in any situation. Yoga, tai chi and qigong, are all ancient practices that incorporate breath as a central component.

As a part of your healing regime, I want to introduce you to a few great healing breathing techniques that are very dear to me. By controlling the breath, you can influence every aspect of your life.

Pranayama:

I found Pranayama many years ago, and was intrigued by the role that it has amongst Indian healers and practices. The yogis of India have for thousands of years had the experience that certain breathing techniques, applied over time, methodically, will give specific healing results. They have a name for their specific breathing science, and it is called Pranayama. The word Pranayama is derived from the two Sanskrit words *Prana* – meaning life force, and *Yama* – meaning control.

By practicing Pranayama, we are clearing the obstructions in all of our bodies. We are allowing the breath itself, the Prana, to flow freely. When breathing is improved, healing is taken to another level.

A regular consistent Pranayama practice is believed to stimulate the parasympathetic system, countering the overstimulation our bodies go through during the so called fight or flight response. When we experience stressful thoughts and our sympathetic nervous system triggers this response, it gives us a burst of energy to respond to the perceived danger. The breathing quickly becomes rapid and shallow. This results in a tight chest, and the body produces a surge of hormones such as cortisol and epinephrine (also known as adrenaline). Now, our blood pressure will increase and the pulse rate will rise. We are in a state of constant alert, burning our adrenals from the inside out, which will lead to physical dis-ease down the road. So, again, it is all connected, breath, adrenals, physical health and all. Deep breathing also stimulates the main nerve in the parasympathetic nervous system, the Vagus nerve. This will also slow down the heart rate, lower the blood pressure and calm the body and mind. Are you ready to try some great breathing techniques? These are all standard Pranayama practices, and I hope that you do some extra research, for more in-depth information on all of them.

The pranayama techniques focus on one or more of the four parts of the breath, which are inhalation, internal retention, exhalation and retention. The practice states that the exhalation is the most important part of the breath, as only when we are empty, can we take another breath.

This is my favorite pranayama breathing technique:

This is referred to as the Nadi Shodhanda: It is used for grounding and calmness, to regain balance. The practice has some great claims for those who practices over time, and for around 20 minutes every day. This is also a great way to start any meditation practice.

It is also called *Alternate Nostril breathing*, and is said to:

- Improve the ability to focus and be alert.
- Restore balance in the left and right hemispheres of the brain.
- Support the lungs and respiratory system.
- Rejuvenate the whole nervous system.
- Remove toxins by moving the lymphatic system, and excreting through the breath.

Start slow and build up slowly. Aim for a 20 minutes a day practice, and make a habit of it. The benefits will come from a steady practice. Find a quiet place where you will not be disturbed, and sit in a comfortable position. Sit on the floor if you can, with your spine straight. If you need support, or find it is more comfortable for you to sit in a chair, by all means do so. As you evolve through practice, you can move on to sitting in a lotus position on a yoga mat. The practice of pranayama is best done in the early morning before you eat anything. Make sure the room you will be using has a lot of fresh air. This is all about the breath, the air.

- Make sure your heart is open, and that your intent is of love and healing.

- Put your right thumb over your right nostril, while your left arm is relaxing on your lap

- Inhale deeply through your left nostril.

- At the peak of the inhalation, put your fourth finger on your left nostril, loosen the grip of your thumb, and slowly exhale through the right nostril.

- After a full exhalation, inhale through the right nostril, closing it off with your right thumb at the peak of your inhalation, lift your fourth finger and exhale smoothly through your left nostril.

- Keep breathing for as long as it is comfortable, but try to start with at least 3 minutes. Any new practice will take time to learn, and by doing we get better.

Note! If you are pregnant, have asthma, heart disease, or hypertension, be cautious of any breathing techniques with fast rhythms or breath retention. Please speak with your health care practitioner before starting any new breathing exercise.

Ocean`s breath: This is another great calming practice that you can use if you feel angry, frustrated or irritated. It will calm the mind, and settle the whole body.

- Take an inhalation that is slightly deeper than normal. Keep your mouth closed, and exhale through your nose. We always use our nostrils in pranayama. Try to imagine that you are breathing out as if you were fogging a mirror. That is the type of air you want to come out. Like the sound of the ocean.

- Try to constrict your throat on the inhale as well.

- Practice the inflow breath first, and then slowly use the same technique on outflow. Gently constrict your throat on your outflow also.

Explore the many techniques of pranayama, and experience what they can do for your health both physically, emotionally and mentally.

Rebirthing:

Rebirthing is also called conscious breathing. It is a process that uses the breath under the guidance of a skilled practitioner. It is a great tool for accessing and letting go of what has been hidden from our conscious awareness. It is like opening the door to our subconscious mind and our old programming. We are letting it come forth to heal and be released. Our hidden traumas, our well buried wounds, are gently breathed to the surface. The breath will carry it and transform it, and the method is therefore often used for healing deep emotional pain.

By digging into the subconscious, our emotional software so to speak, we are allowing anything holding us back to come forth. This way we can unlock our fullest potential and see what has not been seen. There is no denial at the core of who we are, and there is nowhere to hide for the well tucked away baggage. We might not even know that there is a trauma there, that there are things that we are choosing to hide from our awareness, but through the connected breath we can invite it to surface. Only by shining the light on any hidden problem, is it able to heal. Most often the light itself will be the healing that is needed. It is natural to feel good and to be healthy, and it is natural to want it all. We are so often not living that experience, and by numbing ourselves down from the truth, the hurts and the traumas, we believe that we are doing ourselves a favor.

By the simple connection through breath, we are connecting to all that is in a soft and vulnerable way. We're letting down the guard, and inviting in the love that we are all made of. The love that we all have for ourselves and everything else that *is,* we just have to remember it. My personal experience with rebirthing has been absolutely amazing. I was guided by a fantastic breath practitioner, a dear friend and a true healer. The session was life changing, and this is why I am recommending this experience to anyone who wants to set themselves free. The process is intense and powerful, and will reveal your inner purpose. It can also release, alter, and reveal anything that is needed for *you* to be able to live a better and free(er) life.

As you lie on your back with both hands at your side, relaxed and comfortable, you breathe in a guided and controlled rhythm of connected breaths. This means that there is no space between breathing in and breathing out. The mind will slowly calm as all your focus is on the breathing. As you keep breathing, memories may arise, and feelings might come forth. From being a person, thinking and planning, you are swimming in the pool of awareness, just observing the emotions and the pictures that arises in your mind. There will be bodily sensations as tingling or pain, and you might experience old wounds hurting and a total loss of time and space. The breath will take you, transform your physical body to a wind of breath, and you become one with all that is. You are triggered into an alert state, completely aware of everything. Completely aware that you are physical, yet not. No emotions or feelings can stay locked in, and your whole being has come full cycle. Your transformation will happen on a cellular level, and the regeneration is inevitable. The removal of obstruction, releasing flow, will accelerate any healing process naturally and freely. Release is done, and as you keep breathing, the cycle will naturally be completed.

After the breath cycle, the body will rest. Now, you will feel a deep sense of relaxation and peace, saturated and filled. As in a deep state of meditation, there is an inner calm and peace. For some, the experience is life-altering, for others, several sessions might be in place. As always, when there is intent, deep breathing and love present, healing has taken place on many different levels. The experience can truly be that of a re-birth.

Make the fact that we are all in this together, connected by our breath, a comforting realization. This way you know that you are never alone, not even for a short breath. Time is an illusion, and we are unlimited beings.

Chapter 14

Fasting

In nature, fasting is a natural part of life. We, the thinkers and the analysts, have forgotten the simplicity and truth of nature. Therefore, the word fasting might seem strange and extreme for some. All depending on which part of the world we live in, we might see fasting as a crazy act of some extremists, or we are seeing it as the number one healing practice there is. In the world where it is so-called "normal" to eat tortured animal flesh, manmade toxins and drink blue sugar drinks, fasting will seem extreme. Natural will seem extreme. The further we walk from what is intended by creation, the more extreme going back will be. What is considered as "normal" will always be what the masses have been conditioned to believe, no matter what the truth is. It is time to stop the story telling, and realize truth. It cannot be outdated, outsmarted or improved. It cannot even be ignored, even though we tend to try our very best. In the world of natural healing, where we *know* that the body is the only true healer, fasting is the absolute top healing practice, period.

Fasting simply means going without, or refraining from. We are fasting from food when we are water fasting, drinking nothing but water. Yes, absolutely nothing but water. The term fasting is used in many different protocols, and in the world of healing there are a few practices that have adopted the word. Through our continuous search for health and vitality, many different practices have been explored and shared. This is a blessing, as they might all lead to Rome. Still, the basics are the same. Detoxification through elimination of obstruction stands solid. Here are what we typically will call fasting:

Juice fasting is not really fasting:

This is when you are consuming nothing but preferably fresh, homemade juices. It can be fruit- or vegetable juices, and there is no general limit on the intake of them. A juice fast can be done for a day as a quick pick-me-up treat, or for a longer period to induce some deep cleansing. A shorter 3-5day juice fast can be done by anyone, and it does not matter if you are working or not. You will still get your energy from the juices, which makes it preferable and easy for many. The body will now have the chance to rest, meaning the digestion will not have to work on digesting any food. The juice will be absorbed directly into your bloodstream and through the lining of your whole digestive tract, starting in your mouth. Many find great healing from juice fasting, and will stay on juices for a long time. I know people who have lived on juices alone for several years. Yes, years! When someone is concerned after a week on juices only, about whether or not they are getting all their nutrition, this is a great reminder and perspective. What we have been told we need, is simply not true.

Since you are still consuming all the nutrients from the juices, you are still letting the body work to absorb, and to utilize, so it is not a true fast. It is still a fast from solid foods though, and will have a great cleansing effect. For those suffering from gastro-intestinal issues, or malabsorption, the juice fast is a fantastic regime. I did a 21day juice fast myself, and was able to transition from a not so good diet, to a better one by doing so. Sometimes we just need that kick, that shift of gear so to speak. We need to get off our "normal" regime, and by jumping right into a few days, or a week or two of juices only, we are kick-starting our system bigtime. All depending on our level of toxicity, some cleansing reactions will be expected. Nothing to worry about, but it might not be as comfortable as you expected. Know this; when we are letting the body do the work, it will do what is needed. Get the brain out of the way. Think less, love more.

The belief of what we need to consume, has been called as un-truth by the bravest of the brave, our pioneers in natural healing. Dr. Arnold Ehret, Dr. Robert Morse, Dr. Jensen, Dr. Herbert Shelton, Jay Kordich, and so many more. True healers have shown us the way, by walking the path of simplicity.

"By letting go of what we do not need, be it food, emotions or old trauma, we are opening the true pathways of healing." - Hilde

Water fasting for the brave and ready:

In the wild, any animal that is sick will first of all lay down to rest. Second of all it will stop eating. By doing so it is letting the body use all its energy on the healing. As the body uses up to 80% of its energy digesting food, this is all about getting out of the way. It shows us that healing was never really about what we put in but what we let the body do. The animal will drink water, or not even that, and lay still until it is better. It is about restoring energy and trusting the body's ability to heal. It will heal through detoxification and regeneration. If we are hurt with broken bones, or torn muscle and tissue, the body will still need all its energy for a speedy recovery.

In primitive cultures, a water fast was often demanded before going to war, or as part of a coming-of-age ritual. Fasting has also played a key role in most of the world's major religions. It has been associated with penitence and other forms of self-control. Judaism has several annual fast days including Yom Kippur, the Day of Atonements. The Roman Catholics and Eastern orthodoxy observe a 40 day fast during Lent. This is the period when Christ fasted 40 days in the desert. In the Islamic culture, the Muslims fast during the holy month of Ramadan. As you can see, fasting is far from new or special. In modern cultures, for the most part, we have turned from being without, to over-eating and indulgence. Abundance turned to greed, power, constipation and illness.

What I am talking about here is therapeutic fasting. This is when fasting is used as a therapy for better health. It is used as tool and a practice, to better oneself physically, emotionally and spiritually. It can be used to heal or prevent, as a prolonged part of the protocol, or as ongoing shorter intermitted fasts. When we use fasting as a part of a steady protocol, like fasting one day every week or every month, we call it intermitted fasting.

As we are undergoing a water fast, the body moves into the same kind of detoxification cycle that it normally enters during sleep. The toxins are removed, energy is spent on healing and regeneration, and it even looks for old wounds to heal. As it is not getting any food from the outside, it will start to eat away on dead and sick cells. It will consume anything that your body does not need. It can be viruses, bacteria, fibroid tumors, build ups around the joints and stored fat. Fasting has been done for as long as we know, all over the world, it's done by animals and has a healing effect on the organism. This is true power, and still, it is something to treat with great caution. Why would that be? Because today, we are so clogged up, constipated, toxic and poisoned that we have an overload of acids in our bodies. Together with a weak elimination system/organs, we must really slide into the fasting world with respect and knowledge.

This is why it is never advised to do a water fast for more than 3-5 days without proper supervision. I embarked on a 16day water only-fast myself, and even though I was already eating a raw food diet, it was quite a bumpy road. We need to be educated about what is happening to the body and the symptoms that might arise. It is important to be trained in listening to the body`s signals. I am not just talking about physical symptoms and signals, but emotional as well. As we know, healing is never only physical, it is all connected.

When we know better, we can do better, and when we know, we cannot ignore what we know. We can try, but truly not.

Preparing for a water fast:

To prepare for a fast is very important to the outcome. Even if you are doing a 1day water fast, preparing is a good thing. Both emotionally and physically, we need to be ready. If your diet is still high in fats, sugars or any animal protein, leave them all behind and eat lightly the days before the fast. Do not eat any processed food, and enjoy some fresh fruits and vegetables instead. Also, make sure that your bowels are moving. You do not want to go into any type of fast, when constipated. Read about fasting, and make sure that if you are taking on a fast that lasts longer than 3 days, to talk to your health practitioner, and discuss if this is a good timing for you.

Remember that this is your journey, and no-one else`s. Always honor your body's language and messages, and know when it is time to break the fast. You will know, your intuition will tell you. Use this whole healing period to polish your awareness so that you can listen better. Usually, when we have been sick and tired for a long time, we have gone deaf, and are not used to listening to the physical body.

Hilde Larsen

During the fast itself:

Make sure that you rest a lot. Make room in your calendar to take care of *you*. Some will advice that one rests completely, as in bed rest, and some might tell you to do as you usually do, except for doing any strenuous exercise. I am all for the resting. Do as little as you feel like, but always think that your body will need its energy for detoxification and healing. Find a good book, and a great movie, put some calming oils in your diffuser, meditate and find the stillness within. Healing is always about the whole being, and emotional detoxification is as important as the physical one. Be prepared to feel extra emotional at times, extra clear and extra tired. Anything goes, so let go and let be. Drink as much water every day as you feel comfortable with. For most, that will be around 3-4 liters/quarts. The type of water is a whole separate issue, and personally I would go for distilled. It is the only true pure water there is, and it has served me well for many years now. I used to drink alkaline ionized water, but found the inorganic minerals were obstructing my elimination of impurities. They can accumulate in the body, and we do not want that.

Feel free to do some stretching and yoga during the fast. It is great to help move the lymphatic system. Some deep breathing exercises will also be very beneficial. Skin brushing is a great aid to stimulate the lymphatic system, and to move things along (see chapter 21), and you might choose to use the enema bag. I did not, and it is my only regret. When toxins are being released and not eliminated, they will be reabsorbed, and that is not what we are looking for at all.

There are specific changes that the body will go through during a fasting period. This is described in many books and articles, and they all agree on some simple basics. Many of the most important processes actually happen during the first three days. The body will switch from one fuel source to another. Let us look at a very simple setup of the different stages the body will experience during a water fast:

Day 1-2

You might feel some cleansing already, and some glycogen is drawn from the muscles. The tongue might become coated, and you might feel hungry. Not real hunger, but a craving to feed the addictions and the parasites.

Day 3-7

The body will go into what is called ketosis. This simply means that it turns from using sugars/glucose as its main fuel source. It now has to use fat. As soon as there is no more storage left in the liver, this change will happen. This shift generally begins on the second day of fasting and is completed by the third. The body will still need its glucose, but will now, during this katabolic state, convert it from two sources; From the fat store of the body, and from breaking down some of the amino acids in the muscles. When the ketone production is sufficient to produce what the body needs, the protein becomes strongly conserved. This means that the body will actually use very little muscle mass during fasting, but some. The desire to eat will become less, and the hunger will for the most part go away almost completely. The body is adjusting to the fasting, and the digestive system is going into a rest-mode. A cleansing and discharge of mucus is very common.

Day 8 to 15

This is a stage of the water fast when many people report a clearer mind and a raise in overall energy. Some even say they feel better than ever. The body is now working on some deep healing, and old wounds might become painful again, or old ailments might show themselves again. There might be issues that you have not even thought about for years, that will come up to heal. This goes for physical and emotional issues. During fasting, the body's healing process is at an optimal efficiency. The body is now searching for damaged tissue and cells. The lymphocytes enter the damaged tissue, secreting substances to dissolve the sick and damaged cells. The pain is always short lived, as healing is not the same as disease or injury.

Day 16 to 30

The longer one fasts, the more adapted the body will be to the process. More energy will arise. This is quite the opposite of what one might believe. It is important to note though, that this reaction will very much depend on your body's ability to get rid of its waste, and also the level of toxicity present. This late stage of any fasting on water only, should always be monitored by a professional adviser. Also, it is for those that have mastered cleansing for quite some time. The healing work of the organs is being completed. Once the body has focused on the detoxification process, the cleaning-the-house process, more time will be spent healing and regenerating organs and glands. The longer the fast, in general, the more healing will take place. After day 20, a heightened clarity of mind might be experienced. While a short fast will reduce the symptoms, a longer fast can completely heal. Homeostatic balance is at optimal levels. The lymphatic system is clean except for a rare discharge of mucus through the nose or throat. After day 20, the mind is effected with heightened clarity and emotional balance. Memory and concentration improves.

According to Dr. Sheldon, the great master of water fasts, one should break a fast with the return of genuine hunger. To be able to do that, one has to be an experienced faster.

Breaking a fast:

It is very important to break a fast properly. It is said to be even more important than the fast itself. The digestive system has been resting, and by not honoring this very important step, you can really hurt yourself. The longer the fast has lasted, the longer the period of transitioning back will last. I would say that for every 3 days fasted, take one day on a gentle all-fruit diet. The first day is always best to leave with the juices only, then move to some high water fruits like melons or mangoes. You can also include some fresh coconut water. It is very important to stay hydrated.

Slow and steady wins the race! I know from my own life experience that jumping right in can seem tempting. I also know that for some of us, that is how we learn and experiment. That being said, when it comes to water fasting, be humble, and start off slowly. Do a one-day fast at first, and slowly build up to a few three day fasts. This will give you a chance to see what your body`s reactions are. As you get cleaner from eating better, cleansing your liver, colon, eliminating parasites etc., your body will handle a water fast easier and easier.

> IMPORTANT NOTE: Water fasting is not always appropriate!
> As we are sometimes very toxic, we know that a water fast might be too much too soon. The symptoms that arise during the first two days, might be frightening. The more toxic you are, the more intense the symptoms will be. There are several fasting clinics around the world, that specializes in guiding and monitoring people during this process.

Fasting is not for:

- *People who are very thin, or in a state of starvation.*
- *Those who are anorexic.*
- *Pregnant women.*
- *Nursing mothers.*
- *Those suffering from severe anemia.*
- *Those with porphyria. Porphyria refers to a genetic metabolic defect that affects the body's ability to manage porphyrins.*
- *Type I diabetics.*
- *Those with insufficient kidney function*

- *Those who are extremely afraid of fasting.*
- *People with a high toxic contamination level of DDT, (a pesticide chemical). It is stored by the body in a highly concentrated form in fat tissue. When the fat is dissolved, the DDT can be released into the blood stream in a high concentration. This is due to the rapid detoxification.*

After the fast, go back to your regular healing regime, or healthy way of eating, and feel enthusiastic about doing it again. Intermitted fasting is a wonderful part of a healing regime, and I strongly believe that 1-3 day fasts are very beneficial. You can do one day every week, or one day every month. Some do three days in a row, at the start of every month, but you must find what works best for you.

Dry fasting:

This is the absolute deepest form of cleansing there is, and is not at all for beginners. It is extreme, ingesting absolutely nothing. No food, no water. It is usually done for 16 hours a day, a whole 24 hours, or for the absolute maximum of three days. I know people who have gone much longer, but that is not the norm. The literature says that it was used in ancient times, but perhaps among already healthy people. Today, a dry fast might release too many toxins too quickly, and should therefore only be done when you are already well on your way to a clean, well-functioning body, and only for a very short period of time.[9]

It is not advisable for anyone to dive into dry fasting without having practiced cleansing for a certain length of time. Support and guidance is also recommended. Never dive into any fasting from a Western high-fat and protein, cooked and processed foods diet. Practice a transition diet and go slow.

---

[9] «Quantum Eating», Tanya Zavasta

A personal experience with dry fasting:

Ever since I shared that I was exploring the deepest and most profound levels of healing through dry fasting, people have asked me to share my experience. I love to share, but remember, we are all in different places, and have different levels of health. This is why proper guidance and knowledge is very important. Detoxification is an art, and it is important to know when to hold them and when to fold them.

After eight years on a raw food diet, and the last four on a high-fruit, low-fat path, I was called to start to dry fast. I have done water fasts and juice fasts, but had never done a dry fast. It seemed a bit out there, and looking back it was just I who was not ready. Now I am!

I started slow:

I had been reading about dry fasting for a while, and I always recommend to read up on your health and protocols. **It is our own choices that will take us to where we are going,** *always.* Remember this, and know where the responsibility lies. Recieving some good guidance on your journey to health is also a must. Experience and compassion is invaluable support. I always say, when you are ready to go, we need to talk. I love being the support that gets people to really take their health and life to a whole new and brighter level.

I started by doing a 24 hour dry fast. I drank my last glass of juice at 7pm in the evening, so that was my starting point. As a preparation, I had been eating grapes and adding lemons for about 10 days prior. Well, not really as a preparation, but that was what I had been doing. This made that first dry experience extra powerful I believe. I really did not have to do anything to prepare really, as I am already on a fruit based diet. I would soon find how much that means when dry fasting. We are talking about hydration, *bigtime.*

By detoxification, alkalization, *hydration* and regeneration, I had prepared my body to dig deeper. Through detoxification my body had hydrated to the point where going dry would not leave me dehydrated, not on a cellular level. Not for the duration of days with no water and no food.

The second attempt was a 36hour dry fast. It was fairly easy as well, nothing major happened, but I was not prepared for no thirst at all. No dryness in the mouth, nothing. This is what hydration looks like. We really do not hydrate by drinking water the way that we have believed. Hydration comes from within. The body, when hydrated, will make its own internal water to make sure that all organs are well taken care of.

I was building up slowly, and about five days after my 36hour fast, I went for a 48 hour one. This one was harder. My heart was skipping some beats, and I knew my stomach and GI tract was doing some deep cleansing. I did some deep breathing to calm the system, and it worked wonders. Sleep was a bit uneasy, but I was prepared for anything, and the observation was exciting. My body was cleansing on a much deeper level than before, I could really feel it. The detoxification symptoms that I had been experiencing on the grapes, all went away. I am talking about acid build-up in the tissue, manifested as stiffness and sore muscle and tensions. This was amazing to me. It was like a floodgate had opened, and in a few days it all cleared out. Everything my body had been releasing was flushed out in an instant!

I broke my fast with a glass of freshly made grape juice with added lemon, and immediately I had to use the bathroom. I was releasing a lot of burning sulfur from my intestines. Wow, I now *knew* this was the real deal. My eyes have appeared to be brown my whole life. They are getting lighter every year, and by releasing that dark sulfur I am even more confident they will at one point turn blue, their natural state. More on that on a later post. I now had a new sense of energy, a lightness and a brightness of thought. *Everything appeared more crisp and clear.*

Three-day dry fasting bliss:

About five more days after my 48 hour fast, I decide I am going for a 72 hour one, a whole three days and nights. I am so pulled towards this, I cannot stop myself. I have to. I am confident and calm, and feel no fear at all. Only an eagerness from my body.

The first day was great, nothing much to report. I had been eating my normal fruit and herbs diet prior, and felt content going in. Day two was the toughest one. I was hungry, I felt emotionally uneasy, and my stomach was bloated and nauseated. I kept busy by working on my latest book, and pretty much stayed focused on that. Remember, when detoxing, the emotional release can be heavy and strong. Be prepared for anger, tears and sadness. It is all okay, your cells are releasing old memories and toxins. I had no dryness in the mouth, and not real weakness at all. My head was super clear, and my confidence was very strong. Day three was a much better day though. Except for some weaknesses in my legs and some dizziness when getting up a bit too fast, I felt fine. I went for a short walk, but stayed close to my home. This was new ground for me, and we must always play safe. I have been at this for a number of years, so I know my body pretty well. Fear is the largest obstacle to healing, so until you are out of fear, do not dry fast, that is my recommendation.

This time around my heart was beating fine the whole time. The pulse stayed steady, and the hunger subsided. I didn`t sleep to well, but that was okay. It is all okay. This is another thing. When you are detoxifying your body, remember what that *is*! It is the release of toxins, and it is *normal* to feel it happen. It is okay, you do not have to feel well Now, on this three-day dry fast my kidney filtration was amazing. Go to my Facebook page and see the pictures that

I posted. WOW! Dry fasting really opens those puppies. After two days in dry, I saw the same filtration that I have only seen after 30 days on grapes only. This is how powerful this is.

After the three-day experience I have felt better than I can remember. I *know* and feel that deeper healing has taken place, not only on the physical level, but on a spiritual level as well.

I kept going, and what happened was not expected!

Two days after ending my three-day dry fast, something happened that needed a bit of processing on my part.

I have pondered for a while if I should share this so openly, and came to the conclusion that my experience might help many realize how full of shit we really are, and how much work is needed to completely rid ourselves of what is residing within. You might have guessed that I am referring to parasites. Yes, indeed I am. The ones that I often refer to as uninvited guests.

I am not easily freaked out…but this time I was… After my dry fast, I felt amazing. I had experienced some nausea the last two nights, but I am used to detoxing, so that was fine. As you might already know, I am a very clean eater, and I mostly feel fantastic. I am feeling the freedom of having gone from Hell to living my dreams.

About eight years ago, I did extensive parasite cleansing, and I expelled loads of parasites. We all have them, don`t freak out, I mean it. Yes, we *all* have them. I saw many different parasites leave me during that time. A few ascaries, which are the large roundworms that can grow to be, about 12 inches long. I saw thread worms and flukes. Some that I never identified, and loads of eggs. I have some old pictures, but at that time I was so ill, so very sick, that documenting was the furthest from my mind, and this was before the iPhone.

Now, after all these years of cleansing to restore my health and my life, I have been using herbs and done some sporadic parasite cleansing. It has no longer been my focus to kill anything, only to keep creating the best environment and health there is. I have not done a longer parasite cleanse since my 52 liver flushes and my two years of killing/warrior time. I have focused more on the terrain and have seen stone turn to gold, and transformation beyond my wildest dreams. My journey has been the most amazing travel, and still is. Now I have a different view, that is all. We are all travelers, all just passing by, having this experience.

Back to the parasites. They have not been on my mind for many years, and this day, something happened that blew my mind. It blew the lid wide open.

I am lying down to go to sleep (Stop reading now if you are going to freak out), and for some reason I reach down and feel something that makes me tell my husband I am going to the bathroom. I felt something moving, and I freeze and get out of bed holding my breath! I get to the bathroom, close the door, and literally pull out a 12 inch ascaries! It was crawling out of me, fully alive! I am standing there with a living roundworm in my hand, by its tail or head, and my heart skipped a few beats. My thoughts are spinning, what the heck! During all these years I never saw anything like it. This worm was running for its life, actually leaving me! My inner terrain is no longer livable, and that is a *good* thing. Still, I was blown away by the fact that it was actually still in there! I know I was crazy sick for a long time, but this confirms to me that they are very resistant, *and* that we all have them.

This shows us that it is all about the terrain. It is about the cultivating medium, and it is about how we as humans live today. This might seem extreme and scary, but the only difference between this and not seeing anything is that this one *actually came out.*

This is not for the faint, and I have wondered if I should post a picture or not, but I decided, hey, *this* is truth, and this is life. I hope that reading this will inspire you to keep on working on your own health. Better out than in, people. Much better out than in.

I will keep dry fasting in my life, and I will keep sharing what real health looks and feels like. When we have been sick we need to take this cleansing to the top of the mountain. This is evolving and this is walking lighter. Letting go of everything that is holding us back. One step at the time. I am happy to report that the host of this uninvited guest is in great shape, and that any other small or little one is welcome to leave should they pass by my territory.

Detoxifying and cleansing the body is lifesaving, it is absolutely what is needed to regain great health. There is no way around it. No matter what you are feeling, this is what is needed.

True freedom is being on top of your own health, and knowing that you have the full responsibility.

> Any attempt on a dry fast should only be done after a prolonged detoxification period, and by gaining experience from other types of fasting first.

By this short introduction to fasting, I hope you are inspired to do some research of your own. Fasting is all about letting go, both physically, mentally and emotionally. It is about self-love and self-healing. For your road back to health, include intermitted fasting and some longer fasts when needed. When you need to dig deeper, when you feel you have hit a plateau, go on a juice fast for a few days or a week. If you feel amazing on the juices alone, keep going. When you are ready for even deeper work, try a short water fast and so on.

Chapter 15

Grounding

Have you noticed that when you are outside in nature you feel calmer? Have you noticed how a beach vacation is soothing you, and giving you more energy? There is nothing like a long swim in the ocean, or a hike in the woods. The sand and ocean water are both naturally conductive materials. Perfect for grounding the body, removing excess positive electrons. I know, we all need some extra "vitamin sea", and a hug from a large pine tree.

My passion for grounding/earthing is deeply rooted, together with my love for nature. On my own healing journey, I have found that being grounded is more than important. I studied grounding sheets and mats, and I even slept on a grounding sheet for years. I have shielded my computers and telephone with EMF protectors. I have consciously done what I have found best to let me live in this crazy electromagnetic noise with the least amount of negative impact. *But*, and this is a huge but; There is nothing that will do what nature does for us. There is nothing that will reset our cells and clear our energies as a barefoot walk and a tree hug will, so get ready to lose your shoes and socks!

Many with me will state that grounding is one of the most fundamental things we can do for our health and wellbeing. One can be grounded physically or spiritually, and both are important. Being physically grounded simply means to have direct skin contact with Mother Earth. That is all. Be it a tree, the ground or the ocean, by connecting directly we are grounded. We can walk barefoot on the beach, in the grass or anywhere it is safe to walk without shoes. A swim in a lake, a river or the ocean is like embracing the earth with our whole being. Our bodies are meant to come into contact with Earth on a regular basis.

We are suffering from being around electromagnetic waves, Wi-Fi and mobile phone waves, and many of us have a high amount of positive electrons built up in our bodies. Take a walk on the *wild* side, and take an electrical load-off. Throughout history, humans have spent time outdoors and connected with the soil. Today we are separated through shoes and high-rises. From walking on the ground barefoot, to gardening and digging in the soil, humans have always touched the earth. Now, the Western world has moved away from nature in so many ways. We live in houses, wear rubber shoes, are exposed to EMPF´s, eat chemicals and genetically modified foods, and drink un-pure water.

Grounding is simply putting yourself in the environment in which you were designed to be. Simplicity is a common rule for success.

Let us look very simply about how grounding balances and recharges the human body. There is much more to grounding that electrons and ions, of course. Much more than we know, and that is ok. We do not need to know, we can *feel* and sense how healing coming home to nature is. The earth is charged with negative electrons. A negative ion is defined as an atom that has more electrons than protons. A positive ion is defined as an atom that has more protons than electrons. We look at the positive ions as not being healthy to the human body. Positive ions are toxins, electromagnetic pollution, such as EMF's, polluted air and general stress. This can be a bit confusing, as the negative ions are what is positive for the body, and the positive ions are harmful. The ones that we want are outside in nature, where the negative ions are in abundance, especially around waterfalls, by the ocean and in the mountain forests. Wi-Fi modems and Wireless Internet routers use dangerous electromagnetic radiation to send their signals to your computer. All of us that are using these very typical devices are exposed to EMF radiation. This is most definitely a soup of positive ions, which in itself will need balancing from Mother Earth. We got rid of the microwave ovens, and we need to be more cautious about our inner electric charge.

The amazing thing is that these negative ions neutralize free radicals. They provide an antioxidant effect. They enhance the immune function by being detoxifying, they purify the blood and they revitalize cell metabolism. On top of this, they are found to calm the sympathetic nervous system, which supports our heart rate variability. When we support heart rate variability, this in turn promotes homeostasis, or balance, in the autonomic nervous system. The negative ions are also told to clear the air of any airborne allergens like pollen, mold spores, viruses and bacteria. Nature really is perfect! The negative ions simply attach themselves to the positive ions, making them too heavy for you to breathe in, so you are protected by negative ions.

In our polluted cities, industrial areas, in schools, in any crowded area like an airport or a shopping mall, you will find the highest concentration of unhealthy positive ions. We are electrical by nature and the positive electrons in the form of free radicals will easily build up in our bodies. Putting ourselves in direct contact with earth balances this out with its negative grounding charge. When we are constantly bombarded with positive ions, this becomes a must for good health. We simply need to balance out this energy, to promote healing and regeneration. Being balanced and grounded is one of our basic needs. To live as healthy individuals on this planet, we need to do what we can to find our balance.

We ground our appliances, and by putting our bare skin directly on the earth, we are physically grounding our bodies too. This will prevent the buildup of electricity in the body, and any obstruction and ill health that might arise down the road. In a healing situation, when the body is already weak and low in energy, being grounded gives the body a head start and an upper hand.

Simply put:
Positive ions are associated with dis-ease and degeneration, over-acidity, immature ageing and imbalance.
Negative ions are associated with healing, energy, vitality, youth and regeneration.

Mother Earth is a limitless source of negative ions, the electrons and the energy that we need. They stream into the body when we are grounded. People experience less inflammation and more mental clarity after spending time outside in nature. The longer we stay outside, the more benefits we receive and experience. The Earth is alive, and will never stop emanating the free electrons. Connect the skin of your body with the skin of the Earth, and the flow will not stop. By doing this, every day, the electrons restore, the positive/negative balances, and a natural electrical state in the body is maintained. You now have a natural electrical state in your body. Every cell and organ in the body works electrically. We can think of the heart and the nervous system as great examples of that. We are fired up by this electric charge, and we will hurt when it is not balanced.

The best part is that it is free, it is available and it is simple! By jumping in the ocean, taking off your shoes on the grass, touching a tree, or hugging it, you are performing this amazing health promoting act, *and* you will have fun doing it! Watch your step if you are walking barefoot, to make sure you do not hurt yourself. If you are reluctant to walk, you can simply find a nice spot, and stand there for a while. You can even sit on a bench in a park with your shoes off. Try to do this for about 30 minutes every day. There are some earthing sheets to be purchased for indoor use, but nothing beats the real thing. The benefits of being outside are so many more than we can perceive. I am sure that you will notice a difference in your body from practicing grounding for a very short time. It doesn`t take much of the flooding of the balancing ions to make you feel better. Let the rubber soles go, and let those toes breathe! And yes, even if you are in a colder climate, like myself (Norway), there is no excuse for not grounding yourself. During the winter, I even walk barefoot in the snow. Not for long and I am using caution, but still, very doable. One small step at the time, that is all you have to do.

I love standing by a tree. That way I can connect to the earth through my feet, and the tree through my hands. Double power!

I am a very enthusiastic tree hugger, and have found that trees are not only great huggers, they are wise and healing. Yes, they emanate this beautiful energy, this vibration that is very healing and grounding to the human body. Different trees have different frequencies, and in ancient cultures, tree hugging was a common healing practice. To be in sync with nature was natural and sacred. Everything vibrates, everything is literally vibration. Different vibrations affect biological behavior. That means that when one touches a tree or is in the general vicinity of a tree, its different vibrational pattern will affect various biological behaviors within our bodies. I am following an old tradition that has been observed all around the world. Maybe the day will come when doctors will prescribe a day in the forest to those in need of healing. Trees are natural processors that can help us transform our body's sick or negative energy into positive, vital life-force energy. As we connect our energy with the tree, we facilitate our own physical and emotional healing.

The Taoist theory is that because trees stand very still, they are better at absorbing the energy from the Earth and the energy from the Heavens. Trees and all other plants have the ability to absorb the light frequencies and transform them into physical food, and it is told they do the same with energetic food. Science is now presenting several studies on health benefits from hugging trees, but really all you have to do is try it. Go outside, and find a tree that looks inviting. Ask it kindly if you can hug it, then embrace it and breathe deeply. I take my shoes off for some extra grounding. There is nothing like a great hug!

We have lost our contact with that which we are a part of, and are suffering the consequences.

Grounding is nothing more than us, again, getting out of our own way. We need to stop what is hurting us, and embrace what is not. By simply doing that, the body will do the rest. When something as simple as this becomes an obstacle, something that seems overwhelming, strange or crazy, we *know* how far we have wandered. We have kept walking on that path towards disaster for longer than we can remember, and the way back is completely forgotten. By simply re-connecting with where we came from, our senses will sharpen, and the memory will come back to us. We will remember truth and feel the desire and the power to act on it. The key is always action, as without it there are no results. Every time we take a breath of air, which is absolutely vital for life, we are connected to the grander part of Creation. I am humble and in awe at how grand nature really is.

Leather-soles will also keep you grounded, and woolen socks straight onto the ground will do to. There are some specific grounding shoes to be found also, so you might want to look into that.

"The true level of healing that is accomplished, is the level of awareness gained on the journey." Hilde

When we are walking barefoot, this will be a grounding surface:

- Grass
- Sand
- Ceramic tile
- Unpainted concrete brick
- Stone
- Bare soil
- Wool
- Cotton

This will NOT be a grounding surface:

- Wood
- Asphalt
- Rubber
- Plastic
- Vinyl or any synthetic material
- Indoors

On top of walking barefoot, hugging trees and swimming in the ocean, I know that eating the wild herbs and edibles will connect us even deeper to the healing power of nature. This is all so perfectly connected, and every bite, every step, every breath, all beautifully knitted together, simple and effortless.

Chapter 16

Sunshine

Every time you are exposed to the sun you are also connected to nature, one of our vital life-forces. No sun, no life. Now *that* should really make us reflect on some basic rules of healthy living. Sunshine is a life-giving energy, and it is crucial to our health. Not only for the production of the well-known vitamin D3, which in fact is a hormone, but for the Prana, the energy of life itself.

Most of us love everything about the sunshine, me included. Those of us that live up North, eagerly await the spring, when the sun starts to feel warm again. We instinctively love the daylight-hours, and both people and nature are responding to the cycle. We are amazed at the sunrise, and also the sunset. The show can be spectacular, and we never seem to tire from watching nature's canvas in the sky. We crave the sunlight, and are affected by it in so many ways. Those long summer nights, filled with light and communion. The feeling of wellbeing that arises from being outside in the sunshine is well known to all of us. A day of sunshine is always a better day it seems, and the blue sky is a sign of lightness and happiness.

Now that you are looking to raise your vibration so that the body can thrive and glow, being outside in the sunshine is an important part of the plan. Without the sun, we would not be able to see, and without the sun the plants wouldn't photosynthesize, leaving us without the oxygen we need to breathe. In many ancient cultures, the sun has been the symbol of consciousness, and in the older religions the sun was worshiped and honored. They knew that it was the life-force itself. In Greek mythology, Helios was the God of the Sun, and drove the sun across the sky every day. The father of medicine, Hippocrates, was also a great advocate of the sun's healing properties. In the Third Century, A.D. though, Christianity made sure that sunbathing was no longer allowed through most of Europe, and for the following thousand years, sunbathing was restricted almost entirely to the Jews and Arabians. Sunbathing was considered a sin, and was prohibited like other practices of the Hygienic System. In later days, there have been Nobel Prizes awarded to people that have studied the rays of light and their healing effects. We love to tear things apart, suppress and control them. In the same way, we tend to ignore the simple truth. We will relate a lot of different diagnoses to the lack of sunshine through analyzing the blood. Still, we do not see the truth behind our findings. The balance within the body is never from the lack of a vitamin, a hormone or a mineral. The imbalance comes from the *cause* of the findings, and that is what we need to address. We are over-acidic, and therefore need to alkalize. Although the sun will help us do that, through giving us the energy that we need to detoxify, heat in itself is acidic.

I am sure that you have noticed that when you are ill and not feeling well, or have an infection, you will seek the shade. You will also most likely shy the heat itself. This is because it is acidic and will also make us swollen and more inflamed. Bacteria don't like heat so they will get upset, and the same goes for parasites. The sunshine will kill bacteria, and a reaction to that will feel uncomfortable. From being a sun-lover, I felt better out of it when I was very sick. It made me feel weak and drained, and that is exactly what it will feel like. The sun will feel draining when we are not healthy. Still, the benefits are so great, that we need all the exposure that we can handle. Not only from the direct sunlight, but from the indirect also. The sun is not the problem, it is not unhealthy to be in the sun, it is *we* who are imbalanced and of ill-health. *We* are the ones that need to adjust back to nature, and this leads me to a very important sunshine topic, the sunscreen lotions.

We are led to believe that we should use sunscreen lotions to protect ourselves from the sun. The life-force, giving, nurturing sun. We are led to believe that we actually need to put chemicals on our skin to protect ourselves from what gives us life. We actually need to put products that are easily absorbed into the bloodstream on our skin. This is to be able to be outside in the sunshine! WOW! *No*, the Creator/the Universe/Nature did not make a mistake! Again, we need to listen for truth, and stop closing our inner ears. Did we ever stop to think about what made sense, or were we so eager to pay for a sunscreen that it did not matter? Today, the sun is considered the main culprit for causing skin cancer, certain cataracts leading to blindness, and aging of the skin. This is what we have been scared into believing. We are being told that being in the sun "un-protected" is a risk to our health. It could not be further from the truth. Staying *out* of the sun is what is the health risk, like every other act of intellect and not one of intuition or inner guidance.

Yes, I know, it can be hard to know what is what, and we are used to following guidance from the authorities. Still, it is time to take that full responsibility and stop to smell the roses. It is time to wake up and think about what we are doing to ourselves and our children.

The UV-rays in sunlight stimulate the thyroid gland to increase hormone production. This in turn will increase the body's basal metabolic rate. It aids both in weight loss and in improving muscle development. We have seen that farm animals fatten much faster when kept indoors, and so do people who stay out of the sun. Sunshine therapy even has a name; *Heliotherapy*. It was used to heal all kinds of ailments, and especially tuberculosis back in the 1900`s. Infected children were sent to special homes and hospital retreats to spend as much time outdoors as possible. This is but a small part of a large picture and a fun observation, I think. Now, we do not use sunshine therapy anymore, we use antibiotics, and we are living the consequences.

The hemoglobin in our red blood cells actually requires Ultraviolet light to bind to the oxygen. This is needed for all cellular functions. The UV light is also known to activate *solitrol*, a skin hormone that influences many of our body`s regulatory systems. Together with melatonin, the pineal gland hormone, it also changes our mood and our daily biological rhythms. These are profound processes for health and vitality, and merely just a few of the things that sunlight affects. We do not need to know, really, we only need to be aware that sunshine, sunlight, and being *in* it is important to our wellbeing. More than we have ever been led to believe. This is the sort of truth that will heal and restore. It is free and it is ours.

We absorb the sunshine in many different ways. Through the skin, the eyes, water, air and food. The entire bloodstream of the body passes through our eyes, and it recharges by the energy of the sun. This is why it is so important to leave the sunglasses at home. Another gadget that has been made by man, and that might actually be hurting us. Take the glasses off now and then, and let the sunshine in! We know it is absorbed by the skin, and it is stored by our cells. By drinking water, we are also ingesting the sun energy. We can supercharge some water by leaving it outside in the sun in a glass container. You can really taste the difference! We breathe the nutrients of the sun, and supply the digestive and excretory system with this vital force. It is therefore very powerful to do the deep breathing exercises outside. Celebrate life by breathing in the sun-force! Now, that we know the healing magic of the raw living foods, the sun-ripened fruits, we can see that the sunshine-force is a vital force for their nutrients. I call it Vitamin Sun!

When we are deprived of sunlight, we become weak and depressed. We can see that this is true by observing how we live and act. In the Northern parts, where there is little to no sunshine half of the year, people are suffering from what is called a Winter depression. We also see more irritability, fatigue and alcoholism. Even the suicide rate is higher in these countries during the dark season. This information also takes us to the thyroid. The thyroid is the gland of depression, and has a major role in hormone production. This is very interesting; People living in the Northern Countries also have a *higher* rate of skin cancer. Yes, they do! *And* they wear the most sunscreen. We see that when we look towards the sunny climates, people tend to act happier and more vibrant all year round. Also, it is to be noted that the plants and animals are usually more highly developed where the climate is warmer. Cause and effect.

We *are* supposed to be in the sunshine, as it *is* giving us highly beneficial nurturing and energy on so many levels. We really need to wake up from this craziness. We are killing ourselves slowly, creating disease and suffering. Stop all sunscreen usage, and at least stop spraying it around. Going to a crowded beach today is like going to an open-air gas chamber. My heart bleeds when I see little babies being sprayed with pure poison. The skin is absorbing every little bit of it, and it goes right to the bloodstream. Yes, if you put it on your skin, you eat it. Are we still wondering why we are sick? On top of this, the sunscreen is hindering the skin from absorbing the nurturing sunlight, the rays of healing, leaving it depleted of Prana and sunshine love.

If you wear it, you eat it. If you smell it, you eat it. If you eat it, you live and feel it. Cause and effect, always.

Use organic cold pressed coconut oil on your skin, and if you have a fair skin tone, be in the sun less, and build up. I have not worn sunscreen in years, and I am most certainly fair-skinned. I used to get sun rashes, and guess what, not anymore! This is very important information, and this is nature calling. It does not matter how old you are, or how your skin tone is, do *not* wear sunscreen on that beautiful skin of yours. I used to have sun rashes every summer growing up. I burned very easily, but as I cleaned myself out, and healed, my skin healed too. All that congested lymph that was hiding under my skin, found its way out. I am no longer the toxic red nosed puppy while in the sun. That being said, burning is never a good idea, and until you can tolerate the sun, spend more time in the shade, or wear some light clothing.

Try this if you got too much sun:

First, put some apple cider vinegar on the burn, and let it absorb.

Then, blend this together and gently put it on your skin.

- *1 tablespoon fractionated coconut oil*
- *2 drops peppermint*
- *3 drops roman chamomile*
- *3 drops lavender*

It is time to see beyond anything and everything we were ever taught, and connect with Source itself.

We will burn more easily when we are acidic, that is why staying in the shade can be a great idea. All we need for the body to benefit from the healing rays of the sun is about 30 minutes with our full bodies exposed, every day. There is no need to stay in the warm sun for hours at end, unless it feels comfortable. In the colder climates it will feel different, and just being able to have your face in the sun will be beneficial. It can't compare to a full-body exposure, but some of the benefits are still there. We have to do the best with what we have available, always.

Some simple health benefits of sunshine:

- *It increases blood circulation*
- *It enhances energy endurance*
- *It might affect the blood sugar levels.*
- *It will kill off bacteria.*
- *It stimulates the secretion of uric acid.*
- *Any infection and wound heals faster.*
- *It aids our cells' ability to cleans and detoxify.*
- *The liver is stimulated and strengthened.*
- *It lowers the stress level in the body.*
- *Hormones are balanced.*
- *It is a vital nutrient.*
- *It is crucial to vitamin D production.*

Sun gazing:

This might sound strange, but the ancient practice of sun gazing is believed to have many health- and healing abilities. By understanding the power of this life-force beyond the physical, we can open up to the higher realms of healing. The sun holds amazing power for those who seek to obtain it. Once we open up to the endless possibilities, let go of what we have been confined to, and stay patient, new wisdom will arise. We need to access our motivation to change, and our ability to consciously choose life and abundance. We are so much more than we can imagine, and are more powerful than we might want to accept.

By listening to our bodies, to our inner voice and spirit, we will always know truth, we will always know who we are and what we are a part of. We will know that the body is capable of compete self-healing, and that our spirit is eternal. Our body is merely that of flesh, designed to live and recycle. By honoring that, we can use the energy of the sun to connect even deeper, to raise our awareness even more, and to find deep peace and inner healing.

So, the sun gazing, also known as *sun eating*, is a practice of letting the sun into your eyes. This takes place during sunset and sunrise. I came across sun gazing while I was searching for a deeper spiritual practice, and I have found that it has given me many moments of peace and calm. This old practice has seen the light of day again, as younger earthlings are curious and willing to explore. For me, I wanted to see what it was all about, and now maybe you will also.

It is told to dramatically improve sleep quality, improve eyesight, aid the whole endocrine system, and even decalcify the pineal gland - the gland of awareness, also referred to as the third eye or the seat of the soul. It is located deep within the brain, and produces melatonin. It is no larger than a grain of rice, yet so important to our wellbeing, both physically and emotionally. It is an endocrine organ, and the quality of sleep is often related to the state of this little friend. It also regulates stress levels, as well as the physical performance. One might say that how you think and feel depends on this gland. The sun gazing is an important way to re-activate the pineal gland, as it has been slowly calcified through fluoride exposure, food additives, artificial sweetening, alcohol, pesticides, radiation and through general intoxication.

We can activate the pineal gland through sun gazing, meditation, being outside in the sunshine, detoxification with raw fruits and vegetables, and sleeping in the darkness. Isn't it amazing? Know that we know we can *do*!

The practice:

- Find the perfect time of day, either sunrise or sunset.

- Stand barefoot on the ground and gaze at the sun for no more than 10 seconds.

- Do this practice every day.

This is something that you need to read up on, as one should never stare directly at the sun. Make sure you are not hurting yourself. This information is for you to explore further, and not to be taken as medical advice.

Chapter 17

Move and sweat

I have to tell you, I really missed my ability to move! From being a very active and athletic being, I became bedridden and was in constant pain. I could not walk on my feet, my knees were doubled in size, I could not lift my arms, make a fist or bend my elbows. I tell you, and so will everyone else out there who are unable to move, it is not fun. It is obvious to me that we are meant to be active, that it is natural for us.

Running, walking, swimming, jumping, dancing, riding a bike, climbing and skiing, yes most of us love to move. When the opportunity arises, we spend our free time moving our bodies. Well, actually the healthiest ones do. It seems that the healthier we get, the more we like to use our bodies. The stronger we get, the more we like to use that strength. On a healing journey, when we are less than healthy, lack of movement is very often present. It might be that we simply cannot use our limbs that much due to an accident or a disease. Other reasons can be weakness and fatigue, depression, anxiety, vertigo and breathing problems. There are so many issues that will eventually restrict us from moving, yet we need to keep moving along.

Think of little children, how we as toddlers are constantly focused on moving around. We are eager to learn how to crawl and to stand up and walk. Once we get to the running part, we are hard to stop. A child is constantly playing around, if it is a healthy one. Yes, indeed they know, so for most children, only a health issue will stop them from being active. Does this mean that all these children that do not want to move, that would rather sit in front of a TV-screen playing a video-game, are not healthy? Yes, I believe it does, plain and simple. Sadly, they are obese, constipated, depressed, diabetic and asthmatic. Being physical is fun, and it is necessary. We know that everything is connected, we are aware of the mind-body-connection. You might have heard the term "Your brain is in your gut", and it is true. The body *is* our brain, as it is the endocrine system that is the government of the body. If we stop a child from being active, it will restrict the whole learning ability of that child. The relationship between our bodies and the way we use them is either one of healing and thriving, or one of degeneration and decay.

If you don't use it, you lose it!

Movement has always been a part of any ancient culture. Before cars, trains, air-planes and bicycles, we were on the move. Running, swimming, climbing and lifting were all a part of the daily routine. Gathering food, delivering messages and dancing were a part of the life that we were designed to live. By wandering off to the corner of sedentary and a standard Western diet, we brought on sickness and despair as our companions. When eating the food that is hurting us, numbing us down and making us tired, it becomes natural to move less. It is hard for someone that are already constipated and tired, to find the inner *and* the physical strength to do any form of exercise or activity. It is a circle that is hard to break, and the sofa becomes a friend.

In nature, every single animal actively uses their body, and it is never to look better or to build muscle, it is for purpose and joy. Play includes movement, and so does living. Think about when you are happy, really happy. I bet you will want to jump up and down. Moving is an expression of joy.

Why is it so important to include movement in your day?

- First of all, the lymphatic system needs help to move around. It does not have a pump, like the blood does. The heart pumps the blood all through the vessels of our bodies, but the lymphatic system is moved by our physical motion and our muscle contractions. Our diaphragm and rib cage, as well as the blood flowing through our bodies, all contribute to the movement of lymph. even our breathing does, but exercise is our primary method of lymph-moving. Did you know that a sedentary lifestyle can decrease the lymph flow by 94%? Well, even if it is not that high a number, you get the idea. Being active is *in*, sitting still is *out*.

- Being active, like walking, strengthens your heart. Our most vital organ needs to be trained, to be strong and fit. It increases the blood circulation and oxygen to our cells and tissue.

- Muscle tone is very important to our skeletal health, and on impact we not only build stronger bones, but we massage our joints.

- Our lungs are cleared and exercised, which also leads to more oxygen to the cells.

- When we move the body, we aid the whole detoxification process. The lymph, the digestive tract, the lungs, the

- sweating through the skin, are all important elements of the body`s ability to self-cleanse.

- • We also tend to be happier when we are more active, and anyone who has gone for a run, knows the good feeling when endorphins are released.

The general feeling of wellbeing, the physiological, the mental and the emotional benefits from being active, are more in number than we know, but we can easily get the bigger picture.

I don`t want you to think that even though you might not be able to move much at this time, that you will not be able to do what is needed, or that you will never get there. No matter where your starting point is, your *now* situation, you can and will move forward. If you are not able to move at all, right now while reading this chapter, visualize that it is you doing the tasks, the exercises and activities. There is no greater power than your mind. Through thinking it, seeing it, feeling it and smelling it, you are reprogramming your cells. Every cell has a memory, and every cell has awareness. Your body is your vehicle, and by showing it what you want and desire, you will change the course of its health and strength. It is never too late to create the life that you want, and it is never too late to get strong and fit. You are already on the right path, and I will tell you how to move, one step at the time, through taking action.

"Through our actions, the momentum of movement, change and evolvement appears. We tend to analyze and talk about our visions more than actually walking our talk. If we truly want to serve, to give, and to empower ourselves and others, we need to act upon our visions. Being the change you want to see in the world, means acting accordingly to your ideal situation. Any change starts with a thought, a feeling, but only when connected to action will true manifestation happen." – Hilde

Move from where you are:

Like I said, no matter your current situation, you can always shift forward. Through simply moving what you can, when you can, you can work from there. Always be thankful for what you can do. Being grateful, creates more to be grateful for. I was bedridden, and moving anything at all, was very painful. All I could do was sit in a rocking chair, so that is what I did. I could sit in the chair, and I could lie on my back. While lying down I also managed to do sit-ups. I figured it was movement, and it *is*! So, you see, anything you can do, *do* it. There's something called Chi machines, which will move your legs while you lie on the floor, and they are wonderful for those that are not yet able to go for a walk. Below are some suggestions for how you can make sure that you get the active motion you need every single day. Stretch and do whatever you can, and then some. Rest when needed, always, but move when there is energy. During a healing path, while detoxing and healing, strenuous exercise is not recommended. It will create an extra acidic burden to the body, as movement actually *is* acidic. Lactic acid, a byproduct of movement, and a burden for the body. Always go light and be persistent. I have found that anything that is done over time, and not given up on, will produce results.

"Little effort, little result, large effort, large result" - Hilde

Chi machine:

This became a life saver for me, and I am sure it will benefit anyone who is unable to go for daily walks. It is very simple to use, and you can get one online. The original is a Japanese so-called "Passive Aerobic Exerciser." It oscillates from right to left, about 144 times per minute. It is said to give the body the oxygen benefit of 1.5 hours of walking, in only 15 minutes. While you lie effortlessly on the floor, with your ankles resting on the machine, it will move them from side to side. This creates what is called a figure-8 motion of the spine, and is similar to the movement of a goldfish. The movement is believed to have a great effect upon the body, in relaxing nerves, improving energy flow, relieving tension and moving lymph.

Rebounder/Trampoline:

"I remember jumping on trampolines, from childhood. Back then, the only place to get a chance to jump on one, was in gym class at school. Now, they are available everywhere, in all different sizes. My eagerness was always way ahead of my physical ability, and this time was no different. I ordered a small trampoline, or rebounder, on the internet. It had a handrail, a hand bar. That way I could hold on while jumping. We got it all set up, adding yet another equipment to my regime. I was going to jump. I could smell freedom from just thinking about it. I must say, those little things are genius. I was able to start out by walking carefully onto the rebounder, holding on to the handrail, and then not jumping, but softly doing an up and down motion. My feet never left the canvas. I counted every day. I counted how many times I could "jump" up and down. Progress is fun. I then moved on to how many minutes I could do, then actually letting my feet and myself lift and flow. Anytime you think "I can't do that", just walk towards it and take the first step. Then, think again!" – from my first book, "From Hell to Inspired".

Get on a trampoline or a smaller rebounder every day. It is a great place to start. Like me, start slow if you need to. The up and down motion is great for moving lymph, but also for creating bone mass. The impact is what the bones need, and it will also help you to build some muscle.

A full body vibrator:

This is another potential movement life-saver. You stand on it, and it will do the rest. As the machine vibrates, it transmits energy to your body, forcing your muscles to contract and relax dozens of times each second. To me, that sounded like a great idea, and it was. The first time I went on it, I thought my bottom was going to fall out. I had so much acidic waste stuck in my feet and legs that it hurt, bigtime. It was like shaking an open wound. I was on it though, every day, 3 times a day. I was shaking it, and the pain left little by little. If you can stand up, this will work for you. Step by step, finding what works, as *not* moving is not an option!

True freedom is knowing that every moment holds great value, and that it never is about any goal or destination. It is all about each moment of movement, on the path called life.

Walking:

My daily walks will always be what I will treasure the most from my road back to health, and the day that I could start walking past the mailbox, or the day I could put my feet in a pair of normal shoes and go outside, was the best day ever, so far. When it comes to movement, nothing beats walking. It is gentle, natural and healing. Once you are able to walk, you walk. There is nothing that is more nurturing for us than walking. It is a perfect match to our physiology. Work up to walking 30 minutes a day, and feel how much energy you are getting. Walking has everything that you need and nothing that you do not. Move the arms when walking, and get into the brisk-walking-gear when you can. Take deep breaths and enjoy being outside.

"It was a huge milestone to be able to actually do what can be considered a walk. The forest behind our house has a trail. Several really, but a main one. It is not that long, but to me, for years it was unreachable. What seems normal to most, can be the largest obstacle, and also the greatest wish of another." – "From HELL to Inspired"

Running, climbing, riding a bike and swimming:

These are all just a few of many ways to move your lymph, build muscle, expand your lung capacity, release endorphins and so much more. Running is great for building bone mass, and we are definitely made to run, but running on asphalt will take a toll on your skeleton. We were made for running barefoot, on Mother Earth, so running on a beach is a great option. Remember, this is not the time to get too vigorous, but rather the time to do some short easy runs, some swimming, bike riding and some walking. No heavy weight-lifting for now. Building comes later, as healing requires detoxification/cleansing.

Moving forward, little by little, is what makes the journey so colorful and awakening. Remember to stay in the now, and to cherish every single moment. Life is made of those moments, absolutely *all* of them.

When we are able to exercise, or to break a sweat, we are opening another doorway of benefits. This is often the culprit for many, to be able to move or work out hard enough to sweat. Sometimes we do not have the strength or the energy to do so, and even to try would set us back even more. Easy does it, and slow and steady wins the race. Most often when we are so called chronic, or has been ill for a while, the adrenals are so down, they really need the rest. That's why the Chi machine and the easy rebounding is a good place to start.

Sauna:

"The sweating, most likely, is what made me able to survive the heavy detoxification I was putting my body through. The skin is the third kidney, and as my kidneys were down, slapped, not very happy, the sweating saved the day. My sauna, since then, has been my good and trusted friend. From being that first portable one, with my head sticking up, to a used one-person wooden stationary one, and finally a brand new state of the art shiny FIR sauna. I am still in love with my sauna, even though I only use it about once a week now."- "From HELL to Inspired"

Sitting in a sauna can be a great asset to a detoxification regime, and I definitely promote it. There is always a caution though, as the body will need to use some energy, and sometimes with very low adrenals, that too much heat is not a good thing. Remember heat is also acidic in nature. *But*, then there is the kidney connection and our need to move that lymph. The skin is our third kidney as we know, and if we are not filtering, moving toxins out through the skin can be a lifesaver. I use a FIR sauna, and you can use the type that you have access to and are drawn to. Far infrared rays are invisible energy waves that can penetrate all layers of the body, the tissue, muscles and bone. The rays are used to heal, detoxify and relax the body. The sun, our hands, and our bodies all emit FIR energy at all times. Perhaps this is an explanation of palm healing? The FIR sauna operates on low temperatures, and is said to be more gentle to the body than a regular sauna.

I had so much belief in the FIR energy, that I also added a Bio-Mat to my regimen. It is a great way to start moving some energy, and to start sweating even. Yes, you can lie on the mat and sweat. It's a high-tech negative ion and infrared ray treatment system that emits negative ions and Far infrared rays. The gentle warmth of the Bio-Mat will give an overall massaging effect, and will aid in detoxification. It is a very heavy mat, filled with amethyst crystals. I always loved the crystals, and I'm never too far from the healing energy that they emit.

Although the guidelines are easy, and the road back to health is fairly obvious, we all come from a different standpoint. This means that sometimes, working with a practitioner, someone that is trained in detoxification and health and who has the experience you are looking for, is a great idea.

This was what I was longing for the most. Being so active all of my life, all the way from childhood, it was the greatest loss. With movement comes the sense of freedom, and let me tell you; If you cannot move as you want to, keep working on it, and do what you need to do to get to where you want to go. If you are able to move, you go and do so, and if you feel there is any reason at all that you cannot, or that you do not know where to start, let it go. Let it all go and just start, today.

"Let your heart guide you, and your feet lead you, and do not be afraid to follow that tune. Don't wait until tomorrow, there is only today. Do not skip a single beat, as this life is happening right *now*. This is the time to let all fears and hurts go, and let yourself express all that you are. *You* are the amazing artist, the empowered lead performer in *your* life." – Hilde

Chapter 18

The mind game

B eing able to think is what we tend to believe makes us superior to other beings. Not that we don`t believe that other species think, but we do it so much better. We resonate, analyze and contemplate. We keep pondering and pondering, using the mind as if it was who we were, and the most valuable asset of any human being. On the contrary, when thoughts are present, true connection cannot flow. Thoughts are often interfering with being in the *now* moment, and only by stilling the mind can we listen to our divine truth. Our innate wisdom will come through, and the feeling of calm will rise. We are thinkers, and even though the ability to think is a great tool, it is also a constant creator of stress, noise and worry. The mind has a tendency to keep going, even though we are not fully aware of this. We spend our days lost in unconscious and unproductive thinking – addictively replaying the same mental patterns, the same old stories, over and over in our heads like a broken record player. *Monkey-mind* is a Buddhist expression which refers to the incessant chatter that goes on in our heads.

Like a restless monkey, always moving around, the mind is always busy, producing up to 100,000 thoughts per day. It is estimated that our brains are bombarded with seven times as much stimuli as our grandparents experienced. Add to this the rising stress levels caused by increased working hours and longer traffic jams, and it is a wonder that many people can cope at all. Everything we look at, experience, and hear and feel the vibration of, is something our brain wants to process. We tend to take with us the past, and invite in the future in this constant soup of mind-food. The thing is, that everything we think, all the mind-chatter, is holding us locked in the place we are in. We know that we think mostly the same thoughts or thought patterns every single day, like an old broken record. This is a great part of why changing seems so hard to do - it is something to think, rather than to do.

It all starts with the mind. We need to reset and reshape our way of thinking, to be able to do things differently. To be able to do differently actually means to be able to think differently.

I want to let you in on something that I have found quite interesting. To quiet the mind though meditation and yoga is fantastic, and are great practices. They are ancient methods of clearing the head, and moving from the head/thought to the heart. What I was not prepared for, was the fact that the more I detoxified my physical body, the clearer and calmer the mind got. The more raw-living fruits and vegetables that I ate, the more aware and clear-minded I got. The connection became super obvious to me. Detoxification is an all-inclusive experience. Together with a clear intent, a true wish for healing and spiritual connection, reprogramming that old chattering monkey on the top floor will be inevitable. Even that which we call old programming, what we have been told over and over until we believed it, is mostly a subconscious pattern. It always starts with a thought. A conscious thought was always there first. It was there together with a feeling, and then with a belief that was later confirmed over and over again until it stuck. Believe me, getting something to stick in a child's mind is easy. As children we are like sponges, and we are constantly seeking to learn and to find our safe and loving place. We look towards authority for guidance, and as we learn to be followers and not different or special, we keep looking for new authorities throughout our whole lives. It's like we lost our bus and ended up on the route to helpless and overwhelmed – joined the school of followers, and signed up for life.

As adults, we like to believe that we are our own authority, when in fact we are not. We, in the Western world, the freedom fighters and know-it-all intellectuals, are following many - from governments to doctors, completely leaving our sovereign state. We have been programmed to believe that we need constant guidance when it comes to our health, our financial affairs, our education, and our ability to choose in general. From vaccination programs to drugs, from chemicals in the water to genetically modified food. Toxins are everywhere, and they have a great influence on our ability to think and to stay of a clear mind. The inseparable mind-body-connection at its best. Everything from ingesting non-foods and breathing polluted air, to being injected and medicated while being fed fear-based information, will acidify us. Now leaving us with a calcified pineal gland, the little gland in our brain, the one that is our third eye and are connecting us with the higher realms. That one, a gland that is a part of our very own internal government, the authority which always has our best interest at heart, always. Only someone with a calcified pineal gland will automatically be a follower. It is natural for us to be wondering and curious. Look at how children keep exploring new things. Trying and failing. We lost that eagerness and boldness through toxicity and mind-games.

For the purpose of healing and restoration of health, we need to look at what is holding us locked in this position. This is personal, and we need to take it as such. It is our business to stop this pattern, the sooner the better. The old programming is very easy to spot, there is never a doubt what program goes with which person. If you are the one not loving to be with yourself and not speaking highly of your own wonderful being, you are not programmed to love yourself, period. Let me tell you, when we find ourselves in ill-health, the programming that is there, is most likely not that of self-love.

"When you want something to change, change something", is an old but good statement. It is obvious and it makes sense. "Health is a choice", is another one. This statement might not ring as true right away, but it truly is. Those simple statements, hold the key to your healing and transformation, though they might stir up some unhappy emotions at first.

If health really is a choice, am I saying that people are choosing to be sick? No, of course not, and yet, yes in a sense they are. We, you, me, we *are* on a non-conscious level choosing to live what we are living. Right at this moment, our life and our bodies are simply responding to our inner terrain and programming. Conscious or subconscious, it does not matter, a belief is a belief. As long as we are thinking what we have been thinking, we will keep experiencing the same old thing. As long as we keep eating what we have been eating, feeling what we have been feeling, we are simply validating our thought-form. This will manifest in many different ways. Yes, we see it in the life that we are living. We live what we believe we can, must, are capable of and so forth, but we also live the life that we fear and love. Our lives reflect what we talk about the most, who we choose to be with, and how willing we are to change. The old programming is not going to give in easily, as it took time for it to settle. It might trick you into believing that it is right, but it's not. A healthy and blossoming inner talk and mindset, is not often to be seen in a healthy physical body.

In this amazing life of yours, you are the conductor of this fantastic orchestra of cells and events. You are the one in charge, even when it does not feel like it.

Choosing to live, to thrive and be healthy, is also choosing your thoughts. It is letting go of everything that is not serving you, absolutely everything that is not serving you. And why wouldn't you? Well, the fear of change again, and the old programming's tight grip. Change would be easy and the path would be obvious, was it not for this very thing. The road would be clear as day, as it is natural to do what is best for the body, and it is natural to say no to toxins and needless drugs. It is absolutely healthy and sound to change what is not serving you. Only old programming will stand in the way. It *is* obvious, you might say, yet still hard to do. My point exactly! As long as you can see clearly what you need to do, yet find it difficult to follow through, you are not of sound mind, so to speak. You are not of a detached, free, and self-loving mindset.

When I talk about the mind game, I am referring to the stimuli and non-truths that we are constantly bombarded with. Our minds are fed and nurtured through our education, the media, our parents, and our bosses. Authorities are feeding us what is serving the cause you might say, as there is always an agenda. To be a free-thinker, a self-serving and authentic human being, takes courage and strength. To free ourselves from the belief systems that we have embraced and adapted, takes time and persistence. Luckily, through cleansing and rejuvenation, bull-shit does not stand a chance, only truth does. The truth shall set you free, but first it will piss you off.

We want our thoughts to be of a constructive nature, meaning positive for our health and life in general. We want our thoughts to reflect and draw forth the feeling-good emotions, which in turn will be healing to our cells. For a thought to have any impact on our cells, it has to be associated with- or connected to a feeling. The

183

feeling is what has the vibration, and the vibration is what connects with everything that vibrates, which means absolutely everything there is. This means that what we feel is the most important thing of all when it comes to programming our cells. The feeling is the language you might say. The feeling is what speaks the language which the cell will understand and respond to.

Feeling good is something we associate with certain outside events, externally created events. Although our conditioning has made us believe that is how it is, we can break free from that belief. Feelings are not us, and we can choose, through practice and letting go, how we want to feel. Feeling good is a choice, and our life is created one thought, one belief, one feeling, and one bite of food at the time. The direction can be changed at any given moment.

The mindset of a healthy you, is the mindset of a winner. Now is the time to let your true power shine through, by taking control of your mind and emotions. When you know that you are in charge of your thinking, you are on your way, and as one thought changes, the rest will follow. Time is on your side, as the journey is the real destination.

How do you know what you have been programed to believe?

This is very easy to answer: The old programming will show up as your need to speak about the disease, the broken relationship, or the terrible job and boss. Every time you feel the urge to tell a story of something that you would rather change, you know that you are in the mind-game-mode. As long as you keep telling that same old story of what you do *not* want, you are heading down that same old road. When we have the need to talk about what is not serving us, we know that we need to change. What we resist, persists, and what we talk about the most, we will keep creating more of.

Now, there is a very big difference between letting someone know how things are, and to keep indulging in sickness and tragedy. Even though something appears as a truth, does not mean we need to keep telling it. If you do not like your story, tell a different one. "Yes, but...", you might say, but there are no but`s. If you keep telling the same old story, that is what you will be seeing more of. The broken record will keep on playing for as long as it is not stopped and replaced.

How do you condition yourself for true healing?

- *First of all, you must realize that the old programming is there. It is important to acknowledge the way that you have been thinking. The thinking might not be obvious, but your life is. So look at your life and see what you are living that is not what you would like it to be.*

- *Realize that the past is the past, and now is now. What has been has been, and now is when change can happen.*

- *Know that you, and only you, are the one in charge of your thoughts and feelings. This is a must. You really need to know you are the Head of operations.*

- *Be your biggest fan, and do not be shy. Once you realize how amazing you really are, you will wonder what you have been thinking. Bond up with you, your new best friend!*

- *Know that you are not a victim, and never really were. You are a co-creator and a master of your life, so feel, think and live like one.*

- *Get ready for the ride of your life. The rollercoaster ride will be a trip, so be prepared. Prepare your mind and your environment. Make up your mind, pure and simple. Simply decide to do what you need to do and go do it. Once you have made up your mind, there is no looking back. There is no trying or maybe`s, there is only moving in one direction, forward.*

- *Get to know Mr. Trust and Mrs. Faith. If you have any doubts that you can do this, that your body can heal, thrive and regenerate, keep reading until you don`t. Trust and faith are great friends and followers until you know by experience. From then on, everything changes.*

- *Do not worry about what other people might say. They are all conditioned by their own programming and beliefs. Most of the time they only want what they think is best for you, although they might not know what that is. You do not need approval from anyone. This is about you, and your life.*

- *Be committed to the plan. Once you have made a protocol, either by yourself, or together with your practitioner, stay with it. Your health is worth it. You are worth it. There is no reason that is good enough for you to not succeed, not a single one.*

- *Be fearless of change, and welcome it like an old friend. Fear of danger is different, and must not be confused by the fear we are conditioned to have towards anything out of the norm or so-called "accepted" conduct. Stepping outside the box, most often, will be challenging for people around us. Lose the whole concept of there even being a box. Act like the free and sovereign being that you are.*

- *Be unstoppable on your quest for health. Let nothing stop you from getting to where you want to go. If you fall, get back up.*

Everyone has their own path, their own journey, and the one that does not believe it can be done, should never interrupt the person doing it.

There is nothing out there to wait for, and the best time to take the first step is always now. You are the one you have been waiting for, and no matter what you have experienced up to this point in time, the full responsibility is now on you. Only you can change the outcome of your future. How amazingly great is that? From feeling that life happened to you, that you were somehow a victim, you can now *know* that you are the one with the truly wonderful power to change everything. Realizing you have that ability can either make you or brake you. The fact that you are part responsible for the state of your health, does not make you at fault, as this was never a conscious choice. There is never blame involved, only the realization of solution. Being responsible does not mean that you did something wrong, it only means that you are in fact on top of the game.

Health and healing is always about the solution, always. Do not look back unless you are going in that direction. Even so, we might want to go back at times, to understand how we got to where we are at. But this is only to reveal a valuable lesson or insight on how to move forward. Every single experience has a valuable lesson to teach us, so in term, everything is always as it should be. We are here, right now, to learn and to move on. Every person we ever meet is our teacher, even though it might not feel like it at the time.

Start by conditioning your whole being for success. Talk, think and feel like the winner that you are. Your cells are listening to absolutely everything. To every thought and emotion, you have an audience, and it is what is called your life. When you think about your health, think about being healthy. When you talk about your health, be positive and enthusiastic. As your old programming loosens and a new mindset replaces it, what you are sending out will also be changing. This might result in some change in friends and associates, but that is ok. When friends leave, you know you are moving ahead. You will naturally be drawn towards those that have the same creative, positive, solution-based, loving mindset as yourself. New like-minded friends will eventually knock on your door, so don`t worry. Only those that were not of support to you will leave.

The process of healing will include every single part of your life. You cannot heal the physical body without healing the emotional one. It is all connected, and therefore you can start with a few single steps, and the rest will follow easily and effortlessly. You can change your diet, and your emotional body will start its detoxification process as well. You can start your meditation practices, your deep breathing and your letting go routine, and your will start loving yourself more and more. This will soon lead to taking better care of yourself by choosing food that nurtures. As your physical body is healing, your mind is getting clearer, your emotions are balancing out, and your relationships are changing for the better.

Do not worry, nothing is under control. It is all aligning just as it should, and out of chaos comes order.

As long as you let go of the need to control the outcome, life will be created to look and feel like magic. Do your very best, and order health from the menu of the Universe. Try not to give a dang about what that looks like, and let Mr. Trust take care of the rest. You do *your* part, the Creation will do it`s, you can count on it. Your ride, your journey. It will be what you let it, and you are never alone.

Let go and let live, and give the old programming of lack and suffering a kick in the butt. No more attention to old fashioned belief-systems, and no more engaging in fear-based information and behaviors. No more buying into not being great and amazing, and no more chasing validation from others. *You* are in charge, and your mind is under *your* control. Take the steering wheel, and keep your eyes on where you are heading, to healthy and happy.

By realizing that we are powerful beyond belief, we are re-creating every little part of our lives. The enthusiasm and willingness to do good, will light up the path towards more of what life has to offer.

Chapter 19

Stillness and meditation

Meditation has become quite a household name, but are we sure we know what it means? Some people use the word meditate, when they really mean visualizing or daydreaming. Some breathing techniques might also be called meditation, and so is sitting still and feeling content. These are all great practices, and stillness is a great part of a healthy lifestyle, but the word meditation has a specific meaning. It is a technique used to rest the mind, while altering the state of consciousness. The inner awareness will lead to the experience of a completely calm and clear state of being.

Simply put, when we are in a meditative state, we are alert and aware, yet not of anything external, and not of any thoughts. The focus goes inward, and the mind is silent.

As we already know, the mind can be quite a deceiver, and it can keep us locked in our old ways of creating. To be able to get out of the mind will require practice and diligence. Yet, by simple methods we can train ourselves to tap into the healing-space of being. It is not at all about controlling the mind, but rather about letting it be. Our true awareness is not the thinking mind, although our thoughts often seem to deceive us to believe that it is. Being aware simply means to be alert in perception, not with thoughts and chatter. From thinking comes the analytical, critical, and fearful experiences. From just being in stillness comes true love, bliss and peace.

Our lives are constantly bombarded by outside stimuli. From the day that we set our foot in a kinder garden, and all through our school-years, we are taught to focus on the outside. Through colors, language, sound and smell, we are told to evaluate and analyze. We are conditioned to compare and evaluate ourselves to other humans. Our lives are programmed to mostly strive for an outside accomplishment, from when we are very, very young. No-one teaches us to look inward, and to be in our own ocean of knowingness. Meditation is a practical means of getting out of the way of our mind. We are able to explore our inner dimensions, and if we are really committed to this practice, to ourselves and our healing, great benefits will be seen. The practice of calming our whole physical system, will open the door to a new level of wellbeing.

Simply sitting still, is a challenge for many. From running around all day, always on the go, stillness is foreign and might feel un-easy. In my own experience, this was a great challenge. If you are anything like me, you know how hard it is to get the mind to stop jabbering. Cultivating stillness will therefore start with the physical body. The body needs to be conditioned for stillness also, you see. Through simple relaxation techniques, the body will find ease, and the mind will follow. You can sign up for a yoga class, which is a great place to start. Any practice that will still the body and mind will be a great addition to your daily meditation routine. Meditation will acquire practice like any other skill. It will take persistence and patience, but it will be worth it. Trust me, once your inner being opens to the bliss of silence and stillness, your life will change on every level.

To become an experienced meditator takes years of practice, and even then, deeper levels of wholeness will be experienced as time goes by. Luckily, getting started is very simple. No special tool is needed. All you have to do is to show up with an attitude of healing and pure intent. You are going on a mind-vacation, and joining a retreat of the joyful cells. By connecting to all that you are, through the portal of your inner being, your cells will sing and dance. Stress-free, and self-loving energy will embrace them all.

Start your own meditation practice:

Find a space where you will not be disturbed. As you are able to master the practice more and more, this will matter less and less. You can sit in the midst of an airport or a train station and still find the deepest peace in meditation. Imagine the true freedom right there. It is entirely up to us to free our mind of any outside clutter and trauma, and through the inner journey we can do so. For now, make your space of meditation a beautiful and peaceful one. Light a candle and diffuse some essential oils like Frankincense and Myrrh. Make sure that fresh air is available, and that you are sitting in a comfortable position.

- *Make this time your time by clearing your schedule for at least 30 minutes. Practicing meditation and stillness requires a persistent practice, and a true commitment. Make this time a daily routine, and a top-of-the-list priority in your protocol.*

- *Show up with pure intent. By this, I mean find a loving, healthy focus in your heart. Say a prayer, or simply feel what it is that you desire. You can also ask for clarity and healing.*

- *Sit comfortably on a bed, or in a chair. Make sure that your spine is straight, and that your arms are resting comfortably on your lap or along the side of your body. Close your eyes, and relax all the muscles that you do not need to sit up straight. Spend some time just paying attention to your muscles, as you are feeling more and more relaxed.*

- *Pay attention to your breath. As you do so, relax your muscles, and feel all the tension leaving you.*

- *When a thought comes by, just let it come. Don`t react or respond to it, but don`t push it away either. Just let it pass on by. The thought is just that, a thought, and is not a part of you at all. Go back to focusing on your breathing.*

- *As you are focusing on your breath, be aware of how deeply you are breathing. Are you using the shallow breath, or are you breathing all the way from your diaphragm? At first, the breath might be shallow and irregular, but as you keep going, it will settle and become smooth and deep.*

- *Sit for as long as you feel comfortable, constantly connecting with your breath, letting your mind go in complete silence.*

As time passes, the meditation will be deeper, and the experience will be richer and fuller. Explaining the experience in words can be challenging, but the evolvement of inner connection will set you free from the attachment to trauma, and condition you to be an observer instead. By observing life, being detached and centered, we are allowing life to flow without the struggle and resistance. Any situation that we encounter is nothing but a chain of events, until we give them a reaction and a color, so to speak. Even our thoughts are not disturbing, stressful or hurtful, until we give them a reaction. When we give them a meaning, and attach them to a feeling, we are lost in the ups and downs of action and re-action.

When we experience anything from a hurtful comment to losing a business deal, how we react is our own business. We can either look at the situation with a creative, solution-based attitude, or get lost in frustration and hurt. We can stay unattached to the trauma, by simply being the observer.

Once we lose ourselves in the feeling, the reactions and the hurt, we are attached. We are clinging to the emotional roller coaster. Our reactions are always colored by our inner fears, judgments and resistance. This is what I mean by being attached to the trauma. Practicing meditation and stillness will allow us to let go of that attachment, and the emotional upsets are replaced with a balanced observation. Being the observer means to be the one watching, without having the need to react. Now you can stop reacting and start responding. You can and will start to respond openly and creatively, and without judgment. You know that there is nothing to judge, and that you are in fact the one creating your inner *and* your outer experience. This alone is a very healing shift, and will take you to a whole other level of true healing.

True progress is noted over time. Our calling is to always learn and do better, and by allowing who we really are to arise, growth and a higher awareness is inevitable.

Meditation is therapeutic in many different ways. It will teach patience and balance. Your immaturities will be exposed, together with your habits and your inner complexes. The way you see yourself will change, and you will be invited to heal and let go of some old not favorable habits and beliefs. Stick with it, and practice systemically. That way, you will experience the benefits. It is not possible to not receive benefits. Even when you are not noticing, you are receiving. As you sow, you shall reap. Often it will take time to see the benefits, and they might be subtle. Keep your attention on your goal, on your healthy life, and in the *now*.

As meditation simply means awareness, whatever we do with awareness is a form of meditation. A walk in the woods, painting, listening to the birds sing, can also be meditation. Swimming in the ocean can be meditation, and so can running on the beach. As long as there is no distraction to the mind, or any form of mental interference, we could call it meditation. Mindfulness is another word, which means being in the now, completely aware and present. Slightly different in its energy, yet we are looking at the same idea. Stilling the mind, being in silence, and going within. One can be aware of the outside world, yet go within.

Visualization and guided meditation is slightly different, as now, the focus is from the mind. We are forming thoughts and pictures to create a desired inner world. It is much like daydreaming. A guided meditation can be quite useful though, and very pleasant. The subconscious mind will be challenged to reprogram its old patterns, and the body will most definitely listen to the inner picture and its accompanying emotions as if they were "real". What you see with your inner eye, and feel as a result of that inner created "movie"; is as real to your body as what you see with your physical eyes. Your cells do not know the difference.

The constant and inner unchanging part of our being is the Source of all peace and contentment. Learning how to meditate will allow you to deepen your connection with the silence within.

It is easy to forget that we are the controllers and co-creators of our reality. As we go about our days it is easy to forget that our lives are made from our beliefs, thoughts, emotions and mindset. [10]

As we meditate we are able to move from a higher frequency brain wave, to a lower frequency. This will activate different centers of the brain. By learning about the different brainwaves, we can see that the deeper we go, the more we will be able to get in contact

---

[10] www.centerpointe.com

with our subconscious mind. The slower the brainwaves, the more time we have between our thoughts. This means that there will be more time to choose which thoughts are worth keeping, and what actions to take as well.

Meditation offers healing in the form of allowing. By simply accepting the now, and moving away from the mind, we are inviting the truth to enter our awareness.

There are five major brainwave categories. They are each corresponding to different types of activities. They are measured in cycles per second (Hz), and as you can see below, they each have a very specific place in our consciousness. The cycles mentioned below are the ranges most commonly used. The numbers may vary some, from teaching to teaching.

Gamma waves (above 40Hz):

This range is the fastest frequency. The waves have been associated with the highest form of processing information, and also our cognitive function. The Gamma waves are associated with bursts of insight and high-level information processing. These brainwaves are important for learning and processing new information.

Beta waves (14-40hz):

These brainwaves are what we use in our normal awakened state. We are alert and resonating. Beta waves are associated with critical thinking and mental activity. They are necessary at times, as we do the tasks that require quick and accurate thinking, but we operate from this state way too much. This leads to stress and anxiety, and should not be the constant frequency of your brain. You can think of the Beta wave as the very fast brainwaves that you exhibit throughout the day to address and complete our conscious tasks like writing, reading, studying, being analytical and social.

Alpha waves (8-14Hz):

These are the brainwaves that will let us slip into a deeper sense of relaxation. When we close our eyes, we automatically slow our frequency, and we go from Beta to Alpha. You will also visit these waves during a calming daydream or visualization. Any form of deep relaxation will slow down the cycles per second. This frequency also bridges the gap between the Beta and the Theta. Being in an Alpha state will also heighten our imagination and enhance our memory. The closer you get to the lower end of the Alpha scale, the more in-tune you will be with your intuition. We are moving away from the critical analytical mind.

Theta waves (4-8Hz):

During sleep and deep meditation, we are in the state of Theta. The REM dream state is experienced on this frequency. REM means Rapid Eye Movement, and is important because it is the restorative part of our sleep cycle. It is also the realm of your subconscious, and is only experienced at shorter intervals throughout the night. We drift off to sleep from Alpha and wake from deep sleep, the Delta wave. It is believed that a deeper sense of spiritual connection can be found through the Theta wave. It is believed to connect us to the Universe. Theta is connected to our deep and raw emotions, and our heightened state of creativity. At the border of Alpha and Theta, the creative power of our minds begin. We can visualize and create at a deeper level.

Delta waves (0.5-4hz):

This is the slowest of the frequencies, and we experience this state when we are in deep sleep, and in transcendental meditation. A very deep form of awareness. Delta is found most often in young children and infants. We tend to produce less of this healing deep sleep as we age. The more Delta waves we produce, the more rested and rejuvenated we will feel. Delta is also the realm of the subconscious mind, where information is available, and the universal mind can be accessed. This is the much sought after wave for healing and regeneration, and told to be what the most experienced meditators will experience.

By simply moving closer to nature, to the natural way of living, we are altering our conscious awareness. By detoxifying our physical and emotional bodies, we are lessening our mind's chattering and constant activity. From simply walking towards a healthy and joyful life, we are closing the gap between what we believed we were, to seeing what we really are. By going within, the process of letting go becomes effortless.[11]

---

[11] «Super Brain», Deepak Chopra & Rudolph E. Tanzi

PART THREE:
LIVING THROUGH
DETOXIFICATION

Chapter 20

The healing crisis

A healing crisis, also referred to as a healing event, is what we call the cycles of symptoms that arise from the cleansing, and therefore the healing and regeneration. The body will detoxify in cycles, like peeling an onion. So, when you are experiencing a typical reaction like a runny nose or a headache, it is a healing event or a healing crisis. You are experiencing the symptoms that the body makes to be able to clear out the toxins and the acids. Each so called cycle will last from 3-5 days in most cases, but sometimes longer. Very seldom will an event last for longer than 2 weeks. After an event, you will feel better than you did before, until the next crises or event arises. Your body decides when and how it will throw out the toxins. This can be discouraging, but now you know. You might experience feeling amazing for a week, and then BAM, you are feeling like crap. No, you are not getting worse, and no, you are not getting your old symptoms back.

The healing crises is showing you where your weaknesses are, and that is both important and interesting information. If your kidneys are not filtering, you will see some rashes, swelling and pain. Your skin will filter out what the kidneys cannot, and your body will produce edema to buffer the acids that are on the loose. Your lower back might hurt, and you might feel fearful. These are all signs of kidney weakness. If your liver is impaired, you will feel a different set of symptoms, like pressure and pain under your right rib cage. Your body will let you know you need to do a liver flush, or jump on some herbs or liver-healing foods. Your runny nose and mucus-discharging eyes will show you that your head is backed up, and that you are in need of some upper drainage. The fever will show you that your body is raising its temperature to kill off some bacteria and microbes. All for your benefit, always. I will share all my healing crises aids and soothing tricks in the next chapter.

The waves of healing and cleansing will change in length and strength. Anything goes. The symptoms can be completely new to you, they can resemble what it is that you want to heal from (the most discouraging ones), or they can be the same as what you have been experiencing previously. I have found that once you take the fear out of anything, the whole reality of the situation changes. The more we know our bodies, the more at ease we can be with symptoms of cleansing. Be brave, but also humble. Know when to fold them…

Retracing:

This is a term which is used about symptoms that are not of a cleansing nature, meaning they are not a direct symptom of the toxins that are leaving. It is used to describe the old hurts and traumas that are coming forth to heal. You might have had several urinary tract infections as a child, and now you are experiencing that same scenario. The fact is that you are only healing what was not healed the last time around, and any remaining bacteria that were suppressed by medications are now being released and healed. An old injury might also show itself. Maybe you broke your foot, and there is some more healing work that needs to be done. Now, after all this time you might experience some pain and discomfort for a few days, while this is being fully healed. Do not freak out, the body is on your side.

If you are walking through HELL, keep on walking, that is *not* where you want to stop!

What are the typical detoxification symptoms?

As we allow our bodies to start eliminating, the symptoms will be very individual. You now know how we are different only through our weaknesses, thus they are the ones that will determine the severity of your detoxification or cleansing symptoms. The symptoms are a reflection of the health and strength of these elimination organs, the glands, and the general energy level of the body. The strength, or the number of symptoms that you will experience, will also depend on the level of detoxification that you are aiming for. This will be reflected through your efforts and how deep you are digging. If you are making only smaller changes, your body will not be able to do that much cleansing. If you are making severe changes, your body will be able to do some heavier house-cleaning, and the symptoms will be much stronger. It also depends on the present state of your health and toxicity. It is a given that a very toxic, heavily constipated body is going to experience more and longer standing cleansing symptoms than someone who is less toxic.

When you are weak and sick, the symptoms of healing and elimination will also feel stronger than when you have more energy in your body. The symptoms often feel the strongest where you are the weakest. Another thing to take note of is that during the times when you are feeling better, and stronger than ever, is when another boost of cleansing will happen. The body will put that newly acquired energy to good use. This might feel frustrating at times, but know that it is as it should be. The body will make no mistake, and walk you through this in the best possible way. You are a team, and a very potent and highly skilled one.

Not all symptoms while cleansing, are detoxification symptoms. Some are what I would call more of a healing symptom. Any old wound will resurface to completely heal. Any old symptom, even an old infection will seem like it is coming back, but it is not. You have simply suppressed the symptom in the past, and now it is coming forth for true healing. This can be experienced as painful, and that can be scary. Stay faithful, and rest in the faith that you have in yourself and your journey.

When the body is given the chance to clean its house, it will do so, and once the cleaning is done, it will go on repairing and rebuilding. So we clean first, then we can repair and rebuild.

Mucus coming out everywhere: A typical symptom that the body is loosening up old mucus and transporting out old waste, is the release of mucus. It can be new mucus, made to carry out bacteria or toxins, or it can be older mucus, that the body has been holding on to for years. Any opening can and will be used for excreting toxins from the body. The nose, the throat, our colon, our ears, the kidneys, and the eyes, are all available for the body to use. Next time you need to blow your nose, celebrate! Your body is doing its job, expelling mucus!

Cold and flu like symptoms: You might feel like you have gotten what we call the flu. This calls for a celebration as it is a symptom of cleansing and elimination. Toxins are being stirred up in the body, and through the low grade fever, maybe some vomiting or coughing, the body is trying to eliminate waste. Watery, running and red itchy eyes, are all a part of that same process.

Fevers and chills: The body will raise the temperature to get rid of bacteria and microbes, so a low grade fever is a common detoxification symptom. Although the low grade fever is most common, a high grade fever can strike also. If it does, that is a sign of some deep cleansing, and some well-hidden bacteria coming to the surface.

Headaches and dizziness: These are very common cleansing symptoms. The head sits on top of the gastrointestinal (GI) tract, and will start to drain when you start to clean out your bowels. Ringing in the airs, the red eyes, a blurred vision even, are all symptoms of lymph moving in the head. Anything from hair die to cosmetics will also leave a lot of toxins in our head, and for those of us that are missing our tonsils, the draining job has been impaired.

Hair loss and loss of weak cells: Remember that every weak cell will have to go. Hair follicle cells are no different. Many experience to lose some hair, only to regrow new, beautiful, stronger hair.

Itching and rashes: This can be a tough one for many. The skin *is* the third kidney, and we know by now that most of us have some weaknesses in our kidneys. Once the cleansing starts, the skin will expel what the kidneys cannot. Rashes in all forms, from itchy, bumpy skin, to hives and boils. There might also be itching with no rash, as the acids are coming to the surface.

Gas and bloating: These are very typical symptoms with very obvious causes. First of all - parasites will excrete toxins when dying, known as *die–off symptoms*. This will create gas and bloating in itself. Fungus and mold are leaving the intestinal tract feeling like a warzone when leaving. On top of that we are pulling on the lymphatic system to release acids through the intestinal wall, and that will also feel like an acid bomb. Sulfur is released, and we know what that smells like.

Constipation and diarrhea: Constipation often fluctuates between complete stagnation, and what we call diarrhea. It is the same thing, it's just the body's attempt to get rid of what has been obstructing and intoxicating the system. When it detoxifies it is different. The constipation is a reaction to too many toxins building up, and too much waste trying to leave at once. We are impacted with mucus and old fecal matter, and we are allowing it to be released. It might not feel comfortable, but it is very necessary.

Swelling and inflammation: There might be swelling around old injuries or traumas, as well as edema and inflammation during this time. The body is holding on to water-weight to dilute the acids being released. Inflammation is also used as an aid in healing, together with edema. It will dilute harmful substances, and bring in large quantities of oxygen and nutrients.

General pain: Old injuries might show themselves to heal, and old hurts will re-surface. Acids are being released into the tissue, and might create a temporary stiffness and pain all over the body.

Fatigue and weakness: The body will use its energy where it is most needed. If you have a weak adrenal gland, you might also feel extra week in periods while it is rebalancing. Cleansing takes a lot of energy, and it is being used wisely.

Anxiety and depression: Cells hold memory, and once you release those old cells, the emotions that they hold will come forth. Expect to revisit some old hurts and emotional upsets. Know that it is all good. Also, as the endocrine glands are healing, so anxiety and depression-like symptoms might arise. The adrenals are the glands that mimic what we call anxious symptoms, and the thyroid is the seat of depression. None of this is the real you. Our organs represent different emotions. The kidneys are the seat of fear, and the liver is the seat of anger. Keep this in mind as you let the body work its way through healing and regeneration. For some, the emotional symptoms of cleansing are often the most challenging ones to live through. The more you know about what is happening in your body, the easier it will be. Fear is a great dominator, and will exacerbate any symptom.

Brain fog and lack of focus:

Anything from bacteria, viruses, heavy metals, old vaccine residue and more is being let go of. This means that the toxins that will be floating around can cause some temporary discomfort. As many of them are neurotoxins, your brain will be affected. Heavy metals from your mouth, and again, together with so many of us not having our tonsils, we are prone to experiencing some cleansing symptoms in form of being less than clear-minded.

The body will get to work on any weak or damaged part of the body. Even an old scar will fade over time. Only healthy cells will be left, and any weak cell will have to go. The whole point is to let the body get rid of everything that is weakened and damaged, and it will. It is so eager to do so, that it jumps to the task the minute it gets a chance.

There are as many detoxification symptoms as there are humans. This is a short list to give you a general idea, but it is by no means a complete one. By letting the body detoxify itself we are not *doing* anything to it, adding anything or forcing any action at all. On the contrary we are stepping back and letting it do exactly what it wants to do. The amazing thing is that every single body seems to want to do the exact same thing. It seems we are not that different at all. To me, that is what *truth* looks like.

A short recap of my own detoxification journey:

"My detoxification symptoms were many, ranging from mild to severe. For years and years, I have been having symptoms that my body is healing and cleansing. I am sure we will have periods of cleansing

symptoms on and off for the rest of our lives, as long as we eat clean and live free. The body will then obtain the ability to cleanse on an ongoing basis, like it is designed to.

I have experienced everything from rashes to blisters, hives and boils. There was so much mucus residing under my skin, I was ready to burst. My skin was always clear, so little did I know, that my skin was in trouble. As I started to detoxify my body, my skin would break out in terrible rashes. Full body itching from hell-rashes. I have had herpes breakouts, lumps on my tongue, and hives that came and went for years. For a whole year my face looked like I had the chicken pox. Pimples, dots, all over my face. Some days less, some days more. Red burning cheeks, that were even peeling. The acids were coming out, and it felt like burns.

I have had high fevers, and low grade fevers, whole body pains and general flue like symptoms. For years I felt like I had a hangover but missed the party. The nausea has been constant for long periods of times, and even my newborn perfect digestion has been set on hold at periods. When the stomach and intestines are releasing sulfur, mucus and acids from the walls, it will be felt. Gas, bloating, acid pain and diarrhea is the name of that game. I have lost nails, and most of my hair. The hair part is probably one of the scariest symptoms that I have experienced. My hair was long, thick and beautiful, and suddenly, it was falling out. Now, that was a freaky symptom! The weak cells had to be released, and my weaknesses were showing themselves. The weaknesses in the body will always come forth when the mask is taken off, so to speak. My head was detoxifying big time, and my eyes, my hair, the swollen lips and the bumpy tongue, all symptoms of toxic waste moving in the head, trying to get out.

I experienced rushes of anxiety and depression. My joints have been swelling and burning, making me wonder if I was healing- or hurting myself. I believe that the toughest symptoms we go through on a healing path are those that look like the symptoms we are looking to heal.

I have told you this before, I was one toxic puppy! I am amazed at what this body has been able to do. Even though it was beat down, poisoned and weak, it was able to get the job done. No matter how much I had tried to kill it, it was still able and willing to get back on its feet. I am in awe at what a body can achieve, once we get out of the way. Nature really is perfect." – "From HELL to Inspired"

A complete detoxification protocol will benefit greatly from including herbs, the botanicals. On my own journey, the day I discovered the herbs was the day I took a giant leap forward. They are tissue specific, and will be able to strengthen the organs and glands that are weak and tired. They are able to kill off any yeast and bacteria, and they strengthen and support the body at the same time. These God created herbs are our gift and medicine, and also our food. They have awareness, and our cells recognize them as healers. Together with the essential oils, they help raise our whole frequency, and they are all able to balance and restore. Tinctures and dried herbs have been used for centuries, and the herbal masters of our time, like Dr. John Christopher, Dr. Bernard Jensen and Dr. Morse, have made sure that the wisdom is passed on to the next generations. The connection with nature, and the genuine search for health and truth, will always connect man and nature. Through simplicity and the obvious remedy of the creation, we will heal and revitalize. Did you know that the body even has a way of showing us what it needs? That there is a perfect map of everything that is going on within?

A note on iridology:

The eyes have long been referred to as the "Windows of the Soul," and that is more true than you might think. By looking at the iris, the pigmented part of the eye, we are shown the entire composition of the body. It is a complete map of our inner organs and glands. Every single part of our physical being, right there in our very eyes.

This is such valuable information. The eye is not a messenger of symptoms, but rather of the weaknesses within. By looking at the eye we can see which organ is weak, congested by lymph, or even deteriorating. We can observe the progress, the changes that are going on within the body, because *yes*, the eyes will change color as you cleanse and restore. How cool is that? According to Dr. Robert Morse, there are only two true colors of an eye, blue and brown. Any other color is simply the mirror of congested lymph and sulfur. We will be able to see how the congested lymph is loosening and draining, and we can even see how our genetic weaknesses are strengthening.

Not only are we able to establish the current situation within the body, but we can also see our future potential. The eye never lies and will show a weakness long before any noticeable symptoms are present. Any accumulation of toxins, sulfur, even drug deposits are right there for us to see. Genetic weaknesses and the strength of our constitution. This is invaluable information for any practitioner, when understanding the whole health history of a client. Anything from malnutrition, cholesterol, an impacted colon, the level of acidosis to a weak knee, all readable in the eye.

There is much science behind the study of the iris, and it has been a diagnostic tool dated back to the 1600's, but modern iridology started in the late 1800's. We discovered yet another gift from nature, in form of a complete visible map and guiding system. Our complete state of health transmitted into our eyes, with perfection. We are able to study a live body, as it transforms from ill health to vitality. We are able to see the changes that are happening on the inside, not only by watching our symptoms disappear, but also by watching our eyes change. It is truly diagnostic.

The main reason why iridology has such an amazing place in real healing, is that it does not focus on symptoms, but on systems. It focuses on the whole person, on the cause of the problem, the underlying issues. The eye knows no symptoms, it knows only what it is told by the body, and that is the weaknesses and the state of the cells. There is no agenda and absolutely no interest to mask any symptoms.

The current state of health is observable by the beholder, but only the eyes can show the real cause that lies within.

All our inner systems are reflected in our eyes. The digestive, nervous, lymphatic, respiratory, skeletal, endocrine, and digestive system. All our organs and glands are represented, together with our level of stagnation and vitality. This is the tool of prevention, yet we usually wait until the symptoms are present before we improve our lifestyle. By using this blueprint and road map we can steer towards to better health. Through knowing how we are put together, we know what needs to be done. Cleansing and detoxification is always what needs to be done, but sometimes we also need some extra help to support our weak organs and glands. The underlying cause of a symptom will also be established, and we can work with the herbs and the essential oils to bring in more balance and healing.

This map will show where you came from, where you are at, and where you are headed. It will show you why you are feeling what you are feeling, and what your body has been accumulating. You might say it is the perfect preventive diagnostic tool, where one can work on the issues before they even manifest.

The eyes are an extension of the mind, the input for the brain, and yet the complete map of our inner world.

Chapter 21

Cleansing reactions and remedy

Sometimes, when we are experiencing a healing event, and we know that the body is doing what it needs to do, some relief is very welcome. Pain and itching can be overwhelming, and from having experienced a myriad of symptoms, I want to give you some great tips on how to calm a raging storm. We never want to stop the process, but to aid the body in the elimination process. Even a gentle relief can be of great help when moving forward might seem hard.

There is a great difference between pain and suffering. Pain is inevitable, suffering is a choice.

Epsom salt bath:

This is such a blessing, and can easily become your best friend when detoxing. The Epsom salt (magnesium sulfate), has its name from a bitter saline spring located at Epsom in Surrey, England. These minerals are very powerful, and can aid the body in cleansing and relaxation. Both magnesium and sulfate are both readily absorbed through the skin and into the body's blood stream. It is believed that by soaking in a powerful mineral base such as Epsom salts, it creates a process called reverse osmosis. This process will pull salt and harmful toxins out of the body, and at the same time allow the magnesium and sulfates to enter into the body. It will replenish the magnesium level in the body, and at the same time aid in building healthy joints, skin and nervous tissue.

When you are in pain, or feeling a toxic overload, an Epsom salt bath can do wonders. It will help with inflammation and pain, and relax the whole body while you are still detoxifying and healing. The bath will also stimulate the lymph, and the pancreas will make more enzymes needed for detoxification. I added some essential oils for further calming and healing benefits. Look in the essential oils chapter to learn how they can be of service.

The bath:

Fill the bathtub with warm water and add:
2 cups of Epsom salt
6 drops peppermint essential oil
6 drops lavender essential oil
Take a shower afterwards

Spend about 45 minutes in the bath, or until you feel you are done. Repeat as needed. This is a great evening practice, as it will relax you and get you ready for sleep.

Skin brushing:

An ancient practice for beautiful glowing skin is being revisited for many health benefits. It is just as simple as it sounds, but don't let

213

that fool you. Skin brushing is very powerful, both as a free standing health aid, and a detoxification helper. It is also called dry brushing, as the brush is dry, and so is the skin. This is a great part of any morning routine, and the 20 minutes will be well spent. Once you get the hang of it, no more than 5-10 minutes will be needed. It is also a go-to practice for an overloaded toxic system, to open the pores of the skin - letting more toxins find its way out.

The benefits are many:

- *Exfoliating the skin will allow the old dead skin to loosen and be removed. This is giving the new skin cells some fresh air and light. Your skin will feel amazing!*

- *Stimulating the lymphatic system is important for detoxification. By brushing the skin with a firm natural bristle, you will assist in improving vascular blood circulation and lymphatic drainage. The body will be encouraged to discharge of metabolic wastes, and deeply stored toxins.*

- *Because it increases circulation, it also increases energy. A side effect will be loss of cellulites.*

- *It will rejuvenate the nervous system by stimulating the nerve endings.*

- *It might even help with muscle tone, and your skin will look and feel firm and fresh.*

You need a soft or firm (see what you like the best) natural bristle brush with a long handle. This will allow you to be able to do your back as well. Some have removable handles with a strap, so that you can find the technique that fits you the best. This is best to do right before a shower or a bath, on perfectly dry skin. You can find bristle brushes in any health food store.

How to skin brush:

1. *Always start with your feet. Brush upwards towards your hips, and use gentle but firm strokes. Do one leg at the time, from under your feet, upwards towards the heart. The lymph is flowing upwards, so this is important. You can do each section about 10 times.*

2. *Do the arms in the same way as the legs. Brush towards the armpit, with firm strokes. Keep doing each section 10 times.*

3. *When brushing the torso, it is said to always brush towards the heart. I have found that brushing towards the kidneys makes more sense. The lymphatic waste is drained through the kidneys.*

4. *Brush the abdomen from the right side to the left. This is the natural directional flow of the intestines. Gently massage the colon.*

5. *Brush over the top of the chest, and make sure you work on the armpits. A large concentration of lymph nodes is found there.*

6. *Brush from the neck down to the lower back.*

7. *Finish around the neck. Avoid the face, as the skin is very sensitive. You can use a soft cloth to gently rub your face.*

The general rule is to brush from the extremities towards the core. Be gentle, and mind any sensitive areas. A very simple, yet great aid in detoxification and healing.

Sauna:

We are again being reminded that the skin is the largest eliminative organ, and how important it is for it to be in good shape. Acting like the third kidney, it will easily get over burdened during a cleansing period. Any type of sauna will do, as long as it is making you sweat. When we are pulling on the lymphatic system, releasing toxins and acids into our lymphatic system, we need some highly functioning kidneys to filter out that extra waste. When the kidneys are not up for the task, the waste will show up as rashes and boils. Through helping the elimination through the skin, we can relieve some of those symptoms.

Castor oil packs:

These are life-savers, I assure you. If this is new to you, you will love them, I promise. Castor oil comes from the castor seed, which is extremely high in ricinoleic acid. This is the active ingredient that holds the benefit of this amazing oil. The seed itself can be deadly, so I would not ingest this oil. The practice has been around for a long time, for thousands of years in India and China. A castor oil pack is simply a cloth soaked in the oil, and applied to a specific area. Most often heat is used to let the oil penetrate easily into the skin and tissue. It is most often used to improve circulation, reduce inflammation, pain relief, to stimulate hair growth and to stimulate lymph flow. The general improvement of assimilation, elimination and circulation.

One keeps the piece of cloth, containing the oil, on the skin for about one hour, and by bringing in the heat, the stimulation will also be enhanced. The stimulated liver and lymphatic function is brought on by the ability that this oil has to improve the circulation, and reduce inflammation. It also relaxes and calms the skin.

How to make a castor oil pack:

You will need a bottle of organic castor oil, some pieces of wool, flannel or unbleached cotton. The size depends on the area of the body that you will use it on. You will also need a hot water bottle, a large piece of plastic or simply some saran wrap. A glass jar with a lid, large enough to hold your cloths. Have a towel and a washcloth handy for after, and make sure that you have the time and space to lie down comfortably for about 1 hour.

- *Soak your cloth in castor oil, using your glass jar. You can let it sit overnight in the refrigerator, to make sure it is almost saturated.*

- *Put the soaked cloth in a pot, and warm it up on the stove. No microwave please. Add additional castor oil until you feel it is fully saturated. Make sure it is not too hot, only warm, as it will be going directly on your skin.*

- *Put a towel on the surface you will be lying on, to not make a mess.*

- *Fill your hot water bottle with hot water.*

Using the pack:

1. *Place your cloth on the desired body part. It can be over your kidneys to relieve pain, over your liver, or over an injury or inflamed area.*

2. *Cover the cloth with plastic. You want to make sure this wrapped tightly, to not make a mess.*

3. *Lie down and put the hot water bottle on top of the pack, to keep the oil warm. This will make the pack more effective.*

4. *Stay in this position for about an hour, with elevated feet if you can. Shorter sessions are also fine if that's more fitting.*

5. *Breathe and meditate, and see your body as healing and regenerating.*

6. *Remove the pack, and wash off the leftover oil on your skin.*

The pack can be placed back into the glass jar, with a lid, to be re-used several times. Store it in the refrigerator. I find it best to use the pack in the evening, so that I am able to rest afterwards. It is also great to put castor oil on your skin before going into the sauna.

Hot/cold therapy:

The alternating between hot and cold has amazing benefits for the body. Nothing new under the sun, as truth never is. It has been used for centuries to aid in detoxification, to increase circulation and to increase the energy flow of the body. Primal practices like ice-bathing and snow-bathing are getting an increase in popularity as healing exercises these days.

Several things happen when we subject the body to this alternating hot and cold therapy. When we subject the body to a very cold external temperature, it will direct its flow of circulation inwards, towards the vital organs. Once we change to hot, the flow of circulation turns outwards, towards the skin. This alternating inwards and outwards motion, will in turn release any blockage, and increase detoxification and movement of blood flow, and enhance the flow of nutrients and oxygen. This way healing is also enhanced. The hot and cold will also cause the muscles to expand and contract, squeezing more waste from the muscles themselves. It's a great way of moving acids.

How to do a hot and cold shower therapy:

- *Get in the shower and start with the temperature that is most comfortable for you.*

- *Very slowly, increase the temperature of the water. Let it get as hot as you can take. Make sure you invite your whole body to the party.*

- *Then, when you can't take any more heat, turn the water down to cold. Turn it as cold as you can tolerate. It can never get too cold. Again, your whole body has to go in.*

- *Turn the water hot again, and this time try to make it a little hotter than the last time. You should not be scalding yourself, but a good dose of hot water is very tolerable when you build up slowly.*

- *Go back to the cold again, even colder than last time, and repeat seven times. Alternate between the hottest you can do, and the coolest you can do.*

We know the cool water has an alkalizing effect on the body and holds more oxygen. Some say the cold water will clear negative energies from our bodies as well. This is such an easy practice with large benefits. Detoxification or not, this is a healthy circulation-booster of its own. It is a great way to start the day, and is often used in repair therapy.

The neti pot:

I am sure you remember this little thing from childhood. When we are cleansing our bodies, the head is often the place that can run into some stagnation and get in need of draining aid. The neti pot to the rescue. You will find it at any pharmacy at a very low cost. The term neti pot derives from an ancient yogic technique of sinus rinsing called Jala Neti. It seems the yogis were on to something, and it has become a much loved technique for clearing the nasal passages. It will do so much more though, as it will contribute to the drainage of toxins from the whole head.

You can flush your sinuses any time of the day, and many times each day also. It is great for relieving head pressure and any blockages in the nose or ear.

How to use your neti pot:

1. *Get your neti pot ready. I prefer a ceramic one over a plastic one.*

2. *You can use it anywhere, but over a sink is absolutely the best. You will have running water at hand, and as you will be spilling, you are all covered. You might also spill on your clothes, so make that a part of your first-time-plan.*

3. *Get your saline solution ready. I highly recommend using distilled water for this. We do not want little critters or pollutants up our noses, so if you can't get distilled, boil your water and cool it. Use room tempered or slightly warmer water. Mix about 1 teaspoon of salt, in 2 cups of water. Stir well, until the salt it dissolved. Use good quality sea salt, like Celtic.*

4. *Lean over the sink, and tilt your head to the side. Insert the tip of the neti pot into the upper nostril, and slowly poor the water into it. Breathe with an open mouth as the water slowly begins to poor out the lower nostril.*

5. *After using about half of the prepared water, stand up and blow your nose.*

6. *Repeat the same procedure using the other nostril.*

7. *Blow your nose again, and clean your neti pot. That is all there is to it!*

Deep breathing and rest:

This is a tool often forgotten when it comes to relieving some symptoms from a healing crisis. No matter the symptom, breathing deeply from the diaphragm will also be of great benefit. From opening blockages and obstructions in the energetic field, to bringing more oxygen to the tissue, it will soothe and relief. The stress that follows discomfort and fear, will also benefit from the breathing. As we center back to our breathing, we relax and restore. Your body will use all available energy to cleanse, so rest as much as you can.

Going to bed by 10pm will ensure the highest amount of quality sleep. During these hours the adrenals function best to recharge the body, and the gallbladder dumps bile at this time. The period between 10pm and 2am is said to be the optimal time to sleep. The period is believed to be when the body is detoxifying at its best, and also when it is regulating hormones and antioxidants. We know that many ancient cultures practice going to sleep between these hours. Try it and see how you feel.

Essential oils to the rescue:

Take a look at the chapter on the oils, to learn how these magical natural healers will benefit you on your journey. Always use a carrier oil with your essential oils. My favorite is fractionated coconut oil. Use therapeutic grade oils, this is very important. Here are some specific detoxification symptom helpers. Choose some of them, or many together:

- ***Aches and pains:*** *Try some marjoram, birch, peppermint, rosemary, lavender, Frankincense, juniper, sandalwood, wintergreen, and thyme on the affected area.*

- ***Anxiety:*** *Try a few drops of lavender and chamomile on your chest, and inhale. Using a diffuser is also wonderful.*

- ***Bloating:*** *Try rubbing some peppermint and fennel on your tummy. You can also put a few drops of peppermint in a glass of water and drink.*

- ***Caughing****: Try melaleuca and lemon.*

- **Depression:** *Try to inhale lavender, peppermint and wild orange.*

- **Dizziness:** *Try some peppermint, cypress and basil in the diffuser.*

- **Diarreha:** *Try using peppermint and ginger. You can put a few drops of each in a glass of water and drink.*

- **Hairloss:** *Try rosemary, thyme and lavender. Use a few drops in a carrier oil and massage into scalp.*

- **Insomnia:** *Try some chamomile and lavender in a hot bath. You can also inhale them, diffuse them and put them on your skin.*

- **Itching:** *Try putting a carrier oil with peppermint, lavender and oregano on the affected area.*

- **Leg cramps:** *Try clary sage, cypress and lavender. Massage the blend with carrier oil into the legs.*

- **Nausea:** *Try ginger. Apply topically behind the ears, and above the navel as needed. You can also diffuse them and put them under your tongue.*

- **Rashes:** *Try lavender, Roman chamomile and sandalwood Dilute with carrier oil and apply topically to affected area.*

- **Sinus congestion:** *Try melaleuca, rosemary and eucalyptus. Diffuse and inhale several times a day.*

- **Headache:** *Try peppermint, rosemary, eucalyptus and lavender. Dilute a few drops with a carrier oil and rub into chest, neck and forehead.*

Herbs:

The botanicals have a great place in the detoxification remedy tool-box. They are bearers of the healing energy of creation. Healing with medicinal plants might be as old as mankind itself. There are recordings of the use of herbal medicine over 5000years old, and in ancient times, herbalism was mixed with magic and superstition. Many traditionally used herbs have been put to scientific tests, and we see some proven to possess remarkable curative powers. This is one of the reasons that herbalism has a renewed interest amongst many. Nature at its best. We have always searched in nature for healing remedy and medicine. Until the resent decades that is, where the Western world has moved away from these ancient remedies.

I love the herbs, and they will be able to help strengthen any tissue or organ, and at the same time help move and eliminate. I love Dr. Morse`s blends from "Cellular Botanicals", and I use them with all of my clients. A specific personal protocol will be needed, but you can also educate yourself and play with the herbs on your own. The chapter on wild food and medicine gave you some general information about the wild herbs and their powers. During a healing crises, I would slow down on any herbs that are very astringent and pulling on the lymphatic system. This is a generalization, because when working with a practitioner you might find that for your particular situation, moving fast forward is the best thing to do.

Some simple tips on how to remedy the symptoms of the healing crisis:

- **Expelling mucus:** This calls for a celebration! Try the neti pot, and the essential oils to clean the sinuses. We do not want to suppress anything, but let it all come out. You can also try ear candling for your ears, it really helps with any head congestion. Practice some deep breathing to loosen anything that is wanting to come out from the lungs. If you have mucus coming out of your eyes, try an eye cap with some eye-specific herbs. Hot and cold shower therapy will also help to break things loose.

- **Cold and flu like symptoms:** Your whole system is releasing toxins, so make sure you rest as much as you can. Drink some ginger and lemon for the nausea, and stay cool if you have a fever. If not, get into an Epsom salt bath and a sauna to release some of those toxins. Deep breathing is great, and some gentle stretching to open all the lymphatic pathways. Do some skin brushing to open up your lymphatic drainage-paths.

- **Fevers and chills:** If the fever is on the higher side, use a cold cloth on your forehead and neck. Always keep your head/neck cool. If your fever is a low grade one, drink lots of fresh juices, and sleep and rest when you can. If you are getting chills, cover up and stay warm. Drink a cup of warm chamomile tea with some lemon. Chill out.

- **Headaches and dizziness:** The essential oils are great for headaches. Rest and deep breathing, together with a cold cloth and meditation does wonders. If the headache is of a muscular origin, a trip in the sauna or an Epsom salt bath might help bring down the tension. Use the oils above for the dizziness, and lay low. When you are feeling up for it, do some hot and cold shower therapy.

- **Hair loss and loss of weak cells:** This is most often a scary symptom. Remember, it will grow back, better than before. Try using hot and cold therapy to stimulate the blood flow to the head area. There are specific herbs to take for brain circulation also. "Cellular Botanicals" has some amazing ones. Kelp will stimulate the thyroid and also help with regrowth of hair, so you could add the kelp at this time. The castor oil will also stimulate the circulation and promote hair growth, so well worth a try.

- **Itching and rashes:** Use the essential oils described above topically. Focus on your kidneys at this point, and check of they are filtering. Baking soda and water might help the itchy skin, and make sure that it is not dry. Use coconut oil on your whole body, to keep the skin moist. Even though hydration is an inside job, we need to help ourselves along the way. For breakouts of the skin use the melaleuca essential oil.

- **Gas and bloating**: Make sure that you are combining your foods in the best manner. Do not blend any form of fats in with your fruits. You can try to eat more mono meals, meaning only one fruit for each meal. Bananas are very soothing on digestion, so a few days on bananas could do the trick. When in parasite die-off-mode, we have to ride it out, using peppermint and fennel oil on the stomach, eating very simple, and juicing more than eating.

- **Constipation:** Deep breathing will do a lot for constipation. Lie on your back and breathe all the way down to your abdomen. There are specific herbal blends that will help, and also we have the enema bag. Try putting a castor oil pack on your abdomen, as it will bring circulation and soothe. Drink some hot tea with fennel and ginger essential oils. Make sure your bowels are moving every single day, at least once. Make sure you are eating only high water fruits. You can try putting some aloe vera in your morning drink, and try some baking soda in hot water. Make sure you are moving your body, doing rebounding, yoga, walking or running. Skin brushing is beneficial for all obstructions, so give it a go!

- **Diarrhea:** The release of acids and old matter form the intestine, is not your typical diarrhea. This is a deep cleansing, and the body is making sure it is expelled. It should only last for a few days, and the best thing really is for it to run its course. If that is too much, or it gets persistent, here are a few tips to try: The banana has some great binding effects, but make sure that it is ripe. A ripe banana has brown spots on it. Eat an apple, that might also help.

- **Swelling and inflammation:** The castor oil pack is great for any inflammation that might arise. Swelling as in edema might find relief from a sauna session. Both will definitely like a hot and cold shower. Look towards the kidneys, as the indication is they are not filtering. For edema, keep your feet elevated when you can, and get a gentle massage. The essential oils for inflammation will also be soothing. This is all acidosis, and the release of acids into your system.

- **General pain:** For the all-over body pain, I always love the Epsom salt baths. Indulge with essential oils on top, and relax as it does its magic. A sauna session is great also, but keep them apart. Both at the same time can be overwhelming to the body. I would also add the hot and cold showers, to make sure that everything is moving. Pain=acids, pure and simple, so use the essential oils, breathe, and know that this too shall pass.

- **Fatigue and weakness:** The body is saying rest, so rest. There is no way around it. Keep on going on your detoxification journey, and your strength will return. Pay extra attention to your adrenals, as they are the ones firing up the energy. Your nervous system, glands, is showing you that there is much to be done. On top of this, the body is using its energy elsewhere, so do not try to push it. Stay on point, and nurture the adrenals and glands. Try the hot and cold shower, but again, do not push yourself.

- **Anxiety and depression:** The emotional roller coaster ride can be scary. Try the essential oils to balance the experience. Get on the kelp for the depressed feeling, and stay off anything that might stimulate the glands, like salt and coffee. The Epsom salt bath is great as a calming aid, and the hot and cold showers will help energize the glands.

- **Brain fog and lack of focus:** Help the head drainage by using the neti pot. Get some ear candles, and do three on each ear. Use the hot and cold shower, and sit in the sauna. You are looking for anything that will help drain the top floor. It is sitting on top of your GI track, so make sure your bowels are moving. This is very important.

Detoxification is a journey, a period of healing and rejuvenation. It might not always feel and look like it, but it is. Use this time to love yourself even more, and to pamper yourself in the process. Be kind to yourself, and make time for you! This is the perfect time for some deep soul searching. Through patience and the allowing of time to pass, I am sure that you will find every art of this process valuable and interesting. Make this about you, as it is.

Chapter 22

Simple cleansing recipes

Along my own journey, I have noted some helpful tips and recipes. I went through a forest of information, and through trial and error, I have found what has been valuable for me. I do not share anything that I have not tried myself, and that has not been of value to me. Everything that I share, I have felt on my own body. I love experimenting, but I know that if I had known back then what I know now, my journey would have been less painful, and shorter in timeframe. Truth is truth, and it never goes out of style, even though it can be hard to spot when the information is all over the place.

Make sure that your focus is on the healing, and that the search for health is that of enthusiasm and eagerness. Health does not come from the fear of illness. Nothing good ever comes from fear. Focusing on the symptom, on how one is feeling, is not going to shift your perception and signaling to your cells. True healing lies in the connection to health, and the dis-connection from anything not thereof.

"The path of a warrior is that of faith and trust. The power that comes from knowing who you are, is greater than any weapon or shield." - Hilde

When you are experiencing a healing crises, you will want to do one of two things. Slow down or keep going. To slow down means to back off for a bit, until your body can recap and balance. If you are on a juice fast, it will mean to eat some fruits instead. If you are eating all fruits, it means to back off and include some vegetables. Sometimes if the symptoms are too much to handle, this is what we need to do. Also, work with someone who is experienced if you are unsure or uneasy, always. At other times you might choose to keep going, and to use some of the tips below to ease the symptoms of the cleansing that your body is doing. In any case, always stay safe and supported. Know when to hold them, and know when to fold them. Take responsibility for your journey and get support when needed. Doing too much too fast, or trying to be brave and hurting yourself in the process is never the way to health.

Kidney filtering tips:

Let us start with the most important tip first. If you are eating a high fruit diet, 100%, and have added kidney herbs to your regimen, and are *still* not filtering, you might want to try one of these following suggestions. Be patient as your kidneys are awakening, it can take some time to get them going. It took me close to 3 years to get them to where they want to be.

- **Castor oil pack with cayenne pepper:** Make a castor oil pack to put over your kidneys. Before you put the pack on your skin, rub the skin with cayenne pepper. The cayenne is anti-inflammatory and promotes heavy circulation. Put the pack on, with a hot water bottle, and leave it for a few hours. Do this once a day for a week. It might be just what you needed, to see some sediments in your urine.

- **Grapes and lemons:** I found that my kidneys would filter massively after a few days on grapes and lemons only. They are both very astringent, the lemons more than the grapes, but together they worked magic. Eat the grapes, and juice the lemons. For those of you that want to kick it up a notch, a lemon fast or a grape fast is also a great way to help the kidneys to start filtering. I did a 62day grape fast, and it sent me on the deepest healing experience so far. If you can tolerate the lemons, go for it.

- **Essential oils:** Try rubbing some Juniper essential oil over your kidneys, on your lower back. Do this 3 times a day.

- **Parsley love:** The kidneys love parsley. It is cleansing and diuretic, and can be used in many ways. On top of using fresh parsley in your smoothie, try to make some parsley water. Boil 2 cups of water, and set it aside with a small handful of fresh parsley. Let it sit and soak, without simmering. After 10 minutes, strain and cool. Drink 2 cups a day.

Colon cleansing:

If you are raised on a typical Western diet like me, I know how impacted you might be in your entire intestinal tract. Some extra measures might have to be taken, to make sure that you are releasing what is not needed and is in fact hurting you. If you grew up on dairy, you have some serious colon cleansing to do.

- **Juicing:** Nothing is like moving out of the way when it comes to cleansing the GI tract and colon. Ingest nothing but fresh juices for 21 days, to release some old mucus and toxins from your system.

- **Phsyllium husk:** The phsyllium is unique as it will swell up when mixed with water. This gelatin-like substance acts like a lubricant for easier elimination of the bowels. It will also help soften the feces and stimulate better peristalsis. It is the outer hull of the Plantago seed, and has been used for hundreds of years to treat many types of bowel imbalances. Go for the organic phsyllium, and make sure you are drinking a lot of liquids at the same time, or it could leave you dehydrated.

- **Bentonite clay:** This natural clay is very absorbent, hence it's wide use in colon cleansing recipes. It absorbs and binds to toxins in the GI tract, without being assimilated by the body. Any health food store will have this powder.

Colon cleansing recipe:

1. *1 teaspoon of phsyllium husk.*
2. *1 teaspoon of bentonite clay.*
3. *8oz glass of fresh juice or clean water.*
4. *Drink morning and night on an empty stomach, adding another 8oz glass of juice or water to chase it down.*

Herbs:

"Cellular botanicals" has a great blend called the GI Broom. You can find it online, Herbs that are especially good for cleaning the GI tract are Buckthorn bark, ginger root, cascara sagrada, chickweed, slippery elm and senna. There are many more. There are some good ready-made formulas out there also. Herbs are very powerful, and more is not always better. Talk to someone that has experience and knowledge about herbs, before you start any herbal protocol.

Enema:

To own an enema bag while detoxifying is a must. So if you do not yet have one, go get one. You will find one online or in any drug store or pharmacy. Especially when doing a parasite cleanse, you want to make sure that you use an enema bag to clean out the dead parasites. This is simple to use, and I recommend using warm water only. The longer you can hold the water in, the better, so aim for 10-15 minutes.

Colon hydrotherapy:

This is often called colonics, and is a procedure done with a professional therapist, most often a nurse. Although, I am all for doing things the natural way, sometimes we need to bring out the big guns. This is a big gun! It is a gentle rinsing of the colon with warm water. The water is infused via the rectum, while you lie comfortably on a table. There is no pain involved in this procedure, although the loosening of old matter might lead to some cramping, and that will feel uncomfortable. The colonics involves the gentle inflow and outflow or warm water, and will reach much deeper than any enema.

Reflexology:

This practice has been a life saver for me. Reflexology is based on the principle that the anatomy of the body is reflected on our hands, ears, feet, but also on other parts of our body. It is believed that there are nerve endings although our outer body, that collaborate with the energy of our inner organs and glands. That every process within, is reflected to the outside, for us to be able to stimulate and trigger balance and self-healing. You can find charts that tell you where the different reflex points are, and stimulate them gently. Reflexology can help you get some relief from any healing crisis, through stimulating the eliminative organs. Also, it can help strengthen the glands and organs through promoting better flow of energy within them. Find a therapist, read up, buy a book, and see what it can do for you. There are many good charts out there, and the practice is easy to self-administer.

Massages:

It is always a good time for a massage, almost. When the kidneys are not filtering, and we have a lot of acids moving around, a massage can be too much for the system to handle. In most cases, a gentle massage will be of great benefit though. Make sure it is gentle, as during a detoxification period, we do not want to stress the body too much. Aromatherapy is amazing, where you will benefit from the oils also. I always make my own oil to bring. That way I know I am getting what I need, and I am leaving out everything else. So, if you are achy and stiff, try a gentle massage, nothing too deep or vigorous.

Massage oil recipe:

250ml/8.5oz organic jojoba oil
10 drops peppermint essential oil
10 drops Frankincense essential oil
5 drops geranium essential oil
10 drops lemon essential oil
3 drops Melaleuca/Tee tree essential oil
5 drops rosemary essential oil

Cleansing juices:

When you are experiencing a healing crises, nothing is like a fresh cleansing juice. Every fruit and vegetable has its own composition of energy and nutrients. Like the herbs, some are more astringent, and some are more soothing and hydrating. These are some great cleansing juice recipes, to add to your daily diet. Always eat organic when you can, and when not - make sure you peel and wash everything well. A great recipe for washing is lemon, baking soda and apple cider vinegar. Put a tablespoon of each in a bowl of water, and let the fruits and vegetables soak for a few hours. Rinse and peel.

Power up morning juice:

1 cucumber
3 lemons
2inch gingerroot
½ fennel bulb
5 stalks of celery
1tbs aloe vera gel

A juice high in minerals and astringent properties. Hydrating, anti-inflammatory and refreshing. A general detoxifying juice.

Power up the liver juice:

1 beet
1 cucumber
1 hand full dandelion
1 lemon
2 green apples

A great tonic for the liver, blood oxygenator and detoxifier. Beets and dandelions are well known liver-lovers.

Power up kidney love:

1 cucumber
1 green apple
2 lemons
1 handful parsley
2inch turmeric root
2 stalks asparagus

The parsley, lemon and apple combination is a great way to treat the kidneys. The turmeric is highly anti-inflammatory, and the asparagus is slightly diuretic.

Power up lymph buster:

400g/14oz of dark seeded organic grapes
3 lemons

A highly astringent juice, that will pull on your lymph system. Get ready to do some deep cleansing with this one.

Rule number one when detoxifying is always to be kind to yourself. Be gentle and be loving. Honor your body, it is your temple, and it is doing its very best at all times. Try to find peace in your heart and love for the journey. Welcome every reaction and symptom as what it is. A sign that your body is throwing out the garbage. Find community and a helping hand. Never be afraid to ask when you are uncertain about anything. You are never alone. I am walking beside you, and you can always reach me though my website.

Chapter 23

Essential oils

We are all naturally drawn to that which smells good to us. I know you have a favorite smell, or a favorite flower. The sense of smell is one of our highly evolved senses, and if you smell it, you eat it. It is believed that Cleopatra owned the first spa, near the Dead sea, and that she used the essential oils in her personal beauty treatment. The oils are referenced in the Bible, and have since ancient times been used for beauty, pleasure and medicine. We are simply invited to walk in the footsteps of our forefathers, who were closer connected to nature than we are today.

Hippocrates used the aromatic oils, and they have been well embraced in the Ayurvedic medicine. The Egyptians and also the Greeks used essential oils in their practices of therapeutic massage and aromatherapy. The Romans used the aromatic oils to enhance personal hygiene and health. The Persians began to refine distillation methods for extracting essential oils from aromatic plants. We find that the essential oils were even used throughout the dark ages for their anti-bacterial and fragrant properties. Now, in modern time, we are embracing these healing gifts of nature, and learning more about how to use them in our everyday life. The therapeutic grade oils can be incorporated into any healing protocol, and has a place in any home-healing-tool-box.

What are essential oils?

The essential oils are different than fatty oils like the oils that come from nuts and seeds. These are not oils like coconut oil, walnut oil or olive oil. Those have larger molecules, and cannot penetrate the cells in the same manner as these essential oils can. Carefully distilled from organic plant material, these are 100% natural substances. We call them essences, because they represent the essence of the plant. Essential oils are highly vibrational aromatic liquids distilled from flowers, roots, herbs, trees, seeds, scrubs and bushes. They're what give herbs and spices their flavor and aroma, and flowers their scent.

When life gives you the option to choose natures wonders, always do. By allowing the energy of pure essence, we are allowing the cells to bathe in the light.

Being aromatic, the oils contain oxygenating molecules. These molecules act as catalysts, transporting oxygen and nutrients to our cells. Well, they do more than just transport the nutrients *to* the cell, the oxygen is needed for the nutrients to penetrate the cell membrane, to then be assimilated. So, we can say that the oxygenating molecules in the oils actually increase the delivery of nutrients into the cell. The receiving and assimilation of nutrients plays an important role in health and vitality. The essential oils are far from simple substances, as an oil is found to contain up to several thousand chemical constituents. Each of them acting perfectly and harmoniously together, to form the therapeutic property of the specific oil.

Essential oils are gentle yet powerful, and have been used for a very wide range of emotional and physical health and healing applications. They are used on infants and animals. As a single oil or as a more complex blend, the oils can be used in many different ways. The most common usage for health purposes are diffusing/ aromatic, ingesting them orally, or using them topically on the skin.

Take the rind of an orange, and squeeze it. The fine mist that you see and smell, that is the essential oil of an orange. On top of penetrating the cell membrane they also travel trans- cellularly. That means that their unique lipid-soluble structure is so close to the makeup of our cell membranes, that they will travel directly through the cells. This is quite amazing!

Use the oils aromatically:

You might have heard about aromatherapy, which is founded on the body's predictable response to specific stimuli. Aroma -meaning smell, tells us the essential oils are a central part of that therapy. We know that our sense of smell influences many physiological pathways including the stimulation of hormones and other metabolic processes. Diffusers simply disperse essential oils as a fine vapor throughout the air so they can be absorbed into the body through the respiratory system. The aroma will trigger the nervous system to transmit signals to the limbic system in the brain. This is the part of the brain that houses and stores memory and emotions. The brain then responds by initiating these various physiological functions, and we will feel the effect as pain relief, a better mood, or the feeling of calmness.

The oils all have different properties, so when diffused in the air, some can be very stimulating while others will be soothing and calming. Low-heat or no-heat essential oil diffusers are recommended as they do not change the chemical structure of the oil being diffused. This is very important. Make sure that when diffusing the essential oils, you have a good diffuser. Not only will your home smell amazing, you and your whole family will ripe the healthy benefits of the oils.

You can choose to diffuse one single oil, or make a blend to fit your needs and desires. I have a few favorite blends that I use in my diffuser:

The work-time-alert blend 1:
3 drops rosemary essential oil
3 drops juniper essential oil
3 drops peppermint essential oil

The work-time-alert blend 2:
3 drops grapefruit essential oil
3 drops peppermint essential oil
3 drops lemon essential oil

The stress-less soothing blend:
2 drops yang-ylang essential oil
2 drops bergamot essential oil
2 drops lavender essential oil
2 drops vetiver essential oil

The relaxing-nighttime blend:
3 drops lavender essential oil
3 drops chamomile essential oil
3 drops patchouli essential oil

The cold & flu blend:
3 drops melaleuca essential oil
3 drops peppermint essential oil
3 drops lemon essential oil

The optimal healing blend:
2 drops Frankincense essential oil
2 drops myrrh essential oil
2 drops rosemary essential oil
2 drops cedarwood essential oil

Beyond emotional benefits, diffusing essential oils can purify air of unwanted odors and some airborne pathogens.

Use them topically:

This is a very safe and easy way to use the essential oils. Still it is advised to use a carrier oil, such as fractionated coconut oil before applying them to your skin. That being said, many of the oils are perfectly safe to use directly on your skin, and I do this all the time. The application of essential oils can have immediate, localized benefit to the target area. Their restorative and calming properties and can also be used effectively with massage and beauty therapy. I use them in my daily skin regimen, and in baths and oil pulling.

You can put a few drops of any oil in your palm, gently rub your palms together, and breathe in the aroma. The underside of the feet is a very popular application spot. Targeting the reflex point, creates additional healing benefits. Here are a few tips on how to use them topically:

Nighttime sole of the foot blend:
Mix with 15 drops of carrier oil if you prefer.
2 drops lavender essential oil
2 drops chamomile essential oil
2 drops sandalwood essential oil

Morning ready-to-go blend:
Mix with 15 drops of carrier oil if you prefer.
Rub this on your chest and neck.

3 drops wild orange essential oil
3 drops peppermint essential oil
3 drops rosemary essential oil

Flue-be-gone blend:

Mix with 15 drops of carrier oil if you prefer.
Rub this on your chest and neck.
1 drop melaleuca essential oil
2 drops clove essential oil
2 drops eucalyptus essential oil
2 drops lemon essential oil

The uplifted-mood blend:

Mix with 15 drops of carrier oil if you prefer.
Rub this on your chest and neck.
2 drops wild orange essential oil
2 drops peppermint essential oil
2 drops lemon essential oil
2 drops lavender essential oil

Energizing blend:

Put these oils right into the palm of your hand. Rub and sniff.
2 drops peppermint essential oil
2 drops lemon essential oil
2 drops rosemary essential oil

Boost-the-memory blend:

Put these oils right into the palm of your hand. Rub and sniff.
2 drops cypress essential oil
2 drops lemon essential oil
2 drops peppermint essential oil

Calming anxiety-free blend:

Mix with 15 drops of carrier oil if you prefer.
Rub this on your chest and neck.

2 drops cedarwood essential oil
2 drops lavender essential oil
2 drops patchouli essential oil
2 drops chamomile essential oil

Internal Uses:

Essential oils can also be used as dietary supplements supporting healing, detoxification and regeneration. Some of the oils have powerful antioxidant properties while others help support healthy inflammatory response in cells. Many of the oils like lemon, basil, Frankincense and peppermint, are safe to use internally. A few should not be taken internally, so be cautious.

NOTE: Do not use any essential oil product internally that does not have the appropriate dietary supplement facts on its label.

Working with the oils can be very simple and bring a lot of joy. When you first start out, connect with someone who is experienced, and use the therapeutic grade oils only.

You can easily add the oils to your drinks:

Juices: You can add a drop of lemon, lime, grapefruit or cilantro to your green juice. All the citruses are great to use in a juice.

Smoothies: You might add some peppermint, lemon, lime, basil, wild orange or cilantro to your favorite smoothie.

Infused waters: When you infuse water, you add slices of fruits or vegetables to the water, that will give the water some added benefit. The oils are a great addition. Together with some slices of cucumber, a few drops of lemon is great. Apple slices or cucumber and a drop of lime is a good choice also. Add a drop of cinnamon with apple slices, or a drop of peppermint with fresh berries.

Essential oils for chakra balancing:

Essential oils are beautiful for chakra balancing because they can support you on a cellular and emotional level. A little goes a long way. Apply two drops of each oil to the chakra and set the intention for release. Close your eyes and see the shift with an open heart. Set an intent for your balancing. Focus on that intent. Allow any feelings to come up, and release them. Use the oils that speak to you the most for each chakra. You do not have to use them all. Meditate with deep breathing as you express release. Always allow some loving new intent to come in where release has taken place.

Root chakra: patchouli, vetiver and myrrh for balance ad grounding.
Sacral: wild orange, ylang-ylang, sandalwood for creativity and sexuality.
Solar plexus: lime, peppermint, rosemary, black pepper and ginger for confidence and clearance.
Heart: lemon, bergamot, geranium, rose and sandalwood. Give and receive from love.
Throat: bergamot, cypress, peppermint, basil, for communication and patience.
Third eye: chamomile, Helichrysum, lavender, cypress and clary sage for calming purification.
Crown: Frankincense, Helichrysum, rose, cedarwood and lavender for healing, purpose and connection.

Some of the amazing essential oils that are available to us:

Basil essential oil: A great calming oil, also known for its restorative properties. It is commonly used for soothing sore muscles and joints, as a cooling agent for the skin, and to ease breathing. Basil has been used as a natural anti-inflammatory, antibiotic, antiviral and diuretic in traditional Asian Indian medicine practices for a very long time. The leaves were used to treat migraines and chest infections. It was also said to attract possible suitors, amongst women.

Bergamot essential oil: This oil is commonly used in massage therapy and diffused for a sense of self-confidence. It has a lovely fragrance and is unique among citrus oils for its calming properties. Bergamot oil is anti-infectious, antibacterial, anti-inflammatory and antispasmodic. It's said to be uplifting, it improves the digestion and keeps the system working properly.

Black pepper essential oil: A stimulating and highly antioxidant essential oil. Often used to improve circulation, aid digestive system, as well as help curb urges for cigarettes. A little goes a long way, so use it sparingly.

Cassia essential oil: Cassia is a very close relative of cinnamon. You will know it by its amazing smell and aroma. Cassia has also been used for thousands of years for its calming properties, as well as for its effect on the digestion. Cassia oil can be used for cleaning and cooking. It is known to boost the immune system — helping the entire body run properly. Cassia oil improves blood circulation and is used as an antidepressant. It is said to build courage and a sense of self-worth, as well as keeping the mind at ease.

Chamomile essential oil: Most of us know this little white flower, and might know the chamomile from its use as a tea. The essential oil is used widely for its calming properties, to support a healthy inflammatory response, and to relax the nervous system.

Cilantro essential oil: Cilantro comes from the leaves of the coriander plant and is a fresh and tasty flavor enhancer. Therapeutic benefits that may be enjoyed, include digestive, antioxidant, and stimulating effects. It is also used as a heavy metal detoxifier. Coriander has been used for thousands of years to prevent food poisoning and to prevent digestive upset, gas, fungal and bacterial infections. This amazing oil has a very high nutritional value as well.

Cinnamon essential oil: This is a strong one, so use sparingly. Also, never use without a carrier oil. Cinnamon is well known as a spice in flavoring food. The therapeutic uses are also popular, like its cleansing properties and its usefulness with aches and pains. Cinnamon essential oil is often used to balance blood sugar, killing candida, improving skin health and supporting weight loss.

Clary sage essential oil: Known for its uplifting and mood-lightening attributes, and also widely used by women to soothe monthly discomfort associated with their menstrual cycles. It is also a sedative with its soothing and warming components. Known for its antifungal, antispasmodic, antidepressant, antiseptic properties, and many more.

Clove bud essential oil: You most likely know this one from the kitchen. Clove is much more than a popular cooking spice though, and it has been used for its properties as being antiseptic and parasite cleansing. It is also a powerful antioxidant. It has very strong anti-inflammatory properties.

Cypress essential oil: The cypress essential oil is commonly used to clear breathing and as a throat gargle. It is great for easing sore and tight muscles, as well as supporting blood and lymph flow. A blend of cypress and grapefruit is used in spa therapies for getting rid of cellulite. It has a clean and energizing aroma, and is known for its antiseptic, antibacterial, antispasmodic, stimulating and anti-rheumatic properties. A great oil for detoxification.

Eucalyptus essential oil: Because of the many influential compounds found in eucalyptus, it is a well-known ingredient in many cough and throat medicines and chest ointments, this is because it has very calming and clearing properties. This oils benefits are due to its antioxidant protection and the ability to improve respiratory circulation.

Fennel essential oil: The fennel essential oil has pronounced antioxidant properties and is considered a tonic. A great aid for any indigestion, and supports the lymphatic system. Fennel's sweet yet spicy aroma is very balancing and reminds us of licorice.

Frankincense essential oil: This is probably the most precious of the ancient oils. Frankincense is highly sought after by modern consumers for its many uses. It is the essential oil that has gotten the most attention form the medical world. It has great benefits — including relaxation, mood enhancement and immune support. It helps relieve chronic stress and anxiety, it will boost your immunity and reduce pain and inflammation.

Geranium essential oil: Geranium is known for its outstanding benefits in soothing skin, and is therefore a common ingredient in many of our skin care products. Great for any skin issue. Add this one to your shampoo for a glowing vibrant hair. It is also a natural insect repellant. Geranium oil is nonirritant and nontoxic – with therapeutic properties of being antiseptic, wound healing and an antidepressant.

Ginger essential oil: The well know Indian spice, such a valuable component of many dishes, is also a great healer. It is mostly known for its ability to ease indigestion, and also for its anti-inflammatory effects. Ginger's sweet, citrusy fragrance accompanies a multitude of other therapeutic benefits.

Grapefruit essential oil: Grapefruit has a fresh invigorating aroma, which has a very uplifting effect on our mood. It is such a bitter liver-pleaser, and has amazing cleansing benefits. Grapefruit oil benefits weight-loss, and it helps beat inflammation, sugar cravings and is considered a natural stress-fighter.

Helichrysum essential oil: This is by far one of the most precious and sought-after essential oil out there. Helichrysum has traditionally been used for promoting a glowing, youthful complexion. It is also said to be a rare all-round healer. It is distilled from the flower-cluster of an evergreen herb. Another natural anti-inflammatory and antimicrobial. It is a great antioxidant and an antifungal as well. Great for fighting infection, heart problems, digestive issues, supporting the nervous system and healing respiratory problems

Juniper essential oil: This oil has a long history of fighting illness. It is great for the kidneys, and a great protector of overall health, both physical and mental/emotional. It was believed to protect you from witches, and has long been used to fight any bacterial infection. A great remedy for inflammation, infections and arthritis, insomnia and fatigue.

Lavender essential oil: Most likely the most popular oil out there. It has been cherished and loved for its well know aroma and therapeutic properties for thousands of years. It is mostly used for its calming ad relaxing qualities, as well as it`s all-round healing energy. You will find it is widely used in soaps and shampoos. The Egyptians used it for mummification and as a perfume. The Romans used it for bathing, cooking and for scenting the air.

Lemon essential oil: Another favorite that has many uses, and many benefits. It is cold pressed from lemon rinds, to preserve its delicate properties. Lemon is known as a powerful aromatic, and can be used to compliment many other oils. It has magical antiseptic properties and is often used as a cleaning agent around the house. The alkalizing effect of lemon makes it a great detoxification tool. Diffusing lemon in a room can cleanse the air and uplift the mood. The lemon oil is great for any indigestion, as its structure is similar to the juices found in our stomach.

Lemongrass essential oil: Lemongrass has long been used to aid in a healthy digestion and for soothing aching muscles. In cooking it is popular for its lemony flavor and aroma. This oil is known to have insecticidal, anti-fungal, antiseptic and anti-inflammatory properties. It is also used to help regulate menstrual flow, alleviate muscle pain and reduce fever.

Lime essential oil: This oil has a sharp, citrusy smell, and easily becomes another favorite. Lime's stimulating and refreshing properties can affect mood, as well as being a powerful topical and internal cleanser. The aroma is strong and fresh, and it is popular to use on the seasonal bugs. Lime is also, like several of the other citruses, a great joint friend.

Marjoram essential oil: This is one of the most common oils found in kitchens around the world. It has some great calming properties, and can be applied topically to soothe tired muscles. It also has a calming, positive effect on the nervous system. Marjoram is also referred to as "joy of the mountains."

Melaleuca essential oil: More commonly known as "tea tree", melaleuca has been revered for its cleansing and regenerative properties. It is often used to cleanse impurities of the skin, and can be used for anything that needs its strong therapeutic properties. This oil is used to kill mold when diffusing it, and to treat infections when taken internally.

Melissa essential oil: This is a rare and costly oil that has a sweet, fresh and citrus-like fragrance. It is steam distilled from the fresh flowering tops of this plant. Melissa can be used for calming the nerves and addressing stomach discomfort, as some of its wide range of therapeutic properties. It is also used for mood support and seasonal bugs.

Myrrh essential oil: It has been well known in the modern world as one of the oils from the Bible. It has been used in meditation, and embalming in ancient Egypt. Now, we use it for its cleansing properties, especially for the mouth and throat. Myrrh is also perfect for calming the skin. It has a sweet, smoky and bitter smell to it. Most often we see it used for its anti-inflammatory and antioxidant effects. Myrrh is also believed to help us stay emotionally calm.

Oregano essential oil: The oregano oil has been used for its cleansing agents, as well as digestive and respiratory support. It is also used for fighting cavities and parasites. A very powerful cleaner, high in antioxidant activity, phenolic acids and flavonoids. It is often used to replace antibiotics, as the side effects are none.

Patchouli essential oil: Patchouli oil has an easily recognizable fragrance. Very rich and sweet. This oil is widely used for wounds and tissue repair, as well as in skin care preparations for the same properties. It is great for acne, eczema, inflammation and irritated skin in general. It has cell-rejuvenating properties and is considered great for anti-aging and rejuvenation. Patchouli also has a grounding and balancing effect on the emotions, and is therefore widely used as a mood support. It has also been used as an insect repellant and in incense. It has antifungal properties and will heal old scars.

Peppermint essential oil: Everybody knows this one. Popular in everything from toothpaste to chewing gum. The essential oil is used for its amazing aid in breathing, clearing the mind, and keeping alertness and calm. It is also widely used as a digestive aid, and can be used internally. It is also great as an anti-nausea aid. Peppermint essential oil gives a cooling sensation and has a calming effect on the body, which can relieve sore muscles when used topically. It also has antimicrobial properties so it can help freshen bad breath and soothe digestive issues.

Rosemary essential oil: This oil is considered sacred by ancient Greeks, Romans, Egyptians and Hebrews. The rosemary essential oil has been revered by healers for centuries for its soothing effect on muscle-aches and pains, and also for its digestive-balancing properties. This oil also supports the healing of neurological tissue and boosts nerve growth factor.

Sandalwood essential oil: The ancient oil of sandalwood is most notable for its smoothing effect on the skin. Also used as a mood enhancer. Is thought indispensable by the Hindu, and used in anything from soap, beauty products and for general healing.

Thyme essential oil: Thyme is familiar to many as a common seasoning for cooking. The essential oil is a valuable cleanser and has amazing clarifying properties. It is also notable for its broad-spectrum activity for winter-health and healing. Thyme oil is one of the strongest antioxidants that we know of. It will support the respiratory-, digestive-, nervous- and immune system. It is recognized as a great hormone balancer as well as a great helper for arthritis type symptoms, fungal- and bacterial infections, and stroke.

Vetiver essential oil: Vetiver is much loved for its rich, complex and exotic aroma. It has many therapeutic uses, including as an antioxidant and for relaxation. You will find it is used extensively in perfumes as a base note and fixative. Vetiver's woody, almost earthy scent complements many other essential oils. The most popular use is still in scents.

White fir essential oil: White fir is derived from the soft needles of the tree, and is a favorite among essential oil users for its ability to comfort and soothe muscle-aches and pains when applied topically. It heals cuts fast, and has also been used to treat lice in humans.

Wild orange essential oil: The smell alone will lift your mood, and the citrusy smell is a joy to be around. It is cold-pressed from the orange peel, and is excellent for energizing and revitalizing.

Wintergreen essential oil: Most modern consumers are familiar with the aroma and flavor of wintergreen from its use in candy and chewing gum. Wintergreen essential oil, has much more to offer as a therapeutically potent oil for aches and pains as well as treating the flue and cold. It is an antiseptic, astringent and an anti-arthritic. Wintergreen is absorbed into skin quickly and acts like a natural numbing agent, like cortisone. It promotes blood circulation which is calming to swollen skin.

Ylang-ylang essential oil: Ylang-ylang has a naturally rich, floral scent that's considered "romantic" and uplifting. It is famed for this exquisite fragrance and has a long history as a component of high quality perfumes. It is an effective mood uplifting agent as well as having calming properties. It is great for diffusing in the bedroom, or added to the household cleaning products.

Essential oils can also be used as cleansing and purifying additives to laundry and surface cleaners throughout the home. Using essential oils in a diffuser is an enjoyable and effective way to experience aromatherapy in your home. Through air diffusion, a few drops of essential oil can deliver therapeutic aromatherapy throughout one or more rooms while clearing the air and creating a pleasantly fragrant environment

Be sure to use only 100% pure therapeutic-grade essential oils and follow all label warnings and instructions. Essential oils should not be used in the eyes, inside the ear canal, or in open wounds. If redness or irritation occurs when using essential oils topically, simply apply any vegetable oil such as fractionated coconut oil or olive oil to the affected area. Consult your physician before using essential oils if you are pregnant or under a doctor's care.

For further reading and reference I recommend reading the following books on essential oils:

Chemistry of Essential Oils Made Simple- by David Stewart.
Modern essentials – by Aroma Tools.
The Encyclopedia of Essential oils – by Julia Lawless.

PART FOUR:

BREAKING FREE

Chapter 24

The relationship connection

When we hear the word relationship, we most often think about a lover or a romantic partner. That is by all means a relationship, but we all have numerous types of relations to other humans. Be it a boss, a sister, a girlfriend or boyfriend, a wife, a husband, a friend or a business partner, we are connected through our interactions and shared energy. All of our relationships are colored by our conditioning, how we look at the world from a subjective standpoint. They all reflect our inner terrain, our self-worth and need for drama or solitude. We meet people that support us, and those who don`t. Either way, we are exchanging this dance of energy, to either lift ourselves or tear ourselves down. No matter the experience, it is always a part of what we have set ourselves up to learn and to grow from. We are always able to learn from every little thing we encounter.

Most of our personal relationships, which will give us an indication on how well grounded in ourselves we are, are co-dependent. This means that between you and the other person, your most intimate friend or lover, there is an energy of giving and taking. Some are more on the giving side, and some are more on the taking side, or so it might appear. The love and affection that is there, is often accompanied by an attachment to the receiving. We give, and we expect to get "paid". It is the old, "I do for you - you do for me"-game. The pattern and behavior might not even be noticeable until one of the players changes the game-rules. The change can be anything from falling ill to losing a job, or one of you might simply change your awareness and feel the pull towards a different pattern of life. So, when something within the life of one person inside of the relationship, it is easy to see any hidden patterns. Why? Because that is when the pattern is forced to change, and change hurts.

This might become an interesting topic when we are on the journey of healing and letting go. Change happened, you got sick, and now through the work of letting go of what is not serving you, the old patterns of this co-dependency are no longer sustainable. So, what do we mean by co-dependency? All depending on your upbringing and your belief-system, you will use your relationship as a validator of your patterns. If you were brought up by a mother that was constantly critiquing you, you will need someone around to continue where she left off. Most likely, now you have found someone to let you know that you deserved the critique. You have created a situation to match your belief-system. You can keep acting out your lack of self-love and you can keep giving away your power. Not knowingly of course.

Love yourself like you were your own best friend and companion, because you are! Self-love is the ultimate healer and by realizing that, we can set ourselves free.

Let us look at your relationships from a slightly different angle – from the view that says "Hey, who is running this show, you or them?" The ability to stand in your own power, often gets lost through being a people-pleaser and good game-player. What your partner or father believes, might influence you in a grander scale than you believe. You might be depending on them having the same outlook on life as yourself, or you are experiencing not trusting your own decisions, and need constant validation. From early childhood, we have been depending on validation and approval. This is quite normal. This is how we learn and grow. The ability to look towards others for guidance is how we keep evolving into young adults. Now, here is the trick – when do we cut the cord, and when are we able to trust ourselves and our own inner guidance? The indication of self-trust would be to be able to do and act as you wish, even though the people close to you do not agree with your actions. We are not discussing doing anything that would willfully hurt another human, we are simply talking about the ability to stand in one's own energy and power. To break free can be quite a challenge, as both parties are hooked on the patterns and emotional "fix". There might be an abuser in the family, and the family is hiding it, protecting the abuser. They, themselves are addicted to being abused victims. The cord needs to be cut the second you feel you are not doing or living what is optimal for your joy and health. Even though it most often is very hard to detect what is not optimal for us, by spending time to listen to ourselves, we will recognize it. We will know, deep down we will.

When we are dependent on another, we are also addicted to the emotional upheaval that the relationship has to offer. One person might be overly protective and attentive, leaving the other person feeling suffocated and enclosed. This person is continuing the relationship, because she or he is afraid to stand on their own. They have found someone that can validate their belief pattern, and show them that it is true, they need someone to be all over them, constantly. The game will continue for as long as they are both able to continue the familiar pattern of being dependent. The thing is, when one wants out of the game, all hell can break loose. The pattern will crack, and the feelings that are behind the behavior will surface. Now, if the one feeling suffocated, gets really sick and starts to work on their own healing, the need for a sense of freedom will rise as a volcano. The overly protective other will most likely try to keep the status-quo by holding on even tighter. Now, it is easy to feel that the journey of letting go is hurting the partner or the friend. The one that needs their freedom will often not go after it, because the partner or friend will play hurt and frustrated. This is where the self-love breaking-free challenge surfaces big time. Are we ready to stand on our own turf, in our own circle, and be the authentic sovereign being that we are?

There is nothing that you need to do or be to be loved. You can always choose your own path and inner calling. Being together means walking side by side, not one carrying the other.

This same pattern can be seen at the workplace, where one is playing the servant and one is acting out the high, all-mighty part. Both giving and receiving what they think and believe that they deserve. Let us look at a typical family pattern. Father needs little girl to stay little, and the girl loves the feeling of protection and being taken care of. This is all a programmed pattern. The adult might need to feel he is needed, and the girl learns that she needs to be taken care of, that someone else should protect her. Do you see that this is taking away our sovereign ability to live as individual strong, authentic beings? We are simply not conditioned to think and act from the place of inner knowing and desire, but from a place of pleasing and depending.

None of these patterns are who we really are, so let us stop acting and get real. Let us break free from this illusion of being emotionally dependent on another human being, and live as co-creators instead.

Once you let go of the fear of doing what you yourself know is right for you, you can live authentically. Once you are ready to live your life in a way that makes you feel powerful and enthusiastic, you are breaking free from the game. This is an act of bravery and victory. No man is an island, and human connections are wonderful. Nothing is like having someone to rely on, someone that you can trust and walk next to. To thrive as humans, we need to feel a sense of belonging and to be a part of a tribe or community. We need to feel that we are loved and respected. We need to be seen. These are basic human needs, and must not be confused with being dependent or needy. Being human means being in love, with all that is. You, your friends, your family, nature, your job, everything. In a perfect world we would all be in love with it all, and first and foremost ourselves. We would be able to have relationships where there were no dependencies, only unconditional love. Where walking beside one another with no feeling of ownership or conditions attached would be natural.

Being in a relationship of any kind, does not mean that you do not have the ability to walk the path that you need to walk. Your healing is about you, and you alone. Yes, we have to take care of our children, and that is a joy and an honor. Yes, we have to adjust to others to be able to work and function in a corporation. Yes, there will be times where we will willingly and knowingly put ourselves aside for the better of another. This is about something else. What I'm talking about here, is *you* not using or having any reason what so ever that has to do with a human relationship, to keep yourself from healing and regenerating. There is never a reason from outside of you that will be a good enough reason to hold yourself back.

Be authentic, and be clear, that is *your* business!

As long as we can keep our own energy high and focused, the interaction and love from others is nothing but a true blessing. Love in itself is always a blessing, only the mind and the emotional imbalances that we carry can obstruct what we believe is true love. Love has no boundaries or limitations, and it has no rules or expectations. Those are all of the ego, the mind and the emotions. None of which are the true *you*. Being compassionate and engaging is natural, being attached is not. You can be compassionately detached, meaning you can care from your heart, and still not be sucked in to anyone else's drama. Always be the observer and stay in your own center. Do not let what anyone else is experiencing affect you in a way that takes from your energy. Not an easy thing to be able to do, but absolutely something we all need to be mindful of. Sometimes you are being called to be a helper, to serve and to uplift, and that is always from the heart. It is a joy to be on the giving side, but never for wanting return of services, or for the sake of peace or dependency.

It is hard to not lose oneself in another, or to a situation. It is hard to observe someone we love live or act in a way that we do not approve of. Living close to someone can become a "project" of its own. Anything we see in our reality is there for us, as a lesson and a blessing. It is our creation, and does it require attention? The question is, is it any of our business? What others think and feel, is it any of your business? Even what they think and feel about you, is it? Is it really?

During your time of healing and balancing, you need to evaluate all of your relationships. Why? Because they have such an impact on your emotional health. We know that we can't separate our emotions from our physical being, it is not possible. The time has come to take a good look at all of them through looking in the mirror. In the mirror you will find all the answers, as the pattern from which they emanate is all in *you*. Oh, how easy it would be if we could just get someone else to fix our relationships. If only the other person was to blame, and would change to meet our needs.

You are the one you have been waiting for, the one that is going to change all of your relationships.

By walking your talk, staying on your path and being of pure heart and intent, every single human interaction in your life will change to fit your energetic vibration. You really are the one you have been waiting for. By not letting anyone else's world-view clutter your own inner desire and knowing, the people close to you will be of great support. Those that are wishing you well will stick around, and those that will walk alongside you will lift your spirit. This simply means that when you are ready to change your diet, to stop going to the events that are no longer uplifting for you, there is no circumstance that can stop you. You need no validation from someone else, and those around you do not have to agree with your decisions. As long as you are true to yourself, people around you will be too.

Our relationships will always reflect what we think and believe about ourselves, and that is actually the hidden blessing. As long as we are the ones responsible, we can make the change that is needed. By simply loving ourselves more and working on being the observer, we can experience how all aspects of our lives change. Our health is our life, a reflection of how we live, think, feel and speak. Not only our physical health, but every single aspect of our lives. All connected like nature. Pure perfection yet not always obvious to the naked eye.

Start any relationship changes by affirming and by speaking the truth that you want to see. *Faith* it until you make it.

Everyone we meet is our teacher. In some way or another they are all crossing our path to show us something of value. Good, bad, ugly or magnificent, the lessons are of all colors. This is how we grow. There is no failure, and there are no mistakes, there is only life and all that it holds. A lesson learned is a steppingstone for growth. Together we are here to grow and to learn from each other, all carrying our individual stories and experiences. We can never walk in someone else's shoes, and therefore we must never judge another. Judgment is from the ego, from the part of us that feels unloved and hurt. Through real work of detachment and inner evolvement we learn to see another humans path as his own. It is none of our business.

Start your inner transformation by affirming every day:

- *All my relationships are of a loving and compassionate nature.*
- *I love myself like I love all that is.*
- *I am important and worthy of real love.*
- *I AM love.*
- *I am an observer.*
- *I love unconditionally.*
- *Everyone I meet has something to teach me.*
- *I practice detached compassion.*
- *I am always supported.*
- *How can I serve?*

Detached compassion means being able to be of service and support of another, while not attaching or adopting their struggle or imbalances. It means not having to carry their burdens, yet at the same time being able to love and help them. Detaching from someone else`s choices and feelings will leave you completely free to explore your own path. No acceptance is needed. You need no approval to change and to grow, as it is not between you and any other human. It is between you and *you,* or you and God, any way you choose to see it.

All you need to do is to be *you,* and to trust your inner guidance. Do not let anyone interfere with what you have set out to do. Embrace any help and compassion, as walking together is truly a blessing. Together we are stronger, and no man is an island.

Chapter 25

Forgiveness and gratitude

Two really powerful words and healers – forgiveness and gratitude. By working on those concepts alone, we are altering our whole reality of life. Truly transformational and life-altering inner work can be done by feeling the humbleness that comes with being grateful. When we are grateful, forgiveness is easy. They are both compassionate energies from the true source, from who we really are. Words are energy, and they all hold a frequency, an intent and a passion. When we feel gratitude it comes from our heart, and when we forgive someone, it comes from the heart also. One cannot will any of them with the mind. Practicing gratitude and forgiveness is the honoring of love and compassion. Love is the true healing energy, and it always starts with self-love. It always comes back to the self. We, us, you and me, as long as we really love ourselves, will live life from a place of forgiveness and gratitude.

Words are submissions of intent, and even when we are not aware, we are sending out a message to our cells, to the creation, to God or the

Infinite. The energy of gratitude is a pure love energy. It is the vibration of constant positive change.

Whenever we find ourselves wanting something to change, we must start by being grateful for what we already have. There is always something to be grateful for. Even when we are down, feeling lost and depressed, we can search for the inner feeling of gratitude. Being grateful is the same as ordering more to be grateful for. If we want our health to change, we must embrace and love the work that the body is already doing. Feeling gratitude for our breath, our vision, our hearing etc. If we want a better house to live in, we must be grateful for the home that we already have, or the couch that we are offered by a friend. No matter the status of our current shelter - giving thanks for what is already there, is inviting in more to feel grateful for.

The challenge is, that gratitude does not come from the mind. It is not a thought, it is a feeling, a state of being. It is a heartfelt feeling, and it fills the entire body with a nurturing, positive, healing energy. It is very similar to love, but it is directed towards the recognition of all that is. We can be grateful for every single thing in our lives, good, bad and ugly. We can start by being grateful for what is the most obvious to us, and see how our perception towards life changes. Gratitude opens the heart, and it opens the portal for rapid healing and nurturing manifestations. The magic of life will flow towards us, and every cell in our body will align with this vibration.

In your daily life, gratitude starts with mindfulness. Once you are mindful, aware of everything around you, you will be able to see the little things that will create a feeling of "thank you". Those magic little big words, *thank you*. Start by giving thanks for the things that are beautiful around you, that you see every day. The flowers that you pass, and the air that you breathe. The subtle things like - thank you for these comfortable shoes, or the sound of that bird I just walked by. Giving thanks is the ultimate act of gratitude, even though it is merely an honoring of the energy through words. The power is in the feeling behind the words that we speak, and behind the intention thereof.

By being more aware, the gratitude effect will grow, slowly and steadily. From the self-talk and the awareness, there will grow an inner compassion for life as it is. What we put our attention towards grows, and what we hold as our inner energy will draw to itself more that will match it perfectly.

Work on your mindfulness by being more aware in your everyday life. No matter what you are doing, take a moment to soak in your surroundings and feel how grateful you are for what you see. It does not matter if you are walking on a beach in paradise, or you are lying in a hospital bed. There is always something to be grateful for, always. Work on the feeling by starting with something that is obvious. Once you get the hang of it, you can put forth that same feeling towards things and people that you never even knew you were grateful for. Gratefulness is an attitude and a mindset, both of which we choose with our conscious mind. Still, the inner state of gratefulness is a true feeling, and it will grow with the practice. Change will show itself as having a more positive outlook on life, wanting to give more, faster healing, depression and anger disappears and more things to be grateful for keeps showing up.

Now, gratitude becomes a habit and will bring in more amazing healing and blessings. Even if you are in pain right now, focus on your breath, and be grateful that you are still breathing, reading this book and that you are on your way to Joyful City.

- *Thank you for my breath.*
- *Thank you for my friends.*
- *Thank you for the trees and the flowers.*
- *Thank you for being me.*
- *Thank you for my healing journey.*

- *Thank you for my ability to choose my thought.*
- *Thank you for the love in my heart.*

I recommend that you keep a gratitude journal. I have kept one by my bed for many years. This is a fantastic way to reflect on your day. The awareness will open the heart, and invite you to be open to the flow of grace. By being more aware of your thoughts, the ones that are not serving you are easier to detect. Gift yourself a new beautiful notebook and put it beside your bed. Get a special pen to go with it. Gratitude journals are serious business, they are our voice back to the spirit and the Creator. Spend a few minutes before you go to sleep, to write down 5 things you are grateful for that day. It can be little things or not so little things. A hug, a gift, a smile, fresh air and a special meal, are all great things to acknowledge and give thanks for. Thank you is easy and simple, yet powerful beyond our belief.

All of our experiences hold great value, even our less than optimal health, our unhealthy relationships and our seemingly poor career-choices. We are being shown the way to better ourselves and to learn, all as a part of the journey back to our simple state of being. By letting go of everything that is obstructing that simple state of love and gratitude, we are able to grow free. Free from what has been holding us back. The gratefulness will show us forgiveness, the optimal teaching of letting go. It does not matter who did what, or what happened when, forgiveness is an act of self-love, and is absolutely necessary for healing and joyful living. Not forgiving is the same as holding on, and holding on is the same as constipating and acidifying the mind and body.

Forgiving is the energy of self-love and compassion. It is also what shall set you free from emotional baggage.

When we forgive someone, we are putting the energy back where it belongs. By that I mean that we choose to not be the carrier of the event anymore. We refuse to be the one that is emotionally hurting because of what someone else did. The action was not ours, and the hurt or effect of what happened is not ours to keep living. When we are holding on to the memory, we are letting the event continue to hurt us, over and over again. So, you see forgiving is all about *you*, never about the other person. Once you realize this, letting go becomes so much easier. Every day moving forward has the choice of forgiveness. The blame and anger that comes with holding on will eat you up like any other acid. Just like the acids and alkaline foods, there are alkaline and acidic emotions. The anger, blame, sorrow, hopelessness and despair are all corrosive to our organism, and we need to let them be embraced and set free. Through forgiveness and gratitude – love, compassion, thankfulness, joy and enthusiasm will grow and prosper.

You might think that forgiving someone is the same as letting them off the hook and that what they did is now ok. That is not the case at all. You might also think that now that everything is forgiven, you will have to be friends with them again, or interact with them even. No, that is not at all what this is about. Forgiveness is not about validating any action or situation. It is not about making anything ok. This is the act of self-freedom and no longer owning the situation. You are no longer allowing it to hurt you. Trust might be broken and relationships might be over, and that is perfectly ok. Forgiveness is your gift to you, and your doorway to moving on.

The very first step towards forgiveness is acknowledging that it needs to be done. The second step is knowing what it is and what it is not. Once you are ready, give yourself permission to move on with a compassionate heart. That is the heart-felt true you, *and you are reclaiming every single bit of it.*

What is forgiveness and what is it not?

- *Forgiving is the opposite of victimhood. By stopping the continuing blame and hurt, we are refusing to be a victim. We are reclaiming our power.*

- *We can forgive someone even if we will never see each other again. It is an act of energetic dis-connection. By holding on, it does not matter where the other person is, you are still connected by this blame.*

- *Keep walking alongside loving and caring people. Although one can forgive, it does not mean that it is ok to stay in any abusive relationship. Everyone is accountable for their actions.*

- *Forgiveness is knowing that punishment and revenge is not up to you. We are not the ones in charge of justice. Karma is a cosmic law – which means that there is always cause and effect. We do not need to worry about it, it is always taken care of.*

- *The act of forgiving is a choice that is completely yours alone. It is an act of power and sovereignty. You are stepping up to your highest potential.*

- *Forgiving never means that things will stay the same – quite the opposite, it means you will move on without anything holding you down.*

- *No matter what happens, how tragic or seemingly horrible, forgiveness is a process that can start right away. It is ok that it might take time. Grant yourself the time that you need, without indulging in it. There are many meditation and visualization techniques that can help you during this process.*

- *Forgiveness does not mean that you are denying what happened, not at all. Sometimes the offender does not even know he or she did something to hurt another, and sometimes doing one's best just was not ok at the time.*

- *Forgiveness does not have anything to do with repent. Remember, it is not about them, always about you and me. We are walking the path of love and healing, which holds no place for degenerating, debilitating anger and despair. It has nothing to do with their attitude, only with yours.*

- *They might be totally unaware that you are going through this process. They might not even know that they need your forgiveness. They do not at all need to be a part of your healing journey, so this is absolutely something that you can do all by yourself.*

- *Withholding forgiveness is like trying to hold on to pain and power at the same time. Holding it back might give a sense of power over the whole situation. It is the kind of perceived power that will eat you up over time, as it is not true power, it is fear of letting go.*

- *We are not looking for the "forgive and forget" – as we are acknowledging the lesson being learned. Forgetting is something that we see as not validating the event, and that is the opposite of what this is about. Forgive and let go, and let every memory be a part of your embraced and loved journey. Any event, perceived as good or bad, holds the opportunity for growth and learning.*

- *You are always ready to forgive - it is not such a big deal really. It is the energy of letting love back into your heart.*

- *Forgiveness is not about covering wounds, that is called suppressing them. No, on the contrary, you are on your way to healing all wounds. No bandage needed.*

The power of choice is the energy that we use to start the forgiveness process. Choose to do it, and find a way to set yourself free. Your health depends on it.

Although most people will act according to the best of their ability – the act often comes from their own fear and hurts. All of us, the seemingly good, bad and ugly – all of us are doing what we believe is the best we can do at the time. Even though we have the obvious right to feel resentment and anger, we also have the ability to make the choice not to. Now we are refusing to play the victim and we are no longer letting another person hold any power over us or our feelings. Once we give away that power we have lost the control of our health. Reclaim it now by doing some healing forgiveness-work.

Acceptance of life as it is holds a great key to this inner work of healing. Let go of the "why me" and the" but it was not fair". It happened, and it does not have to be fair to be forgiven. Again, this is not about the act or the other person, nor is it about validating or justifying. This is solely about *you* loving yourself enough to not let any past event stop you from living the life that you deserve. Accept and acknowledge everything about it, about the person and the event. This will make you acknowledge that it actually needs to be forgiven. Accepting is not the same as denying, it is taking ownership and responsibility for our own health and life. You are simply calling forth what is not of *you*, or your business to carry around.

Keys to letting go through forgiveness:

- *Commit to moving on*
- *Be willing to let it all go*
- *Accept that it happened*
- *Be patient*
- *Be in the present moment*
- *Love yourself*

Self-love is the catalyst of compassion, gratitude and forgiveness. We all need to look within, and forgive ourselves first. By the simple act of loving ourselves, we are opening the floodgate for the compassion that is needed for forgiveness. You did your best with what you had at the moment, although looking back you might have chosen to do things differently. We *all* know that one, you are not alone – it is called life. It's the same learning path for all of us. Love yourself by forgiving yourself for everything, right now.

Holding on to any kind of resentment has consequences for our health, and it is never worth it. Increased inner peace, happiness and calmness is what every cell in our body will experience once we allow ourselves to move on and beyond.

Set some time to be with your inner emotions, and let any person that will need your forgiveness come forth. Find a pen and paper, and write down any situation or person that you feel have hurt you or done you wrong in any way at all. Look at each situation and feel it in your heart if you have forgiven them. If not, here are a few exercises that will help you during this process.

Cutting the cord exercise:

Sit or lay down in a comfortable position where you know that you will not be disturbed. Look at your notes and decide who you want to forgive. You can repeat this exercise as many times as you like until you have forgiven them all. You do not have to do this all at once, so start slow. It is perfectly okay to do the process on one person at the time. Some situations are harder than others to let go of. We are not focusing on the situations but the person in this exercise. When you are ready, close your eyes and relax your entire body.

1. *Take a deep breath while you count to four. Hold it for four, and release on the count of four. Repeat four times.*

2. *With your inner eye, visualize the person you want to forgive. You are standing right in front of him or her.*

3. *Once you look closer, you will see that you are connected by cords/wires that bind you together. They run from stomach to stomach, heart to heart, head to head and so on.*

4. *The cords might be thick or thin, made of steel or hemp. They might be short or long, many or few. Take a good look.*

5. *Now you are going to cut those cords. Watch them being cut. Some might give in easily, but some might need some more help. I have seen cords that are of metal and will need some extensive work to cut through. If you hit a cord that seemingly doesn't give in, don't worry about it. You will get it next time. Most of the time, they cave easily.*

6. *When the cords are cut, look the person in the eye and say with your inner voice; "I forgive you, as I forgive myself. I let you go in love and I wish you well."*

7. *See a white light opening over the now forgiven person and watch him or her be embraced by this light. Let them go and watch them dissolve into the light.*

8. *You have set yourself free and do no longer have any attachment to them. Repeat until you see no more cords between you and those you have chosen to let go of.*

Setting the stage for a healing and beyond:

This is a different exercise that you can work with. Find a comfortable position and sit in a chair or lay down on a bed. Make sure that you will not be disturbed, and that you have a door or a window open for fresh air to be able to enter.

1. *Take a deep breath while you count to four. Hold it for four, and release on the count of four. Repeat four times.*

2. *Visualize with your inner eye that you are sitting in a theater. You are the only audience, and the person you want to forgive is alone on stage.*

3. *This person has a story to tell you. He or she is telling you how sorry they are, while you are listening with compassion. They are showing remorse and regret, and asking for your forgiveness. You go up on stage and you give them a hug. You realize that it is all ok, that you can grant them their wish.*

4. *See the person happy and free, leaving the stage in joy.*

5. *If there is another story to be heard, go back to your seat and invite the next person on stage.*

The ultimate letting go exercise:

Find a piece of paper to write on. It needs to be a nice piece, as the writing on it will be important. Do not write this on the computer to print, as your handwriting is important.

1. *Sit down in a quiet place and write down everything you can think about that would need to be forgiven. It can be situations or people. It can be your own doings or those of others. Do not stop until you have gotten everything. It does not matter how many pages you write, the more the merrier.*

2. *If you do not feel like you are done with the list, let it be for a few hours or a day, then get back to it and add what you need to add.*

3. *When the list is complete, including everything you can think of and remember that has done you wrong, felt wrong or abusive, fold it together and bring it outside.*

4. *If you can't go outside, find a bucket and go somewhere where you can safely burn your piece of paper. You want it to turn to ashes, together with every hurt and harmful action that is written on it. It can no longer hurt you, as it is given back to the energy of all that is.*

5. *You have let it all go, and can start filling your heart with even more pure love for life.*

The greatest act of forgiveness is that of forgiving ourselves. Often we carry around a self-blame that is in the way of our true happiness. You need to forgive yourself for everything, so use this exercise to free yourself. Take some time to focus on you alone, and go deep within and listen. Write it all down, and set the attention. This is the time for you to rise from the ashes, so dig deep and be proud of yourself.

Everything we are carrying with us from the past is creating our present moment. Let go and let live!

Chapter 26

The power within

The power we all hold within us holds the unlimited power of creation. It all starts and ends with *you*. Your intention holds your true healing mechanism, and as long as you breathe you will be, and tap into that power. You don't get what you want, you get what you are! We all have our own lessons to learn, and our own life to live, but we are not meant to suffer. Suffering is a choice.

The power that I am talking about is beyond the obvious strength to endure – it is a power of creation. We are truly amazing beings that hold a choice to create by living. We are creating with every single thought and feeling, even when seemingly doing nothing we are creating. That is how powerful we are. So much so that we become fearful of it. It might seem or feel safe to be inferior at times – it holds less responsibility and it holds less accountability. But guess what, no matter what you live and create, it is still all *you*. Good or bad, all you. Are there outside forces? Sure there are, and many of them, but do they hold the power over you and your life? No they do not.

I am referring to the free will and magic of choice. The ability that you have, to choose how you let life affect you and how you respond to the world around you. Together with how much you love yourself and what you have, there is nothing that can stop you from thriving in your own world. The magical power is the ability to shift the perception, to own every minute and to love every second of it. Soar and roar. The strength and the creative force that is behind the willingness to live and to give, cannot be stopped. I realized that by accepting that I was the one who held the magic wand, so to speak, I could move forward fearlessly and confident.

Let me share with you a small portion of my own healing journey, from the book "From HELL to inspired":

"I was done being sick, and I was done struggling. I was so filled up on medications, hospital visits, anxiety and pain, that I decided to just stop. I had been diagnosed with severe rheumatoid arthritis several years before, and was heavily medicated - I was told that I was a "severe" case. The diagnosis of Lyme disease, ulcers, anxiety and more, were not helping my suffering soul and spirit. The medical society tells you, you will be sick for the rest of your life, and that medications will be your only hope to live as "normal" as possible. What they do not tell you, is a very different story, and what they do not know - might kill you.

This one day about 8 years ago, I had had enough. I remember thinking, "I will stop all medications and just lie here until I get well, or I die." I really did not care which, as long as what I was experiencing stopped. From being a mother, a sister, a wife, a business owner, an athlete, and a friend, I just became sick. My world changed overnight. I was alone, and I did not know what to do to save myself. As soon as I stopped the medications that made me very ill, I got more ill. Now, my body was showing me just how sick I really was.

A long journey started, a lonely one, filled with pain, fear, and hopelessness. Every day was a battle for survival. My heart did not beat regularly for years. I was bedridden, and could not even go to the bathroom by myself, not for several years. I could not open my mouth or chew foods, as my jaw was too inflamed. I often prayed that I would not wake up in the morning. Watching your body deteriorate, and your joints slowly cripple, is a challenge for the mind, the emotions and the soul.

Something inside me told me that health was there, if I would just let it come forth. I studied all day, every day. I spent all my time searching the internet, reading books and watching videos. Slowly my way of thinking changed, my diet changed, and my connection to my spirit opened up. Friends left, and new amazing souls came into my life. It is hard for family members and friends to understand, and to know how to help when someone gets very sick. Change is often felt as a scary thing, so never blame them for not being there. They do not know any better.

Along this journey I have seen stones turn into diamonds, I have seen life become magical, and I have seen my body transforming before my very eyes. How amazing is that? As I look back, I can see the true gift in my ongoing journey from HELL to Inspired. I made a choice, and I followed my inner guidance. The gift was hidden to me, but is no more. It is now shining as my true purpose.

Now, all these years later, my heart is beating perfectly and the anxiety is gone. My digestion is back to normal after 20 years of ulcers, and my skin looks better than it has in years. I am not stopping until my body is 100% healthy - and beyond! And they said it could not be done! NEVER let anybody tell you that. Not your family, friends, NOBODY! This has been my biggest gift, and I would not be without this journey.

The NOW moment is where the magic is, and for those of you that struggle with health issues, KNOW that it is in your hands to change. Your body is made to be healthy, it's what it is designed to be. It is all vibration, and it's all connected. Stop poisoning it, and start nurturing *it. Change your thoughts, and your emotions will follow. Clear out the toxins from your body, and the mind will clear. Your vibration will raise, and your consciousness will rise. Align your focus with the solution, not with the problem! Speak what you want, and expect it to happen. BE the change you want to see, and love yourself the whole way there. Nobody is perfect, in fact perfection is an illusion, it does not exist. YOU are the perfect YOU!"*

Simply by realizing that you are in charge of, and responsible for your own life and health – you are going to activate your power. It never left you, it is who you are. The life that we live is colored by every single choice that we make, even a thought is a choice. It might not be obvious that it is, but you are not your thoughts.

The power of choice includes:

- **The freedom to choose how to respond to every single situation that arises.** A response is not the same as a reaction. When we respond, we are giving back a balanced analysis or answer to a given activity or outside event. A reaction is an emotionally based response that we see as coming from a place of hurt and lack. The same exact situation can arise in front of two different people, and their perception of it might be completely different. How you respond and react is entirely up to you. You can love or hate, and you can accept or deny. As long as we keep working on ourselves, the detachment from having to live our lives through a reaction pattern will slowly fade.

- **The ability to let go of what is not serving you.** Be it a non-serving relationship or a job that you are not happy with, it is your choice to let it go or let it be. You can change your job, or you can love it as it is – that is how powerful you are. Nothing outside of you can ever demand how you feel or act. Only *you* can trigger that motion. Letting go simply means not letting it obstruct your inner calm and feelings. You can hold on to anything you want, as long as you realize that you are the one who has to live with it.

- **Being able to choose what you eat.** This is such a transformational topic. So simple, yet so hard. Every single thing you put in your mouth is by choice. This in turn means that your health on every level is yours to decide. I know, it might feel like a tough statement to make, but it is the truth. Detoxification is the key to health and healing, and through changing our diet to a supporting and cleansing one, we are changing our whole lives. The physical body is connected to our emotional body, and once that train towards Joy City, on the corner of Health and Happiness, leaves the station, there is no going back, not unless one really wants to. So, choose wisely and know that the power of choice is *yours*!

- **The unlimited choice to change and grow.** Change is perceived as hard, and therefore it will often bring on a high level of resistance. Not only resistance for the obvious reason, being that hard is less desirable, no, this is a much deeper kind of resistance. Letting go of what is, can be scarier than anything, and holding on to what *is* will keep life in your comfort-zone, even if it is an uncomfortable one. Yes, even then, the obvious choice can seem out of reach.

- **The unlimited allowance to take action.** No-one or no-thing is holding you back. The free will to take action is always there. Through the motion you put forth and the steps that you take - you are honoring your freedom of choice.

- **Always having the freedom to love your life**! Loving life exactly as it is, is a conscious choice. From the vibration of love comes more to love, so you see - this choice is a truly

279

powerful one. Find everything that you love about your life and focus on that every single day.

Often we have a "but" coming – as if there is a reason for the above statements not to be true for *us* in particular. You might say: "Yes, this is all well and good, *but,* you see - for me it is not that easy. You see, I have this and this going on and I cannot do this for this and that reason." As long as we keep looking, there will be a reason *not* to honor our inner power. There are as many reasons as there are but's, or rare ends rather. So, what is this all about? If you feel a *but* coming on, know that it is only your own fear speaking. Your mind is trying to reason your way out of losing its hold on you. Taking full responsibility and making your whole life your own business is a very scary thing. The mind finds it's control well worth fighting for – hence it's need for this interference. The inner reasoning is only trying to keep you from realizing that your life is your own business, and that there really is no reason why it is not.

Your power is so much stronger than your mind, and your inner light and ability to heal and restore is grander than you can ever imagine. No person, no event or circumstance can stand in the way of your ability to choose life. The inner strength that we all hold is released when we allow it to be.

Your life is your responsibility and your business. Power up and act like it!

Action is always involved in any part of creation. Everything is constantly moving, changing and vibrating. Nothing is ever still. Every thought that you think is a form of action that puts into motion a whole set of events. These events are what is becoming your life, the story that you are writing. You hold the pen and you write every word. You can turn the page and start again on any given day. You can change your story, even the meaning of your past. The events that have happened are there, but how you perceive them is entirely up to you. What you make of them, how you color them and give them meaning is in your demand.

Your life is your dance and our expression. Health and healing is always there for you. This is *your* time to shine, and *you* are so worth it.

Go get it!

SOURCE NOTES AND FURTHER READING SUGGESTIONS

For further reading and exploring, here are some great books to look into. Life is a journey, not a destination. The flow of information is massive, and only the seeker will know what is right and when.

- "The Detox Miracle Sourcebook" - Dr. Robert Morse N.D.
- "Mucusless Diet Healing System" – Professor Arnold Ehret.
- "Epigenetics" - Dr. Joel Wallach
- "Fasting and Eating for Health" - Joel Fuhrman
- "The Grape Cure" - Johanna Brandt
- "How to prolong life" - C.W Delacy Evans
- "The Amazing liver and gallbladder flush" - Andreas Moritz
- "Reinventing the body, Resurrecting the soul" – Deepak Chopra
- "The Vortex" - Ester and Jerry Hicks
- "A new earth" - Eckart Tolle
- "Re-Awakening the giant within" - Tony Robbins
- "You can heal your life" - Louise Hays
- "The eye of the one" - David R. Hawkins
- "Anatomy of the spirit" – Caroline Myss

- "The Biology of Belief" – Dr. Bruce Lipton
- "The chemistry of essential oils made simple" – David Stewart Ph.D., D.N.M.
- "Hidden messages in water" - Masuru Emoto

To learn more about Hilde, her work and her services, visit her website. Sign up for her newsletter to receive the latest news and recipes: www.inspiredbyhilde.com

Download the FREE e-book *Notes to Power up* here:
http://inspiredbyhilde.com/notes-to-power-up/

Download the FREE e-book *Blessed by Essential oils* here:
http://inspiredbyhilde.com/blessed-by-essential-oils/

Hilde has an easy to follow online detoxification program:
https://zparkl.com/course/about/2/life-transforming-detoxification-cleansing-program/

To request to work with Hilde, visit the website www.inspiredbyhilde.com.

29223562R00167

Made in the USA
Columbia, SC
21 October 2018